Milton & English Art

Marcia R Pointon

Milton &
English Art

University
of Toronto Press

First published, 1970, in Great Britain by
Manchester University Press

and in Canada and the United States by
University of Toronto Press
Toronto and Buffalo

ISBN 0-8020-1708-8

Designed by Max Nettleton

Made and printed in Great Britain by
Butler & Tanner Ltd, Frome and London

Contents

The author and publishers gratefully acknowledge permission to reproduce items in the collections of the institutions and individuals named. They also thank the British Museum, Department of Printed Books, and the John Rylands Library, Manchester, for providing access to engravings. Sizes are given in centimetres, width followed by depth.

Abbreviations

B. Mag.—The *Burlington Magazine*.

J.W.C.I.—*Journal of the Warburg and Courtauld Institutes*.

Boase, *English Art*—T. S. R. Boase, *English Art 1800–1870* (Oxford, 1959).

Bryan—Dr. M. Bryan, *A Biographical and Critical Dictionary of Painters* (1873).

Good—J. W. Good, 'Studies in the Milton Tradition', *University of Illinois Studies in Language and Literature*, I (1915).

Graves, *R.A.*—A. Graves, *The Royal Academy of Arts. A Complete Dictionary of Contributors 1769–1904* (1906).

Graves, *S.A.*—A. Graves, *The Society of Artists of Great Britain 1761–1791 and The Free Society of Artists 1761–1783. A Dictionary of Contributors* (1907).

Graves, *B.I.*—A. Graves, *Exhibitors at the British Institution 1806–1867* (1908).

Havens—R. D. Havens, *The Influence of Milton on English Poetry* (Harvard, 1922).

P.L.—John Milton, *Paradise Lost*.

Schiff—Gert Schiff, *Johann Heinrich Füssli's Milton Galerie* (Zurich, 1963).

Svendsen—K. Svendsen, 'John Martin and the Expulsion Scene in *Paradise Lost*', *Studies in English Literature 1500–1900*, I (1961).

Waterhouse—E. K. Waterhouse, *Painting in Britain 1530–1790* (Harmondsworth, 1953).

All passages from Milton's poetry are quoted from *Milton's Poetical Works* edited by Helen Darbishire (Oxford, 1952, 1955).

Roman numerals refer to the book numbers of *Paradise Lost* or *Paradise Regained*.

Arabic numerals in brackets refer to illustrations.

Unless otherwise stated all works referred to in the notes or the bibliography are published in London.

Preface

Much thought and energy have been devoted to the study of Milton's influence on English literature and works such as J. W. Good's *Milton Studies*[1] and R. D. Havens's *The Influence of Milton on English Poetry*[2] make mention also of the important contribution that Milton's poetry made towards the visual arts, particularly in the eighteenth and nineteenth centuries. However, up to date no comprehensive survey of this subject has been made. This fact is surprising, to say the least, as even ignoring the obvious interest of such a field for the student of the history of English art, one would expect that any topic concerning this much studied poet would already have been exhaustively explored by the student of English literature. In the words of Professor K. Svendsen, 'The critical history of a great literary work is incomplete unless it incorporates inferences from the interpretation put upon the masterpiece by artists. Even when non-aesthetic considerations are demonstrably present, such as obligation to a publisher or a public, they may complicate the question but they do not annul it.'[3]

My indebtedness in writing this book to a great many authorities on the history of English art and literature is evident from my acknowledgements in the footnotes to the text. I should, however, like to make particular mention of T. S. R. Boase and E. K. Waterhouse, to whose work the student of English art in the eighteenth and nineteenth centuries is fortunate in being able to constantly turn. I feel that the work of C. H. Collins-Baker should also be acknowledged here as, although his survey covers the published illustrations to *Paradise Lost* only, this writer may justifiably be said to have pioneered the study of the subject of Milton and English art. I have also found studies on the illustrative work of individual artists by Helen Gardner, M. Y. Hughes, M. Peckham, and especially that by Professor K. Svendsen most helpful and informative. The latter is, despite its brevity, the only article which makes any attempt to establish the fundamental criteria on which the subject of illustrative art may be judged.

I trust that my thanks to galleries and museums which have supplied me with photographs will be accepted without individual specification. The main substance of this book was originally submitted for the degree of M.A. at the University of Manchester in 1967 and I should like to thank the Department of History of Art in that University for financial assistance with photographs. The Directors of the British Museum, the Victoria and Albert Museum, the Slade College of Art, Sir John Soane's Museum, the Fitzwilliam Museum, the Whitworth Art Gallery and the John Rylands Library kindly provided me with facilities for research and photography. My thanks go also to the Librarian of the Witt Library, the Courtauld Institute.

I have received valuable advice and assistance from Mr. Charles Sewter, Dr. T. S. R. Boase, Dr. H. A. Hammelmann, Dr. David Irwin, Mr. Benedict Nicolson, Miss Miranda Strickland-Constable, Miss Susan Booth, Mr. Frank Simpson and Sir John Summerson. My thanks go also to Mr. and Mrs. W. Massey and to my father, J. R. V. Collin, for invaluable help with translations, to Mrs. Kate Turner for assistance with the index and to my husband for his advice and encouragement.

Notes to Preface

1. J. W. Good, 'Studies in the Milton Tradition', *University of Illinois Studies in Language and Literature*, I (1915).
2. R. D. Havens, *The Influence of Milton on English Poetry* (Harvard, 1922).
3. K. Svendsen, 'John Martin and the Expulsion Scene in *Paradise Lost*', *Studies in English Literature 1500–1900*, I (Rice University, 1961).

The great influence that Milton's work has had on subsequent English poetry has long been recognized and the eighteenth-century belief in 'Ut Pictura Poesis' has been frequently discussed during the last two decades.[1] The reverse side of this coin—the question of literary painting—has never received the attention it deserves, although T. S. R. Boase,[2] M. Merchant[3] and Dr. D. Irwin[4] have, to some extent, discussed the question. Comparisons between the arts of poetry and painting abound in the eighteenth century. One eighteenth-century commentator believed that the Greeks 'had no Thomsons because they had no Claudes'[5] and such ventures as Macklin's Poets' Gallery or Boydell's Shakespeare Gallery were based on the assumption that a natural alliance existed between the arts. It was thought that the basic disadvantage of painting as compared to poetry in relating narrative could be overcome by the inclusion as part of the picture's title of long extracts of poetry. Even landscapes, it was thought, and still-life studies could be enhanced and rendered more dignified or impres-sive if a suitable quotation were appended. One need only glance at the Royal Academy catalogues to realize how extensive was the use of long quotations in the second half of the eighteenth century and how this practice became obsessive among nineteenth-century artists.

There was, from the artist's point of view, a great deal to be said for this practice of 'literary' painting. Not least of the advantages was the enlargement of the repertoire of accepted, familiar themes. However, the way of the 'illustrator' was full of pitfalls. Reynolds in *Discourse VIII*, delivered to the Royal Academy on December 10th, 1778, whilst speaking very much from the viewpoint of one who adheres to the classical belief in the parallel between poetry and painting, astutely sees one of the great flaws in the practice of literary painting, one which more than any other factor is frequently responsible for the vapidity and tameness of the endless series of pictures from Shakespeare, Spenser and Milton.

Discussing the qualities exclusive to the sketch (and not found in the finished work) which suffice to quicken the imagination of the viewer, which then develops the remaining detail, Reynolds arrives at the conclusion that because there is no work left for the imagination in a finished painting, we are often disappointed in viewing it. He then goes on to discuss the virtues of a poetic description in which much must necessarily be left to the imagination and the consequent disadvantages of transferring that verbal description into pictorial terms:

These general ideas, which are expressed in sketches, correspond very well to the art often used in Poetry. A great part of the beauty of the celebrated description of Eve in Milton's *Paradise Lost*, consists in using only general, indistinct expressions, every reader making out the detail according to his own particular imagination—his own idea of beauty, grace, expression, dignity or loveliness: but a painter, when he represents Eve on a canvas, is obliged to give a determined form, and his own idea of beauty distinctly expressed.

Most of the objections to Boydell's Shakespeare Gallery and Fuseli's Milton Gallery were raised on these grounds. Charles Lamb, for example, writing in the early years of the nineteenth century said:

What injury did not Boydell's Shakespeare Gallery do Shakespeare. To have Opie's Shakespeare, Northcote's Shakespeare, light headed Fuseli's Shakespeare, wooden headed West's Shakespeare, deaf headed Reynold's Shakespeare instead of my and everybody's Shakespeare.[6]

What Charles Lamb objected to so strongly was most probably caused largely by the lack of any long tradition of pictorial representation. As T. S. R. Boase says:

It was all too easy to follow some conventional pattern that was only vaguely appropriate, or aiming higher, to fall far short of the imaginative power necessary to equal in visual invention the chosen extract.[7]

Nevertheless, the choice by artists of subjects from European literature was unfailingly popular from the middle years of the eighteenth century to the latter part of the nineteenth century when the tradition thus created received new impetus from the doctrine of the utility of art. The subject of literary painting is an enormously complex one, spanning a century and a half. This book comprises a historical survey of the illustrations to Milton's poetry executed in England between 1688 and 1860, including engraved designs incorporated in editions of Milton's poetry and exhibited works. The minor arts are mentioned where relevant and a very general survey of sculpture forms an appendix. An endeavour has been made to assess how—in the case of one poet—literary material is used by the painter as a source of artistic inspiration. At the same time, the problems of method and interpretation which confront the commissioned illustrator are discussed in reference to individual artists and specific works.

The enthusiasm of the early Romantics for the poetry of Shakespeare and Milton is a familiar factor in the history of European art. It was the writers of the *Sturm und Drang* movement in Germany and Switzerland who first sought in the work of these two English writers elements of wildness and of passion and those features that came to be known as 'sublime'. The Swiss painter Fuseli lived in England and, with his circle of associates—Barry, Mortimer, Romney and Blake—nurtured himself on Shakespeare and Milton. This group of English artists may be called early Romantics, but whilst their subject-matter and their attitude towards it may now be seen to exhibit a certain freedom of imagination which justifies their being called precursors of the Romantic movement proper, these artists, working chiefly between 1770 and 1800, regarded themselves (with the exception of Blake) as belonging to the academic neo-classical tradition. This applies particularly to Fuseli, a most distinguished member of the Royal Academy and one whose large corpus of Milton pictures was exhibited outside the Academy not because he felt such works did not belong there, but rather because he regarded the Milton Gallery as a commercial venture and hoped to make money by charging an entrance fee. He hoped for profits and he hoped for fame. In short, one cannot draw a strict dividing line between the Classical artist and the Romantic artist. One can take a key work from the academic camp, Reynolds's *Discourses*, and contrast with it Blake's annotations in his own copy of the work; but this is misleading. An adherence to the classical code is most frequently found co-existing with an interest in certain objects or ideas which later became dominant elements in Romantic art. The two attitudes in the latter half of the eighteenth century were interdependent as R. Rosenblum has illustrated in his most illuminating study of art during this period.[8] In the case of Fuseli, a great advocate of the neo-classical doctrine of art (he translated Winckelmann as well as Rousseau), a study of the antique probably led to a wider interest in ancient art, embracing forms of primitive art; so that eventually he could find himself illustrating Homer and Norse legends concurrently. This was the sort of material on which the Romantics thrived.

What the painter finds worthy of interest in his literary source varies enormously from generation to generation as well as from one individual artist to another. The attitude of the painter to the poet frequently tells us much about the artistic milieu in which the former lived, as well as providing valuable information concerning his creative work in general. In order to attain a more detailed assessment of the artist's position in relation to his poetic source and in order that a general picture of the artistic climate of the age may be achieved, frequent reference is made throughout the book to the opinions expressed by poets and men of letters on the subject of Milton's poetry.

Addison's *Spectator* essays on the imagination, in which Milton is frequently cited as an example, 'laid the foundation of the whole romantic aesthetic in England'.[9] Yet Addison's criticism of Milton, like Lessing's assessment of Shakespeare a generation later, comprises a justification of the poet's greatness based on the argument that his writing accords essentially with the classic canon. The influence of Addison's writing on Milton was widespread in this country and in France. In 1734 Jonathan Richardson wrote: 'Milton's true character as a writer is that he is an Ancient, but born two thousand Years after his time'.[10] This was the light in which Milton was regarded at least until the end of the eighteenth century.

In the work of the 'pre-romantic' artists, where romantic elements are grafted onto the fundamentally classical creation, there sometimes seems to be a reaching out to Miltonic subject-matter in the hope of finding there a compromise between the antique and the modern. The subject-matter accords with the demands of the classical code, but there is a breadth of presentation which to some extent liberates the illustrator. It is significant that many subjects taken from Milton by Fuseli in the 1790s, or by Henry Howard in the 1820s, or William Etty in the 1830s, are not immediately recognizable as Miltonic. In his Milton Gallery Fuseli frequently chose to illustrate the epic similes in *Paradise Lost*; scenes such as 'Ulysses between Scylla and Charybdis', for example. Likewise 'The Gardens of Hesperus' referred to at the end of *Comus* was a popular subject with artists like Howard and Etty.

Further evidence of the wish for a compromise between the antique and the modern may be found in the work of Flaxman, an artist who associated closely with the group comprising Blake and Fuseli and other Milton enthusiasts but who, despite his occasional tentative drawings of falling angels and Satanic figures, never wholeheartedly joined the Milton worshippers. Flaxman's only Milton illustrations were to the selection of his least 'sublime' poems: Cowper's translation of the Latin Poems.[11] Flaxman was a passionate devotee of Swedenborg and it is not improbable that his own religious feelings deterred him from the interpretation of such a biblically orientated poem as *Paradise Lost*. Flaxman was also much accustomed to illustrating genuine classical literature. Attuned to Homer and Hesiod in the original, a direct experience which most of his contemporary illustrators did not enjoy, he found the Milton of passion and violence so much admired by his associates almost impossible to accept.

The attitude of the early romantic artists to Milton's poetry is, therefore, a subtle and difficult thing to assess fully. The gradual development of admiration for Milton's work into the mature and fully appreciative understanding displayed by artists in the nineteenth century is symptomatic of the much wider growth of artistic sensibility in English culture generally at this period, a growth which we are accustomed to loosely name the Romantic Movement. Milton's poetry may thus be said to provide the norm in a study of the development of ideas in the pre-romantic era and during the period of English Romanticism proper. As Professor Svendsen has said in reference to a study of some illustrators of *Paradise Lost*:

As we see more deeply into the poem and into the style, the elements, the method of the illustration, into the bearing of their separate ages and outlooks, we move to a heightened sense of the interrelation of the arts; and thus we are living an experience in cultural history.[12]

European artists in the eighteenth century exhibited an increasing number of pictures illustrating episodes of national history, especially those concerning a struggle for Liberty. Pictures like Reynolds's 'Ugolino and his Sons', West's 'Death of General Wolfe', Wilhelm Tischbein's picture of 'Konradin of Swabia Listening to his Sentence of Death in Prison' (1781) and Fuseli's 'Oath on the Rutli' are all manifestations of this increase. The development of such subjects came to full maturity in the nineteenth century with Delacroix's nationalistic pictures. In England the enthusiasm for themes of national liberty was exemplified in Lawrence's portraits of war heroes in the Waterloo Chamber in Windsor Castle (1814–1819), Wilkie's 'Maid of Saragossa' (1829), David Scott's 'The Russians Burying their Dead' (1832), Haydon's portraits of Wellington and Maclise's 'Meeting of Wellington and Blücher' and 'The Death of Nelson' of the 1850s. However, some of this enthusiasm found an outlet in pictures based on scenes from Milton's life. Though these biographical pictures are not, strictly speaking, the subject of this book, they should be mentioned as being one result of the crystallization of the concept of Milton the man as a great revolutionary, nonconformist protagonist of liberty which was current in the early nineteenth century. The other result was a great wave of illustrations to Milton's poetry.

In 1789 Boydell was thinking in terms of a school of English history painting when he commissioned his Shakespeare Gallery. In the introduction to his catalogue he wrote: 'I believe it will be readily admitted that no subject seems so proper to form an English school of Historical painting as the scenes of the immortal Shakespeare . . .' The extent to which subjects from Milton also provided a great storehouse for the history painter in the traditional, academic, grand style can be seen in accounts of the exhibition (1843) of cartoons by competitors for the decoration of the new Houses of Parliament, the great new national monument. The drawings had to be 'executed in chalk or charcoal, not less than ten nor more than fifteen feet in their longest dimension; the figures to be not less than the size of life, illustrating subjects from British History or from the works of Spenser, Shakespeare or Milton'.[13] The choice of Spenser and Shakespeare as well as Milton is not unexpected and we shall have occasion subsequently to refer to this triumvirate. Evidently Milton was considered by competitors as the most fruitful source of subject-matter. Forty cartoons illustrating subjects from Milton were shown as compared with twelve from Shakespeare and eleven from Spenser. These three writers therefore provided the subjects for sixty-three out of a total of one hundred and forty cartoons.[14] The study of the illustrations to Milton during this period should, therefore, tell us much about the developing English school of historical painting.

Although it cannot be denied that many of the artists concerned with illustrating editions of Milton were minor talents, it is true to say that during the latter part of the eighteenth and the early part of the nineteenth centuries most English artists whose work is now considered of intrinsic interest (as opposed to those who sometimes achieved more fame in their lifetimes) at some time or other painted or drew subjects from Milton's poetry. The examination of illustrations to Milton during this period can thus be amply justified by the consequent broadening of our knowledge of each individual artist.

The history of book illustration is a somewhat neglected aspect of English art. The first illustrated edition of *Paradise Lost* was published in 1688 by Jacob Tonson. This was the time when, due to the efforts of publishers like Hanmer, Tonson and, later, Joseph Johnson and Septimus Prowett, an English school of post-medieval book illustration was established. Although this book is concerned with the artists who illustrated Milton's work, the importance of the publishers who commissioned sets of illustrations to Milton's poetry should not be underestimated.

A study of illustrated editions of Milton's work covers the period from the late seventeenth century, when predominantly foreign artists as well as printers were engaged in the production of illustrated books, to the latter part of the nineteenth century. A maturing of the illustrator's interpretation and technique is seen during this span of time concurrently with a growth away from the tradition of biblical illustration, a tradition which was frequently plundered by the early illustrators of *Paradise Lost*, and progress towards an ability to invent an original design which would not only accompany but also clarify the text. As C. H. Collins-Baker has said, this was not achieved until,

almost all the processes of engraving had been tried, and perhaps the most appropriate method for illustrating Milton's *Paradise Lost* had been found in mezzotint. For heroic figures in close-knit design, and for imperial gesture, no process of engraving could be better than pure woodcut or line engraving. But Milton conceived more than noble figures and majestic action . . . Not until Turner had revealed landscape was the way open to Milton illustrators to create a world in accord with Milton's conception. Then, as John Martin showed, following the lead of Turner's *Liber Studiorum*, the incomparable resources of mezzotint afforded for a Miltonian world what no other process of engraving could have done . . .[15]

In order to minimize the complications attendant on any study of cultural developments during such a large span of time, it must be initially established that we are dealing with three different genres of pictorial art. The engraved plate belonging to a set of illustrations commissioned by a publisher is the most frequently encountered genre. Secondly there is the canvas painted for exhibition, generally at the Royal Academy; and it should be remembered that this type of painting in the nineteenth century was a peculiarly public and ostentatious art upon which, as a rule, an artist's reputation was entirely dependent. Lastly there is what could be called 'private' art: that vast number of drawings and sketches, never intended for public viewing or for sale, which often reveal aspects of an artist's talent not apparent in his exhibited work. These different genres reveal sometimes completely different qualities even in the work of one man. In the case of Romney, for example, one would never infer from his exhibited portraits the qualities inherent in his sketches. Sometimes one genre of work by one man divulges much about another. Stothard's drawings of subjects from *Paradise Lost*, when compared with the engravings after his work which appeared in numerous editions, reveal how much can be lost in the transition from drawing to engraving. Sometimes we only know one genre of an artist's work, whilst in other cases works are known on Milton subjects in all three genres by one artist. Of Burney's work we know only what appeared in published form, whilst in the case of Fuseli we have examples of Miltonic work from all three categories. Prints and drawings are, of course, invaluable evidence for the appearance of lost canvases.

Each of the three types of Milton illustration necessitates a different approach and different standards of evaluation. To consider first the group comprising plates in printed editions of Milton's poems, there are a number of more or less obvious questions to be taken into account. With what degree of care and comprehension has the artist approached the text? Here one comes upon the problem of the numerous possible interpretations of the text, a problem that is aggravated by the fact that the elucidation of literary works tends to fluctuate according to fashions which are often dependent on quite external factors. Does the artist really illuminate the text or does he merely adapt a standard biblical or classical image to suit the context? Does the artist variegate his choice of scene or does he just follow in the tradition of one established scene per book? Are the interpretation and style consistent? Has the artist designed plates suitable for publication or are his illustrations distracting by having been designed or executed in a manner more suited to some other medium? In cases where more than one artist is responsible for the illustrations, have the artists concerned consulted each other over questions of style and interpretation or is the set of plates spoilt by ineptitude and confusion? In short,

we ask a fresh creative act in which the painter either captures the essence of his subject as we conceive it or so transmutes his subject that we are required to see it anew. Our explication of the picture is consequently both dependent and independent. Nor is this an impressionistic response whereby we substitute for the act of criticism our feelings as aroused by poem or picture or both together. Just as we must master the wide and deep vocabulary of the poem, its many parts and their subtle implications from their own time, so must we master the vocabulary of the picture. The elements of the painting are semantic gestures, and like those of the poem are dependent in their relation to the artist's total climate and independent in their nature as acts of imagination—with this difference, that the critic works always within a double vocabulary, the poet's and the painter's.[16]

Works within the categories of sketches or exhibited canvases, may have been created independently of any commissioned series of illustrations and in such cases Milton's poetry may have simply provided a starting point for an essay in imaginative painting. Clearly in this eventuality there is little point in trying to trace too close a relationship with the text. It is more helpful to regard the artist as inspired by Milton's poetry rather than as an illustrator in a strict sense of the word. This makes it difficult sometimes to see clearly the limits of the subject. In the case of an artist like John Martin, who painted a large series of subjects from Milton and who, moreover, was inordinately fond of subjects from the Old Testament, a familiarity with his pictures from Milton renders the critic more sensitive to Miltonic elements in pictures by Martin which have no immediate connection with the poet. In fact the influence of Milton's poetry on an artist who delights in grandiose, sombre scenes is not confined to such an artist's illustrative work. Among Martin's predecessors and contemporaries are artists who painted pictures easily identifiable as Miltonic, many of which, accompanied by long quotations, were catalogued by the Royal Academy. But the fashion for tagging long quotations onto pictures, frequently—it would seem—as an afterthought, tends to confuse the issue. Without foreknowledge one would hardly recognize 'Morning among Coniston Fells' (R.A. 1798) by J. M. W. Turner as an illustration to *Paradise Lost*, Book V, and yet Turner appended the quotation: 'Ye mists and exhalations now arise.' Nor is this an isolated instance. Turner read Milton and extracted quotations which would suit his landscape scenes. Quotations from his own exaggeratedly Miltonic poetry succeeded these after 1813.

The necessity for establishing a clear foundation of criteria on which to work is obvious. Yet at the same time, despite the risk of appearing to desire compromise at every point, it must be said here that the genres and the principles laid down here cannot be applied absolutely rigidly without the danger of misrepresentation. No artist works to rules for the benefit of the art historian. The differences of approach to commissioned illustrations on the one hand and pictures inspired by Milton's works on the other hand are real and necessary. But which group a work is placed in for the purposes of critical assessment must depend on the general nature of the work of art rather than its strict categorical type. This can best be seen in the case of Blake. His illustrations to Milton (though not in fact published until this century) were clearly intended for publication in his lifetime. Yet each one of Blake's illustrations to *Paradise Lost* is so complete and original as a work of art that it would be absurd not to consider it as an independent masterpiece. Professor Svendsen sums up the ideal medium between the pedantic book plate and the imaginative venture, the final result of which bears little recognizable relationship with its source:

A persuasive illustration does not merely or necessarily take account of everything in the passage or conform to the conception of the critic. We cannot confine the success of the illustration to accuracy of this kind any more than we can judge the merit of Shakespeare's image of Cleopatra by his fidelity to Plutarch. The painter is to the poem as an actor is to a playwright or a performer to a composer . . . The true literary painter is a myth-maker. He provides a formulation with which we can precise and amplify our own, or with which we can assert its special features.[17]

J. W. Good has formulated a most helpful table showing the relative popularity of Milton's various writings between 1680 and 1840.[18] Although this table does not distinguish between illustrated and unillustrated editions it provides a general guide to the demand for Milton's writings. Between 1740 and 1820 one hundred and two editions of *Paradise Lost* were published as compared with sixty editions of *Paradise Regained*, fifty-three of *Samson Agonistes*, sixty-four of *Comus* and fifty-six of the *Complete Poems*. The most fruitful years were 1750–70 and 1790–1800. The supreme popularity of *Paradise Lost* is obvious; it was: 'the poem of central interest, far more than the final summary would seem to indicate . . . The truth, whatever its bearings upon the Milton question, is that the English people of this period invested their Milton money pre-eminently in *Paradise Lost*.'[19]

The same pattern of relative popularity occurs in the editions which were illustrated. Excluding reprints of the same sets of illustrations and foreign editions of the *Collected Works*, twenty of *Paradise Lost*, four of *Paradise Regained* on its own, and five editions of the minor poems were published. Of all these, only four editions appeared before 1750.

The question of foreign editions need only be briefly mentioned here. There were a number of editions of Milton's poems which were illustrated by English artists and published, in English, abroad. These are regarded for the purpose of this study as English editions. Nevertheless, the influence of Milton's poetry on the Continent, especially through the medium of John Martin's illustrations, was considerable. This is a case in which a poet inspires a painter whose work in its turn becomes popular with writers. The figure of Satan as conceived by Milton was admired by the Romantics abroad as much as in England. Charles Baudelaire in his *Journaux Intimes* wrote:

Je ne conçois guère un type de Beauté ou il n'y ait du malheur. Appuyé sur—d'autres diraient obsedé par—ces idées, on conçoit qu'il me serait difficile de ne pas conclure que le plus parfait type de Beauté virile est Satan—a la manière de Milton.[20]

Discussing the impact which the paintings of Martin and of the

French artist Leopold Robert made on the imagination of the romantic writer, J. Seznec writes:

Hugo's famous piece *Les Orientales* reads like a description of Martin, and indeed Sainte Beuve brings them together. Michelet, Théophile Gautier, Nerval, the young Flaubert, all refer to those great biblical melodramas. Even musicians are affected: Berlioz has Martinian nightmares.[21]

Statistics relating to all publication of Milton's work, illustrated and otherwise, give us a general idea of the popularity of the poet, but in order to see, more precisely, his importance as a source of subject-matter for artists it is necessary to consult exhibition catalogues.[22] Between 1769 and 1865 one hundred and eighteen works based on scenes from *Paradise Lost* were exhibited. Only one artist exhibited a picture of *Paradise Regained*, but sixty-eight scenes from *Comus*, fifty-eight scenes from the minor poems and eight exhibited representations of *Samson Agonistes* appear. In addition to these, twenty-four pictures illustrating some incident in Milton's life were exhibited. The total number of artists involved in this output was one hundred and twenty-nine, of which only twenty-seven exhibited more than two Milton subjects.

A number of qualifying observations should be made about these figures. They give, of course, no indication of the period before 1769, the year when the Academy was founded. Although there was probably in any case an increase in Milton illustrations after about 1760, the large number of minor artists whose Milton pictures feature in the Royal Academy catalogues and whose work is now quite lost and unknown would indicate that there were probably, besides the well-established figures of Hogarth and Francis Hayman, a corresponding number of lesser known artists of whose pre-1769 Milton pictures no documentation has survived. Of the minor artists working after 1769 who appear in the catalogue, many are impossible to trace as individuals and their work based on Milton has been lost and forgotten. These figures, moreover, do not take into account the work of artists like Burney who were primarily book illustrators and who rarely exhibited canvases, nor do they include drawings or engravings. More significant is the inevitable exclusion of individuals who worked, like Blake, outside the academic fold or of artists like Fuseli who exhibited independently. Decorative schemes involving pictures based on Milton like those at Vauxhall and Westminster Palace, Blake's portraits in the Library at Felpham, Rysbrack's bust for the temple of British worthies at Stowe (1732), De Loutherbourg's 'Eidophusikon' of

1782, William Calder Marshall's drawing-room chimney-piece design (R.A. 1848, described in the catalogue as follows: 'The frieze represents Shakespeare's seven Ages, treated in arabesque; the foliage is budding in fancy, withering in old age; on the pilasters are "L'Allegro" and "Il Penseroso", the whole is surmounted by statues of Cupid and Psyche'), all these are necessarily excluded from the Royal Academy statistics. It is clear, therefore, that the actual quantity of material is much greater than these figures indicate.

Whether a subject derives from Milton or from the Bible is not always clear from the Academy catalogues. Pictures entitled simply 'Adam and Eve' or 'Samson and the Philistines' could be based on either. Unless there is substantial reason for believing the picture to have a Miltonic source (as in the case of a picture exhibited along with a series based on Milton) such works are not included in this survey. Subjects exhibited simultaneously with Milton pictures can sometimes contribute to our understanding. They can give us some idea of the nature of a Milton picture if this has been lost. For example, a scene from *L'Allegro* or *Il Penseroso* might be exhibited by an artist whose usual subjects were nymphs, fairies or anything agreeable, ephemeral and capable of conveying sentiment. In other cases the choice of subject gives some indication of the reason for the artist's interest in the poet. For example, the painter Eyre Crowe (A.R.A.) exhibited in 1859 (R.A.569) a picture entitled 'Milton Visiting Galileo in the Prisons of the Inquisition'. This choice of subject doubtless originated in the nineteenth-century romantic interest in the radical and liberal aspects of Milton's character. The new humanistic concern with freedom of speech and human rights generally, as well as practical contemporary interest in the plight of prisoners, can be seen in the choice of location. Romney, Fuseli and others drew melodramatic prison scenes, and the Inquisition with its legendary evil priests was all too familiar to readers of the Gothic horror novel. The simultaneous humanist, romantic and literary interest is more firmly established when we look a little further and discover that between the 1850s and the end of the century Eyre Crowe exhibited 'Slaves for Sale—Virginia', 'The Foundling Hospital' (both titles which suggest a background full of pathos and similar to that in the Milton picture) and 'Shelley at Marlowe Writing the Dedication of *The Revolt of Islam* to his Wife' (another work of literary biographical interest).

The picture of Shelley and his wife is typical of its period. As the subject of 'Milton dictating *Paradise Lost*' goes well back into the eighteenth century it is fair to assume that the development of this

sort of literary-domestic picture, of which 'Spenser Reading the
Fairy Queen to his wife and Sir Walter Raleigh' (R.A. 1846—a
scene, surely, of doubtful historical authenticity!) by Marshall
Claxton must have been a typical example, probably originates
with the Milton biographical pictures.

A brief look at the pictures exhibited alongside Milton illustrations certainly confirms the assumption that Spenser, in the nineteenth century, was as popular a source as Milton and Shakespeare.
Macklin in his introduction to the 1790 catalogue of the 'Gallery of
Poets by the Artists of Great Britain' says:

> I did not confine my views to any particular author, because I conceived
> that, by embracing them all, a more extensive field presented itself for
> the exertions of fancy, and afforded room for a more diversified display
> of excellence. The sublime and superhuman descriptions of Milton, the
> enchanted regions of Spenser, the pathos and humour of Shakespeare,
> and the rustic scenery of Thomson, presented inexhaustible sources of all
> that could astonish, interest or entertain.

Quotations from Thomson's poetry frequently recur in the Royal
Academy catalogues. The other three writers are the great triumvirate of the literary painter. Milton was preferred by those with
an admiration for the sublime; but Shakespeare was regarded as
supreme. He alone is exempt from the rigid eighteenth-century
laws of 'nature', laws defined by Dr. Johnson and Pope. As Boydell
says in the introduction to his 1789 catalogue of the Shakespeare
Gallery:

> It must always be remembered that he possessed powers which no pencil
> can reach; for such was the force of his creative imagination, that though
> he frequently goes beyond nature, he still continues to be natural and
> seems only to do that which nature would have done, had she o'er
> stepped her usual limits.

It is not surprising, therefore, to find among the household lumber
of busts, enamels and reliefs of British worthies and works of great
literature—like that marble temple adorned with fine scenes painted
from Homer, Virgil and *Paradise Lost* which is described in an
imaginary visit to Parnassus in *The World*[23]—portraits like the one
painted by Joseph Strutt and exhibited at the Royal Academy in
1784. It is entitled 'Shakespeare, Milton and Spenser, with Nature
Dictating to Shakespeare'. Unfortunately lost to us, this picture
must have shown the same propensity for fusing the fine work of
art composed according to the classical canon with the elegant portrait, a fusion most effectively achieved in a work like Reynolds's

'Garrick between Comedy and Tragedy' of 1762. The practice of making oblique allusions to literature was common in portraiture. Hogarth's self-portrait (1745) includes in the foreground three thick volumes, one of which is a copy of Milton. Jonathan Richardson went further and painted a portrait of himself, his son and Milton (Collection, Lt.-Col. and Mrs. W. H. Bromley-Davenport).[24]

R. D. Havens has assessed the relative popularity of Shakespeare, Spenser and Milton in the eighteenth century and it is worth while here to quote what he has to say:

We find that between 1705 and 1800 *Paradise Lost* was published over a hundred times. The wonder grows when we look at the *Faerie Queene* which, we are accustomed to think, had approximately the same number of readers as the epic. If so, they must have borrowed most of their copies, for Spenser's poem appeared only seven times in the same period. Shakespeare to be sure is in a different category . . . But what is our astonishment to learn that the eighteenth century was satisfied with fifty editions of his plays. It is true that a number of these dramas appeared separately; but the most popular of these, *Macbeth*, was published by itself only thirteen times, whereas *Comus* in its original form saw three printings and as adapted for the stage over thirty. Furthermore *Paradise Lost* had the honour of being the first poem to be sold by subscription, the first English poem to appear in a critical edition . . .[25]

In addition *Samson Agonistes* was four times adapted for the stage and was used for an oratorio by Handel, who also wrote music for *L'Allegro* and *Il Penseroso*. *Paradise Lost* provided the basis of Haydn's *Creation*. *Lycidas* was presented as 'a musical entertainment' in memory of the Duke of York and parts of *L'Allegro* and *Arcades* were used as songs in Garrick's opera *The Fairies* (1755). Even if Shakespeare was slightly more popular than Milton with artists, it would seem that this preference did not show itself in the taste of the general public.

The fervour for Milton even spread to the stage, the very stronghold of the Shakespeare protagonist. Mr. Collins-Baker has suggested that the theatre assisted in freeing illustrators of *Paradise Lost* from the restraint imposed by biblical traditions.

In the first illustrations we are still on the fringe of gothic-baroque art, where something of the old unforced acceptance of biblical reality still remains. In the illustrations of the late eighteenth and early nineteenth century we have arrived at the dramatically wrought imaginings of Royal Academicians whose technical equipment was immeasurably superior to that of the illustrators of 1688. But between the academicians and that earlier acceptance the theatre had interposed its rhetoric.[26]

1 After R. Corbould, 'Satan's Return to
Pandemonium'

It is not at all clear just what the writer means by this. Does he
mean live theatre? In this case his point is not very meaningful as
the English theatre was fairly vigorous in the seventeenth century.
Does he mean illustrations of the theatre? These would, to all
effects, be synonymous with illustrations to Shakespeare, whose
plays were by far the most frequently depicted. In either case the
point is quite unacceptable. To begin with, the first illustrated
edition of Shakespeare of any distinction was the Nicholas Rowe
edition published in 1709 by Tonson, twenty-one years after the
Tonson illustrated *Paradise Lost*. T. S. R. Boase says that the frontispiece in the Nicholas Rowe edition was lifted straight from the
1660 edition of Corneille's plays.[27] Theobald's Shakespeare (1740)
was undistinguished and it was not till Hanmer's 1744 edition that
any degree of originality was attained. Meanwhile Tonson had
published in 1720 an edition of *Paradise Lost* magnificently illustrated by Cheron and Thornhill. It would seem, therefore, since

Medina's illustrations to the 1688 *Paradise Lost* show, in general, a fair degree of originality and a high standard of technique, that Milton illustrators were initially more progressive than Shakespeare illustrators.

In fact some of Medina's illustrations (1688) are noticeably theatrical, especially that to Book II in which Satan, with Sin and Death behind him, stands on a very artificial-looking raised foreground reminiscent of the stage. R. Corbould designed an illustration to Book X of *Paradise Lost* (1) which appeared in 1796. Mr. Collins-Baker himself has noted in his catalogue that this scene (in which Satan, with the gestures of a rhetorical actor, from a covered platform addresses his peers who are loosely clad in toga-like garments) resembles an episode from *Julius Caesar* or *Coriolanus*. If the theatre did have any influence on Milton illustrations it was in the early phase rather than, as Mr. Collins-Baker implies, around the turn of the century.

Despite the fact that Milton's work was so frequently adapted for the stage, the theatre seems to have had little influence in general on Milton illustrations. Theatrical portraits, that genre which by the 1740s (the era of Garrick) was firmly established as an essential and very considerable part of Shakespearian literary painting, are scarcely worth mentioning in the case of Milton. Admittedly it would hardly be appropriate to portray Garrick as Satan or Mrs. Siddons as Eve but, in view of the number of dramatizations of Milton's works, one might have hoped for Garrick as Comus or Mrs. Siddons as the Lady. This sparsity of theatrical portraiture is another reason for suspecting Mr. Collins-Baker's assertion. There are only two Miltonic portraits to compare with the Shakespearian tradition; Miss Storace as Euphrosyne appeared as the frontispiece to J. Bell's 1791 edition of *Comus* 'as performed at the Theatre Royal Covent Garden, in the year 1744'. Engraved by Thornthwaite, this was designed by De Wilde who, one may assume, is Samuel De Wilde who exhibited theatrical scenes and portraits at the Royal Academy between 1778 and 1821. Miss Storace appears as a clumsy figure dancing in rustic costume in a rural setting. The other work is known only from a reference in the catalogue of the Society of Artists for 1776. It is by Francis Wheatley, who worked with Mortimer and is best known for his picturesque scenes of peasants and cottages. It is entered as 'Mr. Webster in the Character of Comus'. Some of Milton's poetry lends itself to figure painting, but such works as Angelica Kauffman's 'La Pensierosa' (R.A. 1772), Reynolds's 'L'Allegro' showing Mrs. Hale as Euphrosyne,[28] and all the host of L'Allegros and Penserosos with

which the Royal Academy catalogues abound were primarily intended, for the most part, as portraits with a little additional dignity
and atmosphere rendered by a literary allusion.

Just as not all Milton's poetry was equally popular with artists,
so illustrators show definite preferences for certain scenes within
the chosen poems. Beginning with Medina's illustrations in 1688,
a tradition of iconography was gradually established. Mr. Collins-
Baker has compiled a most useful list of subjects and the dates at
which they occur between 1688 and 1850. His list, however, is a
little misleading as it includes reprints. The first two books of *Paradise Lost* were undoubtedly the most popular, 'Satan Summoning
his Legions' and 'Satan, Sin and Death' being the most favoured
scenes in these books. It is significant that foreign editions, like the
Paradise Lost published in France in 1836 and illustrated by
Flatters, frequently include only Books I and II. The choice of scene
for Book II is not at all surprising. Edmund Burke in *A Philosophical
Enquiry into the Origin of our Ideas of the Sublime and Beautiful*
wrote in 1757 that in Milton's description of Death '. . . all is dark,
uncertain, confused, terrible, and sublime to the last degree'.[29]
'Uriel and Satan' was the preferred subject in Book III followed
by 'Satan Watching Adam and Eve' in Book IV. For the subsequent
eight books the most favoured scenes were as follows: 'Raphael
Arriving in Eden', 'The War in Heaven', 'Raphael Discoursing',
'Adam Sees Eve Approaching', 'Eve Tempted' with 'Adam
Tempted' as a close second, 'Adam and Eve in Sad Discourse',
'Michael in Eden' and finally 'The Expulsion'.

The choice of scenes from *Paradise Regained* is limited by 'the
lesser degree of local colour and pictorial variety in the text, and
most illustrations tend to be biblical rather than Miltonic as a result.
'Sabrina Attended by Nymphs' and 'The Brothers Surprise Comus'
were the most popular scenes from *Comus*. The most recurrent
interpretations from the minor poems are personifications of
L'Allegro and *Il Penseroso*, often with very little reference to Milton.
The titles of these two poems came to be understood as synonymous with Mirth and Melancholy and were used in all sorts of
improbable contexts. Ten lines from *Il Penseroso* were inscribed in
the hermitage at Hagley Park[30] and at the end of a garden walk in
Surrey was 'a beautiful alcove called Il Penseroso'.[31] The sporting
painter John Boultbee exhibited at the Royal Academy in 1783 a
picture entitled 'Pensoroso, a stallion, the property of T. W. Coke
Esq.'. Generalized personifications apart, the most popular scenes
from the minor poems were landscapes to which, in the case of exhibited works, the quotations were often added as an afterthought

in preference to passages from Gray, Thomson or Young. The most extreme example of this practice can be seen in the case of George Lance, a painter of still-life scenes who exhibited at the Royal Academy in 1852 'The Marshalled Feast, Served up in Hall. Milton' and in 1856 the entry reads 'Fruit of All Kinds. Milton'. *Samson Agonistes* was seldom illustrated, but when it was, the artist generally showed Samson sitting alone, a tragic, blind figure.

It was usually weaker artists who chose to illustrate *Comus* or the minor poems, possibly they saw them as less of a challenge than *Paradise Lost*. Undoubtedly the most original and accomplished illustrations are almost always from *Paradise Lost*. Why did this poem appeal so much as source material for the artist? J. W. Good has said of *Paradise Lost*: 'As the embodiment of a powerful mystical conception of life, the poem held a didactic position second only to the English Bible, and was only a little less widely known.' [32] Didacticism and familiarity certainly had something to do with its popularity among artists. They conferred a certain universality on the subject and rendered unnecessary the sort of explanatory note or enslavement to narrative demand that harassed later literary painters like the Pre-Raphaelites. *Paradise Lost* depends upon varied and exotic imagery for much of its effect and from rapidly changing scenes it is possible to extract some poetic source for every mood. Jonathan Richardson, a painter and writer, realized this when, in his *Explanatory Notes* of 1734, he drew up a 'Table of Principal Subjects for Pictures'. These are descriptive passages from *Paradise Lost* suitable for adaptation to painting. Similarly, Samuel Palmer could inscribe in the front of his copy of the poem references to all the descriptions of moonlight. With the whole universe as conceived by Milton for its backcloth, *Paradise Lost* provides endless variety of detail and scenic effect and is thus ideally suited to the illustrator's requirements.

Each individual and each generation of artists found in Milton's poetry a formula for the expression of whatever mood they aspired to convey through pictorial means. The pastoral poetry of Milton appealed to Hayman and Roubiliac for its qualities of cultivated rusticity and to the enthusiasts of landscape gardening for its agreement with the principles of picturesque taste. Horace Walpole was always interested in the scenic effects of Milton's poetry, and in his *Essay on Modern Gardening* (1785) he is full of praise for Milton's Eden. The associations with orientalism in Milton's description of Eden must have exercised considerable influence on landscape gardening. It ranked so high because, as Lord Kames in his *Elements*

of Criticism (1762) observed: 'Milton describing the garden of
Eden, prefers justly grandeur before regularity . . .'[33] What began
as a fashion for the few eventually became almost a law:

Gradually it came to be a matter of common thought that Milton had
furnished a pattern for English gardens, and the adoption of his standards
was even insisted upon. One may find such titles as *Paradise Regained or
the Art of Gardening. A Poem* (1728) by John Lawrence and *Eden or, a
compleat Body of Gardening.*[34]

Just how divergent are different artists' attitudes to the same work
can be appreciated by comparing this mid-eighteenth-century enthusiasm for Milton's landscape description with the incentive to
imaginative naturalism which Samuel Palmer found in the same
passages more than a century later.

Milton's influence was not confined to the fine arts, but appeared
in all sorts of unexpected spheres. It is often difficult to find documentary evidence for decorative arts, but pictures from Milton
most probably appeared on china along with those from Shakespeare. Steele in number six of *The Tatler* describes Mr. Bickerstaff
visiting Sappho, 'a fine lady', who, through breaking her fan
'wherein were so admirably drawn our first parents in Paradise
asleep in each other's arms', has been encouraged to read 'the same
representation in two of our greatest poets . . .'[35] John Howes,
an enamel painter, is recorded as having exhibited two works in
enamel at the Royal Academy in 1787 from *L'Allegro* and *Il Penseroso*. Another such example of the popularization of Milton representations is a sculpture by V. Gahagen, 'Satan in Council, a design
for the end of a garden walk', exhibited at the Royal Academy in
1817. This must, indeed, have been a startling sight.[36]

R. D. Havens neatly sums up the reasons for Milton's popularity
with the general public in the eighteenth century:

In the combination of classicism with romanticism lay Milton's strength.
It was because his work preserved a balance between these conflicting
elements that it was peculiarly adapted to a period of transition; that is
what gave it an almost equal appeal not only to readers of opposing
tastes but to the two forces at war in almost all readers. Robert Lloyd
has summed up the whole matter in his line: 'Thus Milton, more
correctly wild'.[37]

Milton's work appealed to artists during the eighteenth and
nineteenth centuries for much the same reasons. Whilst steeped in
familiar classical and biblical traditions and conforming to the
literary expectations of the public, an extraordinary wealth of

imagery was presented with a quite unusual amount of force and passion, allowing some degree of emotion to enter the interpretation of the artist.

Notes to the Introduction

1. This subject has been thoroughly dealt with by J. Hagstrum in *The Sister Arts* (Chicago, 1958).
2. T. S. R. Boase, 'Macklin and Bowyer', *J.W.C.I.*, XXVI (1963), and 'Illustrations of Shakespeare's Plays in the Seventeenth and Eighteenth Centuries', *J.W.C.I.*, X (1947), pp. 83–108.
3. M. Merchant, *Shakespeare and the Artist* (1959).
4. D. Irwin, *English Neo-Classical Art* (1966).
5. Thomas Twining, 1789, quoted in R. Cohen, *The Art of Discrimination: Thomson's 'The Seasons' and the Language of Criticism* (1964), p. 220.
6. C. N. Talfourd, *Memorials of Charles Lamb* (1848). Quoted by M. Merchant, op. cit., p. 67.
7. T. S. R. Boase, *J.W.C.I.*, XXVI, pp. 148–9.
8. R. Rosenblum, *Transformations in Late Eighteenth Century Art* (Princeton, 1967).
9. G. Robertson, *Studies in the Genesis of Romantic Theory in the Eighteenth Century* (Cambridge, 1923), p. 241.
10. J. Richardson, *Explanatory Notes and Remarks on Milton's 'Paradise Lost'* (1734). Reprinted in H. Darbishire, *The Early Lives of Milton* (1932), p. 318.
11. J. Milton, *The Latin Poems* (1808).
12. K. Svendsen, p. 73.
13. T. S. R. Boase, *English Art 1800–1870* (Oxford, 1959), p. 210. The writer does not give his source for this quotation.
14. T. S. R. Boase, 'The Decoration of the New Palace at Westminster', *J.W.C.I.*, XVII (1954), p. 327.
15. C. H. Collins-Baker, 'Some Illustrators of Milton's *Paradise Lost* 1688–1850', *The Library*, III, no. 1 (June 1948), p. 2.
16. K. Svendsen, pp. 72–3. M. Y. Hughes, 'Some Illustrators of Milton', *Journal of English and Germanic Philology*, LX, 4 (1961), p. 1, writes in reference to Svendsen's statement: 'The case for the illustrator as a catalyst in the precipitation of a traditional myth in whose development the poem behind his illustration may be but a stage can be made very strong.'
17. Svendsen, p. 72.
18. Good, p. 141.
19. Ibid., pp. 141–2.

20. Mario Praz, *The Romantic Agony* (Oxford, 1933) (ed. 1962, p. 72).
21. J. Seznec, *Literature and the Visual Arts in Nineteenth Century France* (Hull, 1962).
22. A. Graves, *The Royal Academy. A Dictionary* (1906); *The Society of Artists and the Free Society of Artists. A Dictionary* (1907); *Exhibitions at the British Institution* (1908).
23. *The World*, no. 121 (April 24th, 1755). Good, p. 30, n. 10.
24. J. F. Kerslake, 'The Richardsons and the Cult of Milton', *B. Mag.* (Jan. 1957), pp. 23–4.
25. Havens, pp. 4–5.
26. C. H. Collins-Baker, op. cit., p. 1.
27. T. S. R. Boase, *J.W.C.I.*, X, p. 86.
28. Mrs. Hale does not seem to have had any connection with the Theatre. She was Mary, second daughter of William Chaloner of Guisborough, Yorkshire, and married in 1763 General John Hale, Governor of Londonderry. See G. Goodwin, *Thomas Watson, James Watson and Elizabeth Judkins* (1904), pp. 107–9.
29. E. Burke, *A Philosophical Enquiry into the Origin of our Ideas of the Sublime and Beautiful* (1756), Part I, Section III. Ed. T. Boulton (1958).
30. Joseph Heely, *Letters on Hagley* (1777). Havens, p. 28. The Hermitage was 'made with the roots of trees with a seat round it covered with matting, and in this quiet, retired spot were engraved Milton's concluding lines from "Il Penseroso" '. See E. Malins, *English Landscaping and Literature 1660–1840* (1966), p. 63.
31. *London Magazine*, XXXII (1763). Havens, p. 28.
32. Good, p. 222.
33. Lord Kames, *Elements of Criticism* (1762, 8th ed. 1807), p. 439. Quoted by Good (who has dealt with this subject in App. I), p. 237. The precedents for Milton's description of Eden (for he can never have known such a scene) are discussed by E. Malins, op. cit., pp. 1–3.
34. *The Critical Review* (Sept. 1758). Good, p. 363.
35. Havens, p. 23.
36. Probably the same as Sebastian Gahagen described by T. S. R. Boase as 'Nolleken's poorly paid assistant'. *English Art*, p. 130.
37. R. Lloyd, 'A Dialogue' in *Poetical Works* (1774). Quoted in Havens.

Early   I
Illustrators
of Milton

1688–1720

The history of Milton illustrations during the period 1688–1720 is pre-eminently an account of foreign artists who settled in England. Flemish and French book illustration in the first half of the seventeenth century was certainly of a superior quality in general to that executed in England. The fact that three out of four of the artists contributing to the two illustrated editions of Milton's poems published in this period were foreigners is no coincidence. The fourth artist, an Englishman, was responsible only for one design. Not only book illustration but English art generally in the seventeenth century was much enriched by the work of Protestant refugees from the Low Countries.

Milton died in 1674 and fourteen years later, in 1688, Jacob Tonson published the first illustrated edition of *Paradise Lost*. All the plates except one are by John Baptist Medina. *Paradise Lost* was first printed in 1667 so that the publisher Tonson (1656–1736), who acquired half the copyright of *Paradise Lost*,[1] was not slow in recognizing demand for an illustrated edition. The 1688 edition proved a sound business venture and went into many reprints. Tonson may be said to have been in the forefront of the growing body of people prepared to recognize the potential popularity of Milton's work. The first *Life* of Milton which contains any sort of genuine critical assessment was John Toland's, published in 1698, ten years after Tonson published the first illustrated *Paradise Lost*. Toland sets the tone of the period's rational yet enthusiastic taste for Milton's poetry: 'The unparalleled sublimity and Force of the expression with the delicacy of his Thoughts, and the copiousness of his invention, are unanimously owned by all ranks of writers.'[2]

John Baptist Medina, who has been called 'Kneller's equivalent in Scotland',[3] came of a Spanish family. He was born in Brussels, where he trained under Du Chatel,[4] and came to London in 1686 as a painter of history, landscapes and portraits. He seems to have spent most of his working life in Scotland where he was knighted in 1706. He died in 1710 and his practice was carried on by his son. Apart from his Milton illustrations Medina's only known surviving work is in the field of portraiture.[5] It seems, however, that he may have been engaged at some time on other schemes of illustration. George Vertue refers to 'several drawings by Sir John Medina for Ovid's *Metamorphoses* never graved'. He adds: 'The prints in Milton's *Paradise Lost* drawn by him.' He speaks as though he saw the drawings for Ovid in the Duke of Florence's Gallery of Painters.[6] C. H. Collins-Baker suggests that since the signature of M. Burghers (whom he assumes to be the same man as M. Burghers or M. Burgesse who engraved most of Medina's *Paradise Lost* illustrations) appears on one of two frontispieces to a Bible printed in Oxford in 1701, perhaps Medina designed and Burghers engraved both these plates.[7] However, there is no conclusive stylistic evidence so that one may conclude that Medina's Milton illustrations are his only certain surviving ones. *Paradise Lost* only was printed in the 1688 edition but there is an edition of *Paradise Regained* published by Tonson in 1713 the illustrations of which may be ascribed to Medina for reasons which will be discussed later. Several plates in the 1688 *Paradise Lost* are unsigned but are clearly by Medina. One plate is signed B. Lens, presumably Bernard Lens the elder (1659–1725), a mezzotint engraver working in London. The identity of the engravers of the Medina illustrations is really outside the field of this study. However, it seems probable that C. H. Collins-Baker's assumption on the single identity of the three signatories Burg, Burghers or Burgesse is correct.

In 1720 Tonson brought out a much grander edition of Milton's *Works* illustrated in elegant and fashionable style by Louis Cheron, a Protestant refugee who arrived in England in 1695. Best known now as a decorative painter he was employed by the Duke of Montagu and was much admired for his drawings. With Vanderbank he founded St. Martin's Lane Academy where Hogarth later studied.[8] Cheron had a distinguished early career, winning the Prix de Rome twice (on both occasions with 'Miltonic' subjects: 'The Expulsion' and 'Adam's and Eve's Punishment'), but he was evidently considered worthy of less distinction in England and was decried by Vertue and Walpole. He is indeed a maladroit painter when compared with Thornhill, Verrio and Laguerre. He collaborated with Thornhill and Laguerre in illustrating the 1717 Oxford *Baskett Bible* and with Thornhill in the 1720 Tonson Milton and Addison's *Works* (1721).[9] Thornhill, in addition to his contributions to the *Baskett Bible*, seems to have planned his own full-scale set of illustrations to the Bible, the pen and wash drawings for which are presented in the extra illustrated *Kitto Bible* in the Huntington Library.[10] It is evident, therefore, that Cheron must have been occupied as an illustrator to a much greater extent than his present reputation would indicate and that he was one of a group of painters combining decorative work with book illustration. These two artistic fields, which might be expected to demand very different talents, appear to have frequently appealed to the same artist.

A brief look at the semantic development of the word 'illustration' indicates, to some extent, the nature of the incentive which directed Medina in designing the plates for the 1688 edition of *Paradise Lost*. In the seventeenth century the word meant strictly to enlighten or to explain. Bullokar, the grammarian, in 1676 uses the word 'illustration' in this sense. It was not until the eighteenth century that the word was applied to engravings and its meaning was then extended to cover embellishment or decoration as well as explanation.[11] It is only in the work of an individualistic artist like Blake that one sees, after about 1730, any real insistence on the original explanatory meaning of 'illustration'. The wealth of closely observed and faithfully translated detail in Medina's illustrations makes it quite clear that Medina saw his function as illustrator to be concerned with explanation and enlightenment. Medina shows himself more familiar with all the intricate detail of *Paradise Lost* than any other artist. Yet this does not make him in any way pedantic in his approach. Apart from the rare occasions on which he was tempted to revert to biblical iconography, Medina seems to have benefited from the lack of a precedent and his designs as a consequence are a great deal more interesting and vigorous than those of many later artists.

Medina had the choice between two methods of illustration for *Paradise Lost*. The first possibility was the old biblical usage of one comprehensive design for each book of the poem, every design containing a number of scenes illustrating different episodes. This was a popular and, in skilful hands, an effective method of illustration especially where the text involved more than one level of reality. If mythical or heavenly personages were to appear it assisted the reader if the page could be implicitly divided to represent the different levels of existence. William Kent used this method to great effect in 1730 in his set of illustrations to Thomson's *The Seasons*. It is evident then that despite the fact that its antecedents lay in medieval art this method was not considered old-fashioned in Medina's day and survived successfully well into the eighteenth century.

The second method involved the choice of one single episode for one picture and was certainly a more effective method of portraying moments of crisis or of heightened dramatic appeal, as it involved little or no progressive narrative to distract from the chosen

2 'The Devil' from *Compendium Malificarum*

episode. Medina varied his method from book to book of *Paradise Lost*, and it is some indication of the artist's sensitivity and intelligence as a reader that he chose the single-episode method for illustrating Books I, II, VI, VII and XII. In these books Milton is less concerned with the subtle stage-by-stage movement towards the moment of crisis than with the grandiose panoramic scene as displayed in the description of Hell in Book I and the Battle in Heaven in Book VI or on the moment of significant conflict in Satan's arrival at the gates of Hell (Book II) or the Expulsion (Book XII). As originally issued the plates were all fairly large (circa 18·4 × 29·9 cm), so that the episodic method of illustration, when employed, was a very satisfactory way of showing the gradual progress of events in Eden. It was only when the plates were reduced in size by re-engraving on a smaller scale in later editions that this method of illustration failed.

Despite Medina's perceptive reading of *Paradise Lost*, his illustrations are more reminiscent of medieval and sixteenth-century manuscript illumination than anticipatory of the impassioned illustrations of the later eighteenth century. Satan, as he most frequently appears in Medina's illustrations—and, for that matter,

in Cheron's thirty-two years later—is a combination of the traditional devil and an Italianate satyr. He has large pointed ears, horns
and a tail and, notably in the illustration to Book IX (3), he has
satyr's legs and hooves and bat's wings. He also appears to have a
goatee beard. This combination is not at all surprising considering
the fact that right up to the end of the seventeenth century encyclopaedic manuals on the detection and prevention of witchcraft were
widely accepted and such manuals were illustrated with woodcuts
which show Satan as a figure who would have been easily recognizable in the Middle Ages. In the *Compendium Maleficarum* (1626)
Satan has the large pointed ears, horns, wings, tail and long claw-
like finger nails that Medina gives him (2).[12] The only fundamental
difference is that in the woodcut Satan also has a large bird-like
beak. The satyresque qualities which Medina's Satan possesses are
likewise not surprising in view of the great increase in Italianate
painting, especially in the decorative field, in England at this time.
The decorative 'Roman' style of Raphael's Vatican loggie was used
to embellish the new classical architecture of Inigo Jones in the

3 After J. B. Medina, 'Satan in the Garden'   4 After J. B. Medina, 'Satan, Sin and Death'

Queen's House at Greenwich right at the beginning of the seventeenth century. This sort of decoration was readily accepted by a public conditioned by the existing decorative tradition inherited from the Flemish pattern books of men like Vredeman de Vries. Scrolls, grotesques and Flemish strapwork were the customary decorative material for the sixteenth-century country house.

The assumption that Medina was familiar with and attracted to decorative work of this kind is borne out by the existence in his illustration to Book II of *Paradise Lost* (4) of a curious feature. Forming a sort of lunette above the three main figures in the scene are three very strange flying forms, hovering in the air. Two are facing the viewer and blowing bugles; the central one faces the cave and has its hands outstretched. All three figures seem to have wings, horns and fish-like tails. Their heads are distinctly diabolical, which suggests that Medina intended them as devils waiting upon Satan. However, there is no justification whatsoever in the text for the introduction of these three alien figures and it is unusual for Medina to depart from the text to this extent.

The central of these three grotesque figures is the least akin to the real animal world. It has great splayed wings like fronds of foliage instead of bat wings and its body terminates in a similar leafy form. The other two have little or no hair, but this creature has a great wavy mass of flowing hair. There is nothing as anti-realistic as this elsewhere in Medina's illustrations, but it does bear an extraordinarily close resemblance to the creatures which, based on the idea of hermae, are painted on the ceiling of a first-floor room at Royston, Thurnalls (1635–6).[13] These creatures have highly decorative wings, hair flowing out in a halo round their heads and distinctly fishy tails. The artist of the Royston ceiling is unknown and in any case it would be unwarranted to suggest that Medina knew this actual room. However, this is a rare surviving example of the sort of painting that was going on in public buildings, inns and such private mansions as Royston all over the country in the middle years of the seventeenth century.

Medina's illustration to Book II of *Paradise Lost* (4) contains another feature which is certainly based on a long tradition. Medina's Death inherits his image directly from the Dance of Death sequences of the Middle Ages. This is particularly evident when one compares the skeleton-like figure, grinning skull and deadly arrows that Medina gives Death with the Greek Fury which was Fuseli's concept of Death in 1776 (107), over a century later. A medieval figure of Death of the type to which Medina's so closely approximates can be seen in the *Hours of Mary of Burgundy*

(Flemish, c. 1477–82),[14] (5). The fourteenth and fifteenth centuries were obsessed with thoughts of death and mortality, but so were the eighteenth-century tomb sculptors and it is worth noting here that, besides looking back to the Middle Ages, Medina's Death looks forward to Roubiliac's monument to General Hargreave (1759, Westminster Abbey) and especially to his monument to Lady Elizabeth Nightingale (1761, Westminster Abbey).

Medina's love of detail is also a part of his inheritance from the Middle Ages. No other illustrator of *Paradise Lost* so lovingly and painstakingly fills in all the minute detail of Eden, except Bernard Lens whose illustration to Book IV (12) includes rabbits, goats, unicorns, a rhinoceros, a deer, an elephant, a dromedary and many other beasts.[15] In Medina's illustration to Book VIII (6) the sun shines forth with a benign, avuncular expression on its painted face, a delightfully unsophisticated touch on Medina's part. With a similar concern for verisimilitude Medina provides Adam and Eve in his illustration to Book IX (3) with a sort of primitive pruning hook with which to go about their work in Eden. In the plate for

5 'Death', from *The Hours of Mary of Burgundy*

6 After J. B. Medina, 'Adam's Story'

Book VI (7) Medina shows Leviathan spouting like a whale in the
lake of Hell into which Satan and his peers are falling. Helen
Gardner wonders whether this portrayal of Leviathan could be a
'rationalization of the familiar yawning mouth in Medieval representations of Hell'.[16] This hardly seems possible. To begin with,
the idea of the mouth of Hell and the idea of Leviathan were more
or less synonymous in the thirteenth century, so that for Medina
to place Leviathan in the lake of Hell is no rationalization but a
reversion to one of the most firmly established iconographic patterns in apocalyptic art.[17] The most natural source for an artist who
wanted to render a picture of Hell more vivid in the seventeenth
century would still be found in the traditional representations of
the apocalypse. Moreover Leviathan was seen from early times as
a figure of Satan whom Christ should overcome, so that his presence
in Medina's lake, in which Satan is to lie 'vanquished, rolling in the
fiery gulf',[18] is to be expected. However, Medina did not have to

7 After J. B. Medina, 'The Battle of the
Angels'

8 After J. B. Medina, 'The Son in Heaven'

look as far as this to justify placing Leviathan in the lake of Hell because Milton twice refers to his presence there, a fact which Helen Gardner seems to ignore. In Book I, writing with extraordinary fidelity to the tradition described above, Milton likens Satan lying 'prone on the Flood' to:

> that Sea-beast
> Leviathan, which God of all his works
> Created hugest that swim th'Ocean stream:

In Book VII, Raphael describing the creation of the birds, beasts and fish, says:

> There Leviathan
> Hugest of living Creatures, on the Deep
> Strecht like a Promontorie sleeps or swimmes,
> And seems a moving Land, and at his Gilles
> Draws in, and at his Trunck spouts out a Sea.

9 After J. B. Medina, 'Satan Rising from the Flood'

10 After J. B. Medina, 'Michael Comes to the Garden'

This is just how Medina portrays Leviathan with two large water spouts shooting high into the air.

It is unlikely that Medina ever studied under Rubens, but he may have learnt how to paint the nude from a study of Rubens's work. There is certainly a vigorous quality about the depiction of Adam and Eve which might be associated with the school of Rubens. Medina seems to have a better understanding of the human form and anatomy than Cheron and many subsequent illustrators whose figures tend to be very stolid and conventional in pose and gesture. Medina provides Adam and Eve with a great variety of poses. They are never just standing impassively in Eden but are constantly walking, gesticulating, acting. One is never in the slightest doubt as to exactly what each little scene signifies in the narrative—even when as many as five or six different scenes are enacted in one of the episodic plates. It is possible that some of the more baroque and mannerist elements in Medina's *Paradise Lost* may be the result of a familiarity with Rubens's renowned Banqueting House ceiling which was installed in 1636. The most obviously baroque device used by Medina is that of placing figures on floating masses of cloud in the upper half of the picture in a way which ensures that these figures are seen from below in a rather exaggerated perspective and hence dominate the scene. This is best seen in the illustration to Book III (8) which shows Christ in Heaven surrounded by an angelic host. There is not a great deal of opportunity for introducing architecture into illustrations of *Paradise Lost*, but in the illustration to Book I (9) Pandemonium appears in the background. We are shown one distinctly baroque wall, concave and broken by two immense round-headed arches. Satan sits under a complicated canopy at the top of a flight of curved steps. The final touch is provided by the statuesque figures silhouetted on the skyline of the building against the flaming sky. This, undoubtedly the most impressive of Medina's *Paradise Lost* illustrations, owes much of its dramatic impact to the extraordinary light effects which Medina has created and in which he has fully exploited the black and white medium. The very bright, white light which emanates from the glowing sky and which glares forth from the burning lake contrasts with the blackness of Hell and, particularly in the violent contrasts of reflected light and shadow on the body of Satan, creates an effect like that of a photographic negative. The sense of abnormal grandeur, of weird unnatural light and of great melodrama make this one of the most successful pictorial renderings of the scene in the history of Milton illustrations.

In the 1713 edition of *Paradise Regained and the Minor Poems* (which was probably illustrated by Medina) Samson, again at the top of a flight of elegantly curved steps, breaks a set of very baroque-looking columns. In the illustrations to the first two books of *Paradise Lost* (9, 4) Satan wears a strange sort of Roman soldier's tunic which must have become firmly associated with Satan in the minds of subsequent illustrators because they invariably show Satan in similar dress. One can only suppose that a Roman soldier's garb was the nearest the artist could get to a celestial warrior's battle-dress. Elsewhere Medina takes a typically mannerist delight in exotically fluttering drapery. In the illustration to Book XI (10) Michael's cloak, as though whipped by a high wind, flows from behind his right shoulder whilst the plumes of his helmet, with the licence for the irrational adopted by many mannerist artists, blows in absolutely the opposite direction. One might prosaically fear that Raphael descending (Book V (11)) is going to have severe difficulty in landing upright in Eden, such is the pretty tangle of drapery around his ankles; and Uriel descending in Bernard Lens's

11 After J. B. Medina, 'Raphael Descending' 12 After B. Lens, 'Uriel Descending'

illustration (Book IV) (12) is in a plight only a little less severe. In the latter illustration the

> Celestial Armourie, Shields, Helmes, and Speares,
> Hung high with Diamond flaming, and with gold

are affixed to the cliff wall with such ease and abandon that one might well expect to find beneath them a mannerist portrayal of Mars and Venus instead of a group of angelic guards at leisure on the borders of Eden.

Although in many plates Medina uses his cloud formations simply as architectonic structures, providing seats for the inhabitants of Heaven, in others Medina seems to be intent upon making his skies reflect or emphasize the drama that is going on below. The latter is best seen if we use Bernard Lens's illustration (12) as a comparison. In this we see a few cotton-wool clouds and one flat black cloud in the top right-hand corner, very heavily emphasized and looking as though cut from paper. This is obviously placed in this position by Lens in order to balance the heavy shadow which runs the height of the left-hand side of the page. Medina's clouds— though far from naturalistic in the nineteenth-century sense of the word—are never used in this purely formal way. Either they are fully conventionalized as in Book XII (26) or they incline towards naturalism and reinforce the mood of the scene. In the illustration to Book V (11), a peaceful scene in Eden, the sky appears calm. Compare with this the sky in the dramatic scene of the temptation (Book IX (3)), and we see, faithful to Milton, a great black cloud hanging over the proceedings and flashes of forked lightning.

Landscape plays an important part in Medina's compositions, a fact which is only fully evident in comparison with Cheron's designs in which the figures invariably occupy most of the space. We know that Medina came to England as a painter of landscapes among other things. Medina's Eden landscape backgrounds with their long panoramic vistas, rocky mountains and wiry trees remind one of the tradition of Northern Dutch landscape. Milton's descriptions of Eden, particularly in Book IV of *Paradise Lost*, must be among the most sensuous and vivid scenic passages of poetry in the English language. Later illustrators, particularly Martin (and Gustave Doré in France), fully exploited the exoticism of these descriptions. But in Medina's illustrations the plants in the foreground are native to the North European countryside, and the trees, though sometimes treated decoratively, tend less toward stylization and more towards naturalism. These landscapes are most closely related to the Dutch seventeenth-century landscape tradition of artists like Ruysdael with the occasional addition of a palm tree to create an Eastern atmosphere. Archibald Alison in 1790 writes of 'common nature . . . embellished and made sacred by the memory of Theocritus and Virgil, Milton and Tasso'.[19] He would not have recognized this embellishment in Medina's landscapes; they lack any such literary refinement. They are designed to be functional with hollows and hummocks where they are required to 'contain' the various episodes and are in no way ideal as one might expect landscape scenes of Eden to be.

Bernard Lens's landscape background to Book IV (12) provides a sharp contrast to the rocky, rather barren slopes of Medina's Eden and it is interesting to note that, although at first sight one might assume the great craggy cliff on the left of Lens's composition to be an inheritance from Altdorfer or Grunewald, Lens relies much more closely on the text in the question of the landscape of Eden than does Medina. He provides a lavish amount of foliage and some very convincing palm trees, and the whole composition is an effective translation into pictorial terms of Milton's lines:

> It was a Rock
> Of Alablaster pil'd up to the Clouds,
> Conspicuous farr, winding with one ascent
> Accessible from Earth, one entrance high:
> The rest was craggie cliff, that overhung
> Still as it rose, impossible to climbe.
> Betwixt these rockie Pillars *Gabriel* sat
> Chief of th'Angelic Guards, awaiting night;
> About him exercis'd Heroic Games
> Th'unarmed Youth of Heav'n, but nigh at hand
> Celestial Armourie . . .
>
> (*Paradise Lost,* IV)

Although there are several unsigned plates in the 1688 edition of *Paradise Lost*, it is clear from stylistic comparison that these are by Medina and that only the illustration to Book IV is the work of Lens. This one plate is certainly more delicate in general effect than anything by Medina, but we must attribute some of this quality to the fact that the engraver was different. All Medina's plates were engraved by Burgesse, Burghers or Burg, whilst Lens's illustration is engraved by P. P. Bouche and this may account for a certain clarity of line that is lacking in Medina's illustrations. Lens's nude figures, on the other hand, even allowing for the fact that they are so small, are inferior to Medina's.

On the whole Medina's illustrations to *Paradise Lost* provide an intelligent interpretation of the text. There are, however, two notable failures, in the illustrations to Book II (4) and to Book XII (20). We have already discussed Medina's reactionary portrayal of Death and the unwarranted presence of the three flying attendant creatures in his illustration to Book II. The scene in which Satan confronts Sin and Death at the portal of Hell is one of the most dramatic moments in the whole of *Paradise Lost* and it became the most popular single scene with later artists. We can congratulate Medina on having thought to leave Satan with certain angelic attributes.[20] Medina subsequently portrays him as increasingly animal and less angel in accordance with Milton's description of Satan's gradual degradation towards the lowest animal status in the universe. This is something essential to *Paradise Lost* but which very few illustrators have bothered with. We can also admire the Hellish and weird contrasts of extreme light and shade which the artist also uses for his illustration to Book I. It is this unnatural light which primarily differentiates these two illustrations from the rest. This is appropriate as the first two books of the poem are very distinctive and have tended always to be regarded as a pair. Nevertheless the illustration to Book II lacks the overwhelming sense of drama created by the single, huge figure of Satan arising in Book I (the only occasion on which Medina uses a figure of this size to dominate the scene). The illustration to Book II is conceived in formal rather than dramatic terms. The problem of how to join Sin's lower quarters to her torso, a problem which baffled most subsequent artists, is not solved. Medina simply draws a torso more or less sitting on a great pile of snake coils and hell hounds.[21] Satan stands on the remnants of a broken door, again a false feature since one of the main points of the scene is that Satan does not have to break down the gate (of which Medina's door would have been a totally inadequate representation anyway) but persuades the guardians of the gate, Sin and Death, to join with him in conquering Eden. Satan is positioned in the foreground with Sin and Death behind. From Medina's illustration one would scarcely guess that Sin throws herself between Satan and the stroke of Death to protect him. The sense of psychological tension and explicit melodrama is totally lacking. We know that Medina can achieve a significant composition if we look, for example, at his illustration to Book VII in which Eve's nervous, self-covering gesture while Raphael speaks to Adam anticipates her gesture of shame after the Fall. Medina possibly would have agreed with Addison that:

Most readers are more charmed with Milton's description of paradise than of Hell; they are both, perhaps, equally perfect in their kind; but in the one the brimstone and sulphur are not so refreshing to the imagination, as the beds of flowers and the wilderness of sweets in the other.[22]

It is clear that Medina did not read the text of Book II with his customary care. Cheron in 1720 renders this scene a little more successfully, but by then it had become well established in the repertoire of the sublime. As early as November 8th, 1717, in a letter to Pope about the relative merits of Homer and Milton, Bishop Atterbury testifies to the sublimity of this scene.

I challenge you, with all your partiality to show me in the first of these [i.e. Homer] any thing equal to the Allegory of Sin and Death, either as the Greatness and justness of the invention, or the height and beauty of the colouring . . .[23]

The other failure among Medina's illustrations is his plate for Book XII (26), a design which is totally foreign to the mood of Milton's expulsion scene. It is upon the idea of the 'felix culpa' that Milton's conclusion to *Paradise Lost* depends. The expulsion for Milton is not a negative, tragic event but a positive and hopeful though still unhappy one. This ambivalence is essential to the poem. Medina (like Bentley, the 'renovator' of Milton's poetry in his edition of 1732) turns to the traditional biblical expulsion scene for his model. Medina's illustration to Book XII is a close copy of Raphael's and Giulio Romano's 'Expulsion' in the Vatican Loggie, which is in its turn based on Masaccio's scene. Medina betrays himself badly in this final illustration. Not only does he ignore Milton's lines:

Some natural tears they dropd, but wip'd them soon;
The World was all before them, where to choose
Thir place of rest, and Providence thir guide:

and substitute a wrathful, tragic expulsion scene for this sad but hopeful one, but he also involves himself in all sorts of minor inconsistencies as a result. Eden as represented by Medina has always been an undulating countryside; why then depict Adam and Eve making their exit through a severe stone portico? The figures of Adam and Eve in this plate lack the natural grace with which Medina endows them in other illustrations. In Book XI (10) Michael appears in warrior's dress with a helmet and lance, in Book XII Medina, following Raphael, depicts him as an angelic figure in loose, flowing robes.

In 1713 Jacob Tonson published an edition of *Paradise Regained and the Minor Poems* with illustrations which, though considerably smaller in size than the 1688 Medina illustrations for *Paradise Lost*, appear to be by Medina's hand. They are all unsigned and no engraver's name appears. This edition of 1713 is inscribed 'The fifth edition', and as Medina's *Paradise Lost* illustrations frequently appeared in reprint without signature throughout the eighteenth century, it could have been intended to accompany Medina's *Paradise Lost*. An edition of the *Paradise Lost* with Medina's plates appeared in 1711 and, as it was common for a second volume of a writer's works to appear two or three years after the first volume, the 1713 *Paradise Regained* may belong to this 1711 reprint. There are many good reasons for attributing the illustrations to Medina. They could not possibly be by Cheron or Thornhill; they are so different in style, and in any case we already have one set of illustrations for *Paradise Regained and the Minor Poems* by Cheron. There was no other illustrator of Milton apart from Medina and Cheron until Hayman in 1749. The quality of the engraving is lower than that of the 1688 *Paradise Lost*, but this could be explained by the fact that it is a reprint. The frontispiece to *Paradise Regained* shows Christ victorious holding a cross and trampling on Satan (13). This scene is, in fact, iconographically very close to the Harrowing of Hell which was so familiar to the world of medieval art and appeared on the west fronts of so many Romanesque cathedrals in Western Europe. The artist has slightly modernized the image by surrounding the head of Christ with a cloud of Italianate putti, but the rendering of Christ remains iconic. This combination of traditionally biblical and modern elements is, as we have seen, typical of Medina's work.

However, the conclusive evidence for attributing this set of illustrations (they are clearly by the same hand) to Medina lies in the fact that Satan has the bat wings, pointed ears, claws and the strange shaggy growth of hair around the knees which Medina gives him in his illustrations to Books IX (3) and III (8) of *Paradise Lost*. Christ, moreover, is endowed with a benign expression and a halo from which points of light radiate. Identical features occur in Medina's portrayal of Christ in *Paradise Lost*, III (8). Medina does not choose one scene from each book, as he does for *Paradise Lost* and as most subsequent illustrators were to do for *Paradise Regained*. This is probably because he found the episodes of Christ's temptation in the desert rather repetitive when translated into pictorial terms. Instead, he provides one plate for Book I, representing the Baptism of Christ, two for Book II, one of which is not actually described by Milton.[24] 'The Temptation of Food' is a choice of scene to be expected, but there is only the slightest reference in the text to 'Christ in the Temple with the Elders' when Mary reminisces, 'when twelve years old he scarce had seen/I lost him . . .'; Medina was presumably attracted by the potential variety of background. Similarly Medina intelligently chooses 'Samson Breaking the Pillars' to illustrate *Samson Agonistes*. This is the only really dramatic moment in the poem. It is certainly the only moment involving real action and yet it only occurs in the messenger's description of the event at the end of the poem. Most subsequent artists chose the simpler task of portraying Samson sitting outside his prison. The poem *On Shakespeare* is illustrated with two portrait roundels, one of Shakespeare and one of Milton, not surprising considering Medina's accustomed *métier* of portrait painter. *L'Allegro* is represented by the personification that was later to become so popular, but Medina's final choice for illustration was a very minor piece of juvenilia, a poem called *On the*

13 After J. B. Medina, 'Christ Victorious'   **14** After L. Cheron, historiated initial

University Carrier. . . . He shows a rather clumsily drawn horse and cart driven by an elderly man of funereal aspect. As far as I know this is the only instance of this poem being illustrated.

Medina's illustrations are frequently both literal and pedestrian, but we have seen how, in most cases, Medina read and endeavoured to understand the passages that he was illustrating. His literalness may perhaps give us some idea of how Milton was read by men of his own century. Medina's plates are, moreover, of great interest as the earliest illustrations to *Paradise Lost* and the only set by which we can fully measure the development of illustrative concepts and the change in men's interpretation of the poet during subsequent centuries.

In 1720 Tonson published an edition of Milton's works containing one illustration by Thornhill and the rest by Louis Cheron. With a larger number of plates than the 1688 edition it is altogether a much more sophisticated production. The chief illustrations are headpieces occupying the upper two-thirds of the title page of each book of *Paradise Lost*. In addition there are historiated initials (14) and tailpieces to each book. The latter tend to be rather clumsy. It was clearly intended as a splendid and expensive edition rather in the manner of the Venetian illustrated book of the period, and this is probably one reason why it was only reprinted once as opposed to the twenty reprints of the earlier *Paradise Lost* between 1688 and 1784. Medina's illustrations evidently had more popular appeal.

The most noticeable feature of Cheron's designs is their lack of detail, the heavy rather fleshy treatment of the figures and the general breadth of approach. Cheron's activities as a decorative painter are probably partially responsible for the large size and monumental quality of his figures and for the rejection of background detail and the sort of episodic composition used by Medina. Each illustration comprises one incident only. Thornhill's illustration to Book I, his only contribution to the edition, can be distinguished from Cheron's only by a difference in his method of composition. Thornhill portraying 'Satan Summoning his Legions' (16) seems to delight in depicting a vast number of figures whilst Cheron prefers small groups of three or four.

The contrast between Medina's and Cheron's illustrations is very great. Cheron's work is most definitely a product of the eighteenth century. Individually Cheron's illustrations are much less interesting than Medina's as they tend to be repetitive in design, more dependent on biblical sources and less closely observant of the text. Yet, despite the historiated initials so reminiscent of medieval art, there is a grandeur, a new quality of sophistication in this edition which serves to emphasize how crucial were the years between 1699 and 1720 for the development of English art. Taken together, Medina's and Cheron's designs provided the foundation on which a tradition of Milton illustration was gradually built. In Hogarth's illustrations to Milton we shall see a fully baroque rendering of the scenes from *Paradise Lost* which when treated by Medina already contained suggestions of the baroque. In Cheron's frontispiece 'Milton Inspired' (28) and in some of the tailpieces (15) we have early examples of the type of rococo frame which was to become so popular later on in the century in the work of artists such as Thomas Kirk. The latter framed his illustrations to *Paradise Lost* with skulls, coiled snakes, doves and all kinds of symbolic machinery. The first signs of an interest in this sort of thing can be seen in the apple-boughs and the twining serpents which embellish the upper and lower parts respectively of the frame of Cheron's frontispiece.

In his episodic illustrations Medina tried to include everything that was of importance in the book he was illustrating. A rejection of the multiple-scene illustration means a reduction in detail. Therefore, we require of Cheron an illustration which has a unity that is more representative than encyclopaedic, a very difficult task for an artist of Cheron's skills. Later artists such as Fuseli and Blake achieve this unity by infusing their illustrations with their own individual and fervent interpretation, not of each individual scene but of the whole poem, so that each illustration is indubitably born of

15 After L. Cheron, 'Satan Disputes with the Angelic Guard'

16 After Sir James Thornhill, 'Satan Summons his Legions'

the whole poem with all its recurrent images and cross references. In the hands of Cheron the result of such a task tended to be some very dull, pedantic scenes. Cheron abandons the attempt which Medina made to convey Satan's gradual degradation from fallen archangel, to wolf, to toad, and finally to serpent. He portrays Satan throughout with a heroic human body, but with wings and diabolic countenance. Death appears as the traditional skeleton holding Father Time's scythe instead of a spear or arrow (17, 22). This again is a legacy from the Middle Ages when the attributes of Time, Saturn and Death became interchangeable.[25]

C. H. Collins-Baker has said that 'Medina may be regarded as having set the subjects to be illustrated'[26] in subsequent editions.

17 After L. Cheron, 'Satan, Sin and Death'

If this is so it is more likely to be a result of the fact that Medina chose to illustrate the most important scene from each book than the result of any dynamically influential quality of Medina's work. It would be interesting to see how closely Cheron follows the pattern set by Medina in the 1688 edition. As many of Medina's illustrations are episodic we shall consider the main scene which Medina chooses. For Book I (9) Medina chooses the line:

Forthwith upright he rears from off the pool.

Thornhill illustrates a later episode right at the end of Book I when Satan, already risen, is preparing to address his host (16). The drummer and bugler seen at the right-hand side indicate that Thornhill's scene takes place after the building of Pandemonium:

And Trumpets sound throughout the Host proclaim
A solemn Councel forthwith to be held
At Pandæmonium,

These lines lead us on into Book II. Thornhill has followed the text fairly closely but disregards the complexity of background in Milton's poem, giving no suggestion of a plain of fire or of the Palace of Pandemonium. For Book II Medina (4) and Cheron (17) choose the same episode when Satan encounters Sin and Death at the gates of Hell. We have already discussed Medina's rendering of this scene in some detail (p. 6). It remains to see whether Cheron was any more successful. The figure of Satan has more vigour and movement in Cheron's picture, but there is still no feeling of conflict. The figures just stand. Sin is a very unconvincing figure with a few snakes coiling around a fully human body, a very poor substitute for Milton's description. The artist shows her as blind although there is no mention of Sin being blind in Milton's poem and one can only think that this is another example of Cheron's confusion of iconography. Cheron's rendering of this scene is a little more successful than Medina's as both Satan and Sin are less static and he does try to show how the gates 'like a furnace mouth cast forth smoak and ruddy flame'. (Medina shows a very slight puff of smoke only.) Nevertheless, the total effect is not very successful. One has no sense of the earth-shaking and prophetic conflict that Milton describes:

So frown'd the mighty Combatants, that Hell
Grew darker at thir frown, so matcht they stood;
For never but once more was either like
To meet so great a foe: . . .

Nineteenth-century and present-day readers generally dislike Book III, reading in the speeches of God the Father to his son an unpleasantly pedagogic and authoritarian trait. Later illustrators generally choose 'Satan Flying' or 'Satan Addressing Uriel' as illustrations to this book. Medina's plate (8) includes Satan flying to Uriel, Adam and Eve, Satan landing on Niphates and, what really belongs to Book IV, Satan addressing the sun from 'the firm, spacious globe of this round world' and Satan seeing the scales tipped against him appear in the sky. However, the choice for the chief scene in both editions is the very passage where Christ offers to save mankind ('Account me man . . .') which modern critics so frequently find sanctimonious and pompous. There is no reference to the cross in the text, yet both, in deference to biblical tradition, include it. Neither shows God the Father though Cheron (18) shows a great light as an indication of God's presence. Medina's scene is a little later in time than Cheron's, when the Almighty has ceased speaking and angels sing to 'harps ever tuned/that glittering by their side . . .' The illustrations to Book IV differ radically. Cheron (19) shows a peaceful symmetrical scene with Adam and Eve in paradise in harmony with each other and with the beasts. The affectionate gestures of the dogs in the foreground reflect the relationship of the man with the woman. Bernard Lens's scene (12) of 'Uriel Descending' has already been discussed in detail so it will suffice here to say that Uriel never became a popular choice of illustration for Book IV. Far more artists follow Cheron's pattern of 'Adam and Eve in Paradise', a very sensible choice since Book IV is the first real chance presented to the illustrator of showing Adam

18 After L. Cheron, 'The Son in Heaven'

19 After L. Cheron, 'Adam and Eve in the Garden'

and Eve as the most important actors in the poem. However Lens does help to establish another tradition by showing in miniature as one episode of his illustration 'Satan as a Toad at the Ear of Eve'. Blake painted a fine interpretation of this scene, and the moment immediately afterwards, when Satan starts at the touch of Ithuriel's spear, was to become one of the most popular scenes in the whole of the poem. Both Lens and Cheron introduce a few representative examples of 'all kind/of living creature', but only the odd palm tree in Lens's illustration reflects the most exotic of all descriptions in Milton, 'Groves whose rich Trees wept odorous gummes and Balme'. He does make some attempt to show 'umbrageous grots and caves/of coole recess'. Cheron's paradise has most affinity with

20 After L. Cheron, 'The Battle of the Angels'

21 After L. Cheron, 'Adam Tempted'

a well-kept park belonging to an eighteenth-century English gentleman.

For Book V Medina (11) uses the scene of 'Raphael Descending' while Cheron shows what takes place later on when Raphael has dinner with Adam and Eve (33), a scene used by Medina for Book VII. The Battle in Heaven is chosen by both artists for the illustration to Book VI but Medina's panoramic view (7) is much more successful than Cheron's clumsily organized group of figures (20). Cheron gives the falling angels horns and pointed ears (Satan being distinguished by his tail), for which there is no justification in the text. The aim of the artist was presumably to distinguish the good angels from the bad. The choices of scenes for Book VII have

22 After L. Cheron, 'Sin and Death in Paradise'

nothing in common. Medina depicts 'Raphael Talking to Adam' and indicates the substance of the conversation in a series of little roundels depicting the inhabitants of Heaven about their business. Medina's vivid imagination is at work in the last roundel on the right which shows two angels tending a unicorn, that favourite of the medieval bestiary and a creature excluded from Milton's carefully considered view of Heaven. Cheron makes a valiant attempt at 'The Creation' (35), which is a scene invariably shown in Genesis illustrations but rarely chosen for *Paradise Lost*. (More will be said of this later in connection with Cheron's Bible illustrations.) Cheron's illustration to Book VIII is a very tedious near repeat of that to Book V. Medina shows 'Adam Recalling the Creation of Eve' in the presence of Raphael, who is not actually depicted though his presence is understood from the text. The monotony and repetition into which Cheron falls is thus avoided. In Book IX (21) Cheron shows Adam tempted by Eve and a dog howling, a foretaste of the savage greed that overtakes the whole of nature as one of the first results of the Fall. It is a great deal too restrained to be a convincing representation of this all-important scene. Medina's treatment is quite different (3) and, although it has less sense of design, his illustration is more convincing. Satan occupies the foreground of Medina's illustration to Book IX. This is appropriate as the book is as much concerned with Satan's triumph as with the fall of Adam and Eve whose activities appear in the background. Cheron's illustration to Book X (22) showing 'Adam and Eve, Led by Death and the Angels, Leaving Paradise' is again very weak when compared with Medina's. Both artists use the same

23 After L. Cheron, 'Michael Foretells the Future'

scene as a basis for illustration but their treatment of the subject differs considerably. How alarming and how evocative of the mood of the poem is the real juxtapositioning of Hell and Paradise which, in Medina's illustration, are divided only by a pack-horse bridge. From Paradise we can see into Hell where Satan's peers are indulging in triumphal revels. The only real weakness is that Medina, like Cheron, does not show Adam and Eve contrite as Milton describes them at the end of this book. It is important to understand their contrition as it is essential for subsequent developments. In Books XI and XII both Cheron and Medina ignore most of the visions that Michael sets before Adam and which comprise a large part of these books. Cheron shows a little more of the events in Eden in Book XI (23) than Medina does (10). Cheron's Expulsion scene (24) differs in composition from Medina's (29) but not in mood. If anything Cheron ignores Milton's 'So send them forth, though sorrowing, yet in peace' more than Medina and creates an entirely pessimistic expulsion scene.

It is evident therefore that Cheron frequently chooses completely different scenes from Medina and even when he is treating the same or nearly the same episode in the poem his approach is radically different from Medina's. One can only assume that if Cheron knew Medina's illustrations he was determined to differ and to create a new idiom. Cheron's illustrations are nearly always more skilfully composed than Medina's and the tailpieces and historiated initials make for a much richer general effect. Nevertheless Medina is the better illustrator, showing greater imagination and closer comprehension of the text.

24 After L. Cheron, 'The Expulsion'

25 After L. Cheron, 'Christ Tempted'

The latter part of the 1720 edition of Milton's works contains a number of illustrations also by Cheron, most of which are not very distinguished. These include a frontispiece and one illustration to each of the four books of *Paradise Regained*. The best of these is the illustration to Book III (25) showing 'Christ Tempted by Satan to Accept Worldly Power' and has rather more local colour with its background of fighting warriors than the other illustrations to *Paradise Regained*. The plate to Book IV is a reminder of *Paradise Lost* with Satan and his associates in diabolical shapes appearing in Christ's dreams. There is one main illustration to *Samson Agonistes* (26) in which we see most clearly the disadvantages of the rectangular design which Cheron invariably uses. This subject is

26 After L. Cheron, 'Samson and Manoa'

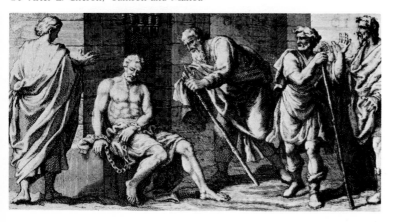

27 After L. Cheron, 'Lycidas'

'Samson Seated in Chains before his Prison with Manoa Pleading', and the figures, occupying the whole length of the plate, appear in one long row with little suggestion of recession to alleviate the frieze-like effect. The illustration to *Lycidas* (27) shows the poet receiving a crown of laurels from a classical figure, probably intended as Apollo, and is very strange in that it is an almost exact replica in reverse of the frontispiece to *Paradise Lost*, 'Milton Inspired' (28). The Apollo figure has exactly the same pose as Milton,

28 After L. Cheron, 'Milton Inspired'

and Lycidas himself has a pose closely approximating to that of the muse in the frontispiece. Cheron was not an artist of great originality and he tends to use conventional compositions as types which may be adapted to fit varying requirements.

The importance for the early illustrators of Milton of the tradition of biblical illustration (and in particular the illustration of Genesis) has been frequently referred to in this chapter. Is there, in fact, any close relationship between the work of Medina and Cheron and that of Bible illustrators of their period? In general the seventeenth- and eighteenth-century reader was very much more familiar with his Bible than was the literate populace in subsequent years. Medina is clearly interested in the religious significance of *Paradise Lost* in a way that is completely alien to many of his successors such as Fuseli, Barry or Mortimer whose interest in the Picturesque, in the Sublime or in Milton's use of classical myth was the basis for the attraction that the poem held for them. By the early nineteenth century Milton's poetry was admired for quite other reasons than the sound moral and religious truths which were thought to reside therein by eighteenth-century readers. The typical gentleman of letters in the eighteenth century admired *Paradise Lost* not only for the classical elegance of its style or the grandeur of its subject but also because it could instruct and elevate the mind of the reader. The Earl of Shaftesbury wrote of *Paradise Lost* in his *Characteristicks* in 1710 that: 'Our most approved heroick poem has neither the softness of Language, nor the fashionable turn of wit; but merely solid Thought, strong Reasoning, noble Passion, and a continued Thred of moral Doctrine, Piety, and Virtue to recommend it.'[27] In 1793 the poet and editor John Aikin wrote to his son that: 'A relish for the works of Milton is not only a test of sensibility to the more exquisite beauties of poetry, but a kind of measure of the exaltation of the mind in its moral and religious sentiments.'[28]

Medina was following the tradition of Genesis illustrations when he chose to illustrate *Paradise Lost* with multiple-scene illustrations. There are many Bibles illustrated according to this method. One such edition of the Old Testament which Medina might easily have known is that published in London by Henry Hills in 1660 with illustrations by an anonymous artist. Medina's concept of the landscape of Eden and Cheron's lack of exploitation of this feature of *Paradise Lost* has already been discussed at length in this chapter. Later illustrators such as John Martin and Gustave Doré concentrated on this aspect of the poem. It is interesting to note that Medina is not alone in his preference for an Eden that is less fertile

and lush than Milton's. A magnificent Bible was published in Cambridge in 1666 illustrated with 'chorographical sculps. by J. Ogilby'.
These are inscribed in Latin, French, Dutch, Greek, English and
German. This Bible was clearly a very superior presentation volume
and it seems unlikely that neither Medina nor Tonson, for whom
he was working, should have known of it. The illustrations are of
an unquestionably high quality, especially those to chs. II and III
of Genesis, which are full-page representations of an exotic Eden
packed with a variety of fruits, flowers, palms and acanthus plants.
That Medina knew the illustrated Bibles of his time there can be
no doubt. He probably contributed illustrations to them himself.
The 1701 Bible, the Old Testament plates of which were executed
by Medina's engraver, Burgesse, has already been mentioned. Far
more conclusive evidence lies in a Bible published at the Theater,
Oxford, in 1682, before the date of Medina's *Paradise Lost*. One of
the illustrations to Genesis (30) is an expulsion scene almost identical to Medina's design for *Paradise Lost*, Book XII (29). Stylistically

29 After J. B. Medina, 'The Expulsion'   30 Anon., 'The Expulsion'

31 Nicholas Chapron after Raphael, 'The Expulsion'

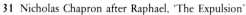

31 Nicholas Chapron after Raphael, 'The Expulsion'

the work is not unlike Medina's, though the other illustrations in the book are certainly not by his hand. It is possible that the illustrator of the Bible based his work on the same engraving after Raphael's 'Expulsion' as Medina used. But as the two plates resemble each other much more closely than either resembles Raphael's 'Expulsion', it is fair to assume that Medina either designed this plate or copied it in his *Paradise Lost* illustration six years later. In either case the un-Miltonic quality of Medina's illustration to Book XII is to some extent thus explained. There are a very few minor differences between the two plates. In the Genesis illustration Eve is turning her face towards Adam instead of looking ahead, and Adam and Eve have no leaves with which to cover themselves. However, the drapery of Michael's garments in the *Paradise Lost* plate is identical to that in the Genesis illustration.

In 1717, three years before the publication of Tonson's *Works of Milton* illustrated by Cheron, a Bible was published in Oxford with illustrations by Thornhill and Cheron. Many of the plates were used by Cheron as models for his Milton illustrations. The

32 After Sir James Thornhill, 'Adam's First Sight of Eve'

33 After L. Cheron, 'Raphael Discourses'

34 After L. Cheron, 'Angels Glorify the Lord'

frontispiece to the Book of Moses, 'Adam's First Sight of Eve' (32), is by Du Guernier after Thornhill and is composed in exactly the pattern which Cheron frequently uses in his Milton illustrations, especially in those to Books IV and V of *Paradise Lost* (19, 33). A triangular structure, built up of three figures, forms the centre of the design. This is reinforced by trees behind and supported on either side by animals, the favourite of which is predictably the familiar and frequently depicted horse. In the New Testament Cheron contributed a frontispiece to the gospel according to St. Mark which was engraved by Van der Gucht, the engraver responsible for most of the illustrations in the 1720 edition of Milton's works. This frontispiece (34) is composed of the same basic pattern Cheron used in his design for Book VII (35) of *Paradise Lost*. The only real difference is that in the Bible illustration there is a curtain drawn back by putti and three more angels. The cross serves much

35 After L. Cheron, 'The Creation'

the same compositional function as that in Cheron's illustration to *Paradise Lost*, Book III (18). The Bible has the same layout of page as the 1720 *Works of Milton*. The illustration occupies the top third of the page, and there are historiated capitals and tailpieces. All that is lacking are the rococo frames which would perhaps have been considered inappropriate in a Bible. This accounts for the biblical overtones in Cheron's Milton illustrations. Moreover, it becomes clear that both Medina and Cheron depended to some extent on biblical illustrations, their own or others', and that this dependence seldom contributed towards a successful illustration of Milton. In writing *Paradise Lost*, Milton was far from re-writing Genesis.

However, despite their inconsistencies and insufficiencies the illustrations to Milton's works by Medina, Lens, Thornhill and Cheron do possess a certain intrinsic interest to students of these artists, readers of Milton or anyone concerned with the cultural history of the period.

Notes to Chapter I

1. Helen Gardner, 'Milton's First Illustrator', *Essays and Studies*, N.S. IX (1956), pp. 27–38. Jacob Tonson was a most distinguished member of the literary society of his day, one of the founders of the Kit-Kat Club and publisher for Otway, Dryden, Pope, Addison and Steele.
2. Helen Darbishire, *The Early Lives of Milton* (1932), p. 179.
3. E. K. Waterhouse, *Painting in Britain 1530–1790* (1953), p. 102. I owe all my information concerning Medina's life and reputation to this source.
4. Dr. M. Bryan, *A Biographical and Critical Dictionary of Painters* (1873). Dr. Bryan states that Medina studied under Rubens. Medina would have been too young at the time of Rubens's death for this to have been possible. The reputation of Rubens in England after the painting of the Banqueting House ceiling must have been such that it would be worth the while of any young painter from the Low Countries to claim that he had studied under Rubens.
5. See, for example, 'George, Earl of Melville', Scottish National Portrait Gallery.
6. The Notebooks of George Vertue, *The Walpole Society*, XVIII (1929–30), p. 46.
7. Collins-Baker, *The Library* (June 1948), p. 8, n.
8. For a full description of Cheron's decorative work, see E. Croft-Murray, *Decorative Painting in England 1537–1837*, I (1962), pp. 243–4. For Cheron's part in establishing the academy, see N. Pevsner, *Academies of Art Past and Present* (Cambridge, 1940), pp. 124–6.
9. Croft-Murray, op. cit., p. 265.
10. C. H. Collins-Baker, 'Sir James Thornhill as Bible Illustrator', *Huntington Library Quarterly*, X (1946–7), pp. 323–7.
11. For a full discussion of the semantic development of the word 'illustration', see R. Cohen. op. cit., pp. 249–58.
12. In connection with the popular idea of Satan, see H. R. Trevor-Roper, 'Witches and Witchcraft', *Encounter*, May 1967, pp. 3–25, and June 1967, pp. 13–34.
13. Reproduced in Croft-Murray, op. cit., p. 117.
14. m.s. 78B12, fol. 221r. Kupferstichkabinett, Berlin.

15. The Creation of the Animals was invariably a favourite scene with medieval illuminators.
16. Helen Gardner, op. cit., p. 32.
17. E. Mâle, *The Gothic Image* (1961), ch. VI (11), writes: 'The mouth of Hell is the mouth of that Leviathan spoken of in the Book of Job. It will be remembered that the Almighty Himself addresses the Patriarch, describes the monster he has created and sternly asks him: "Canst thou draw him out with a hook? . . . Who can go into the midst of his mouth? . . . Who can open the doors of his face?" etc.'
18. Ibid., ch. VI (11): 'From early times the commentators on the Book of Job (of whom St. Gregory was one of the first) see in Leviathan a figure of Satan and all his works, and in the Middle Ages certain passages, interpreted with amazing subtlety had the most singular fortune . . . Honorius of Autun . . . wrote: "Leviathan the monster who swims in the sea of the World, is Satan. God threw the line into the sea. The cord of the line is the human descent of Christ, the bait is His divinity. Attracted by the smell of flesh Leviathan tries to seize it but the hook tears his jaws."'
19. Archibald Alison, *Essays on the Nature and Principles of Taste* (1790) (6th ed. Edinburgh, 1825, p. 64).
20.   '. . . His form had yet not lost
        All her Original brightness, nor appeared
        Less than Arch Angel ruind, and th'excess
        of Glory obscur'd:'
                                    (*Paradise Lost*, I)
21. Milton's description of Sin (*Paradise Lost*, II) does not offer any solution to the problem of pictorial representation of such a figure. This is the sort of description which, whilst very powerful, is almost impossible to fit into a straightforward narrative reading of the poem. Sin is simply not a realistically viable personage.

    'The one seemed Woman to the waste, and fair
    But ended foul in many a scaly fould,
    Voluminous and vast, a serpent arm'd
    With mortal sting: about her middle round
    A cry of Hell Hounds never ceasing bark'd
    With wide Cerberian mouths full loud, and rung
    A hideous Peal:'

Sin's ancestry is of a complexity which matches Milton's description of her in *Paradise Lost*. For Milton's sources in this matter, see: J. Illo, 'Animal Sources for Milton's Sin and Death', *Notes and Queries*, CCV (Nov. 1960), pp. 425–6; J. F. Gilliam, 'Scylla and Sin', *Philological Quarterly*, XXIX (1950), pp. 345–6.
22. J. Addison, *Essays on the Pleasures of Imagination*, no. 418 (June 30th, 1712) (*The British Essayists*, XII, 1823).

23. A. Pope, *Works*, ed. Elwin-Courthorpe (1871–89). Quoted in Havens, p. 17.
24. In 'The Baptism of Christ', a number of the hallmarks of Medina's style are to be seen: notably the baroque cloud formation, the dramatic single shaft of light which illuminates the scene and the fluttering drapery of the attendant angels.
25. For a full discussion of the iconography of Father Time, see E. Panofsky, *Studies in Iconology* (Oxford, 1939) (ed. 1962, pp. 69–93).
26. Collins-Baker, *The Library* (June 1948), p. 3.
27. Earl of Shaftesbury, *Characteristics* (1711) (3rd ed. 1723, I, p. 276). Quoted in Havens, p. 16.
28. J. Aikin, *Letter from a Father to a Son* (1800). Quoted in Havens, p. 23.

Milton & the Artists of the English Rococo

1724–1764

Where MARO and MUSAEUS sit
List'ning to MILTON's loftier song
With sacred silent wonder smit;
While, monarch of the tuneful throng,
HOMER in rapture throws his trumpet down,
And to the BRITON gives his amaranthine crown.
　　　　　Joseph Warton, *To Health*[1] (1746)

Not all writers and artists during the middle years of the eighteenth century made their rejection of the Ancients in favour of the Moderns so explicitly as Joseph Warton in this ode. Many joined Jonathan Richardson in regarding Milton and other great modern writers simply as late products of the Antique World. But most of the Milton enthusiasts of the age were, like Joseph Warton, concerned with upholding the right of the modern poet—in this case Milton—to the dignity of reputation normally reserved for the Ancients.

The artists primarily responsible for illustrating Milton's poetry during the period 1724–64 were all to some extent associated with Hogarth. They, like Warton, were adamant advocates of modern art and were anxious to free the art of their time from what they considered to be the tyranny of the Old Masters. This does not mean that their work was necessarily overtly anti-classical. As they were responsible for most of the Milton pictures of the period, and as their close association and collaboration one with another represents a new and significant phase in the history of literary painting, it is important to establish the exact nature of the relations between Hogarth's group and the current neo-classical views of the establishment at this time. Which aspects of these artists' work represent a protest against the tenets of the time? Which features of their work owe their origins to the coherent pattern of aristocratic, eighteenth-century thought?

It is ironic that the essentially neo-classical doctrine of 'ut pictura poesis' should have reached its culmination by the mid-eighteenth century not in the work of the neo-classicists but in that of the new, middle-class, 'realist' artists. It is strange to recall Pope's lines 'To Jervas':

Smit with the love of Sister-arts we came,
And met congenial mingling flame with flame;
Like friendly colours found them both unite,
And each from each contract new strength and light.[2]

and then to realize that the influence of Defoe on Hogarth and of Hogarth on Fielding was not something dependent on vague ideas of 'congenial mingling', but was a real reciprocation of ideas about life and the social functions of art. It was, in fact, a true alliance of the sister arts and one that was to prove most fruitful.

Hogarth thought most deeply about the relationship between visual arts and literature, for in the advertisement for 'A Harlot's Progress', Hogarth calls himself the author, not the artist. Moreover, the concept of the sister arts held by Hogarth and his acquaintance resulted in the real-life friendship and collaboration of writers and painters. Inevitably this concept and the art that grew from it depended to some extent on patronage and on art forms dominant at this time. A new, middle-class patron appeared in this period and helped to provide a market for the moralist-realist art of Hogarth and his associates. The demands of dominant art forms were one reason for the amazing variety of genres found in the work of these artists. Had Hogarth been accepted in the field he undoubtedly preferred, we should, most probably, have had no 'Rake's Progress' but only a collection of ill-executed history paintings.

Similarly the beliefs of Augustan writers such as Shaftesbury, Dryden and Pope that 'the proper study of mankind is man', and that 'the way to be an excellent painter is to be an excellent man',[3] had never been put into practice in such a literal way as they were by those two notable philanthropists, Hogarth and Fielding. Hogarth's series of engravings, 'The Four Stages of Cruelty', supported Fielding's campaign against murder and robbery and came out in the same year as the latter's *Enquiry into the Causes of the Late Increase of Robbers* (1751). The engravings of 'Industry and Idleness' reflect the view expressed by Defoe in *The Complete English Tradesman*, that idleness is a sin against the Holy Ghost.

This kind of moralistic doctrine of self-advancement is, in turn, reflected in the writings of Voltaire, Rousseau and Diderot in France where Hogarth's prints were sold with great success. The concern with social ills and conditions of life which gave rise to this active association between artists and writers resulted also in actual philanthropic activities. Fielding was a Justice of the Peace and very much concerned with law reform. Hogarth was one of the founders and a supporter of the London Foundling Hospital, which was modelled on the institute in Florence.

The accession to power of the Whigs in the eighteenth century contributed towards a great revival of interest in Milton, who had previously been condemned by many as Cromwellian and Puritan. Although a small section of society has probably never ceased to admire Milton's poetry, an interest in Milton's work and in Milton as a man now spread throughout the populace and was reflected in a variety of portrayals of the great poet. A bust of Milton by Rysbrack adorned the Temple of British Worthies at Stowe about the year 1732.[4] The custom of decorating libraries and halls with busts or portraits of distinguished men was becoming common and Milton was now admitted to the company of Newton and Shakespeare. The name of Milton had not hitherto been permitted to defile the fabric of Westminster Abbey, but William Benson's monument to Milton (commissioned from Rysbrack in 1737) was erected in the Abbey in 1738. William Benson also ordered a Milton medal to be struck and paid William Dobson a thousand pounds for a translation of *Paradise Lost* into Latin verse. This extraordinary edition was published between 1750 and 1753.[5]

Milton's works were thoroughly and widely consulted by the middle of the century and *Paradise Lost* was quoted on any excuse as an authority for such matters as: relations between husbands and wives, astronomy and military equipment.[6] The popularity of *Paradise Lost* reached the proportions of a cult with the publication of books bearing titles such as *Adam's Luxury and Eve's Cookery* (1744) and even Lord Chesterfield, who found himself unable to read Milton through, dared not let this secret be known in England.[7] The storms of abuse and vituperation which descended upon anybody who dared to attack Milton testify to the vigorous enthusiasm of the period for Milton and his work. Bentley's amended *Paradise Lost* of 1732, and the Rev. William Lauder's charge in *The Gentleman's Magazine* of 1747 that *Paradise Lost* was a paraphrase of lesser-known foreign poets, were decried from all sides.

Who then were the members of this group of artists which assembled around Hogarth? Mainly artists associated with the St. Martin's Lane Academy and literary men who haunted Slaughter's Coffee House where the group most frequently met, they formed a close-knit gathering.[8] Roubiliac, Hayman, Fielding, Garrick, Gainsborough and two plasterers William Collins and James Paine were the chief members. Of particular importance was the French artist and engraver Hubert Gravelot because he, more than any other single artist, was responsible for establishing the French rococo style of Watteau, Boucher and Fragonard in this country.

Gravelot came to London from Paris in 1731 and specialized in book illustration and in engravings with very delicate, decorative frames. In 1743 he collaborated with Hayman over the illustrations to Hanmer's *Works of Shakespeare* and he may have taught the young Gainsborough, whose early overmantel pictures executed for the Duke of Bedford in 1755 are executed in a very rococo style. The Duke of Bedford was also the patron of Fielding, another member of the Slaughter's group. Such interconnections are very typical as these artists frequently collaborated and shared commissions. Hogarth was a personal friend of Tyers, the proprietor of the Vauxhall Gardens where the decorations and the entertainments epitomized the English phase of the rococo. Tyers gave Hogarth and his party free admission for perpetuity and a portrait of himself

36 After F. Hayman, 'Euphrosyne Leads the Poet'

37 After F. Hayman, 'Satan Watching Adam and Eve'

by a French painter. It is reasonable to suppose that this friendship was responsible for the many commissions which these artists received for the decoration of the Gardens. Hogarth and his associates seem to have had a virtual monopoly in the execution of this scheme.[9]

An agreeable levity of mood and delight in what the eighteenth century called 'fancy' is easily recognizable in the growing taste for Chinoiserie and for the sort of decorative Gothic typified by Walpole's Strawberry Hill. A similarly rococo atmosphere prevailed in the decoration of the Vauxhall Gardens, which included a Temple of Comus decorated in the 'Chinese Taste' and in much of the other work of these artists. All members of the bourgeoisie, they believed in the vigour and potential of native art, in spite of their associations with the art of French rococo. They were avowed supporters of the Prince of Wales, and in opposition to Burlington's neo-Palladianism, the king and the court. Hogarth's early print 'Burlington Gate' (1724) is a declaration of war on Palladianism and imported art, literature and music. The works of Shakespeare, Ben Jonson, Dryden and Congreve are shown being wheeled away as waste paper.

Only Hogarth and Hayman actually designed illustrations to Milton, but as they worked in such close association with the other members of the group their art becomes more meaningful if something is understood of their associates.

The artistic relations between France and England at this period were complex and fruitful. E. K. Waterhouse has said:

Although at the level of the court there was a marked divergence between British and French taste, the middle classes of the two countries approximated more and more in their likes and dislikes, and the enthusiasm which greeted Samuel Richardson's *Pamela* (1740) in France initiated the period when the products of British culture, now well established at home, began to make themselves known abroad.[10]

This is certainly true, but the aristocracy in general, consisting of men like Horace Walpole, was internationally minded and it would seem to have been the bourgeoisie which was prejudiced against foreigners. Hogarth only went to France once and 'wherever he went he was sure to be dissatisfied with all he saw'. He was, moreover, 'often clamerously rude' in the streets.[11] 'The Gate of Calais' (1749) was designed as the frontispiece to *The Jacobite's Journal*, an anti-Jacobite, Whig periodical, edited by Fielding. Yet against this one must set the fact that Hogarth and numerous other artists of the period employed French engravers. Hogarth also in 1740 employed Jean Rouquet to write a pamphlet to accompany some sets of his prints abroad.

The rococo style is fundamentally French, but in England it appeared primarily in the work of the friends and associates of the xenophobic Hogarth. The paradox is not as acute as at first appears since there is not much sign of direct French influence in Hogarth's illustrations to Milton. The work of Francis Hayman, however, is a different case. Hayman's illustration to *L'Allegro* (1749) (36) shows Euphrosyne leading the poet, and the background is comparable with what we know of his Vauxhall decorative work. A building adorned with statues in niches is seen in the far background and in the middle distance a fiddler is playing and a couple are dancing. A veritable 'Fête champêtre' in miniature, this little scene is Watteauesque in its light-hearted mood and is very similar to the much larger 'Dance of the Milkmaids on May Day' from Vauxhall now in the Victoria and Albert Museum. Some of Hayman's illustrations bear a general resemblance to one of the great rococo book productions of the period, the edition of Tasso's *Canti* that was illustrated by Piazzetta in 1745. Hayman's 'Satan Watching Adam and Eve' (37) has the same pear-shaped composition containing a central tree, foreground pool and group of animals that is found in many of Piazzetta's tailpieces and, particularly, in his illustration to Canto Eight.

Milton was evidently a subject of discussion among the artists and writers meeting at Slaughter's. We know, for example, that Jonathan Richardson read extracts from his *Life and Explanatory Notes on Milton* (1734) 'to all comers'.[12] Although Richardson's work is now appreciated as a real contribution to Milton studies, we are told that the *Explanatory Notes* was greeted with derision by Hogarth and company, who found Richardson's fulsome acknowledgement to his son particularly objectionable. An engraving which caricatures Richardson's pride in his own and his son's Milton scholarship bears the title 'The Complicated Richardson' (1734) and is attributed to Hogarth.[13] However, Richardson's work on Milton is of particular interest on two counts. Firstly his *Explanatory Notes*[14] shows the vital interest that was developing at this time in Milton as a man, an interest which culminated at the turn of the eighteenth century in a series of portraits of Milton.[15] Richardson states that he intends:

. . . not a Panegyrick, not to give my Own Sense of What a Man should be, but what This Man Really was. Not to Plead for the Poet, or the Poem, but for Truth, by giving Light into What hath Hitherto lain in

Obscurity, and by Dispelling Mistakes which have Injured the Memory of a Deserving Man, Debased a Work Worthy of the Highest Estimation, and Robb'd the World of the Pleasure and Advantage it Might have Received, and I presume to Hope Will Hereafter Receive.[16]

Secondly Richardson's work provides a link between the Hogarthian advocacy of the native tradition in art and neo-classicism. Richardson belonged to the anti-Palladian Slaughter's group and, ever faithful to the camp of the Moderns, he employed that favourite Georgian word 'taste' in reference to Milton. Yet he estimates Milton as a classical writer in terms of grace, majesty and simplicity. This brings Richardson's attitude closer to Shaftesbury's and distinguishes him from the pastoralism and theatricality of the Slaughter's group. The following passage from the *Explanatory Notes* clearly illustrates this aspect of Richardson's attitude to Milton:

All his Images are Pure Antique . . . Connoisseurs in Painting and Sculpture can Best tell what is the Difference of Taste in Ancient and Modern Work, and can therefore Best Understand what I am Now Saying; it must Suffice that I tell Others that there is a Certain Grace, Majesty and Simplicity in the Antique which is its Distinguishing Character. The same Kind of Taste is Seen in Writing and Milton has it, I think, to a Degree beyond what We have ever found in Any Modern Painter or Sculptor, not Excepting Rafaelle Himself.[17]

Despite his alleged derision of Richardson's *Notes*, Hogarth was himself an admirer of Milton. The chief qualities of Hogarth's art are summed up in his self-portrait of 1745 (National Gallery). Hogarth created a portrait within a portrait, a baroque device which is emphasized by the majestic drapes of the curtain drawn back to reveal the portrait. Yet the face is full of pungent realism and is treated with the same humour that characterizes Hogarth's dog, which appears in the dominant position in the foreground of the picture. In addition to the dog the foreground also contains a palette on which is inscribed the ogee line of beauty and three volumes of Hogarth's favourite authors, Shakespeare, Swift and Milton.[18]

One may be sure that Hogarth read and was intimately acquainted with the works of these authors. Unlike Pope's subject in the *Epistle to Lord Burlington* he did not indulge in the habit of collecting bindings rather than books, a habit which resulted in the absence of any copy of Locke or Milton or 'any modern book'.[19]

Hogarth made use of his familiarity with Milton in *The Analysis*

38 W. Hogarth, 'The Council in Heaven'   **39** W. Hogarth, 'The Council in Hell'

of Beauty (1753).[20] The title page includes a quotation from Milton, the verbal quintessence of the serpentine line of beauty:

> So vary'd he, and of his tortuous train
> Curled many a wanton wreath, in sight of Eve,
> To lure her eye . . .
> *(Paradise Lost, IX)*

In Chapter XVII of *The Analysis*, in his discussion of the beauty of serpentine lines in the action of country dancing, Hogarth again calls on *Paradise Lost* for a picture of 'the whole idea in words':

> Mystical dance! . . .
> Mazes intricate,
> Eccentric, intervolved, yet regular
> Then most, when most irregular they seem.
> *(Paradise Lost, V)*

It was clearly the baroque exuberance of Milton's verse that appealed most to Hogarth during the very early phase of his career in the 1720s and 1730s. Among the most baroque engravings that Hogarth ever designed are two which most probably were commissioned by a bookseller and never printed. 'The Council in Heaven' (38) and 'The Council in Hell' (39) are both dated about 1724.[21] We know that Hogarth (who in 1739 eloped with Sir James Thornhill's daughter) aspired to be an historical painter and, though he had little success on canvas, some of his book illustrations—particularly these two plates to *Paradise Lost*—are treated in the lofty manner considered suitable by painters in the grand manner for the depiction of noble literary subjects.

The first of these two plates shows Satan summoning thousands of devils to his capital and the second shows God the Father, Christ and attendants seated on a rainbow and looking down towards Earth towards which Satan is flying. According to F. Antal the models on which Hogarth based these very grandiose, 'continental' works are different in each case.[22] Antal sees a relation between 'The Council in Heaven' (with its great orchestra of angels and bold chiaroscuro) and Dutch book illustrations which adopt a French and Italianizing style, as in the work of Luyken. In 'The Council in Pandemonium', on the other hand, mannerist elements can be detected in the theatrical setting which always appealed to Hogarth. Antal describes the engraving thus:

. . . an enormous, dark and wildly ornamented repoussoir arcade completely fills the left side, pushing far into the background, across a vast, unreal space, the large figure of Satan seated beneath a swirling canopy surmounted by a slight variation of one of Michelangelo's Sistine slaves. The space between is occupied by a teeming host of devils; as Milton says, they can reduce their shapes to the smallest of forms.

It is probable that this background originated in Callot's courtly theatre representations, for example the illustration of the 'First Interlude of La Liberazione di Tirreno'.

The scheme for the decoration of Vauxhall Gardens has already been mentioned as the project on which almost all of Hogarth's particular associates collaborated. The Vauxhall Pleasure Gardens played a most popular role in the world of London entertainment in the middle of the eighteenth century. The general idea seems to have been an expanse of elegant garden laid out with fountains and coloured lights, statues and covered colonnades. The only substantial architectural structures were the supper boxes and the temple, all of which were richly decorated with paintings.[23] In style the Vauxhall decorations seem to have embodied the art of the English rococo, providing a 'London equivalent, on a popular and rustic level, of what Boucher was doing in France'.[24] For the first time the tradition of stage-scenery design which was established with Inigo Jones and the tradition of English historical painting were united. C. Mitchell has written:

> For a paradigm of the popular taste which prevailed in West's time and the national pride to which he appealed in the 'Death of Wolfe' we have only to go to contemporary descriptions of Vauxhall Gardens . . . In the Rotunda [the visitor] complacently admired the literary heroes of his country—Shakespeare, Locke, Milton and Dryden.[25]

It was in the guise of a popular, national hero that Milton took his place in the decorative schemes of Vauxhall Gardens. His distinguished face greeted the visitor not only in the Rotunda; Roubiliac, who achieved such celebrity with his statue of Handel for the Gardens, executed a full-length statue of Milton. This was located on one of the heights of the Gardens and represented (in lead) the poet 'seated on a rock, in an attitude of listening to soft music as described by himself in his *Il Penseroso*'.[26] At night the statue was illuminated. Roubiliac in the 1750s also did a terracotta bust of the poet.[27]

The architectural showpiece of the Gardens was the Temple of Comus. A. Dobson describes the Temple and its adjoining buildings thus:

> The new room was entered through a Gothic portal or temple, which contained portraits of George III and Queen Charlotte, and also formed the starting point of a semi-circular piazza or colonnade that swept round to a similar terminal temple at the end of the arc. Between these two, in the middle of the semi-circle, was a higher central structure denominated in old prints the Temple of Comus. This is said rather vaguely, to have been 'embellished with rays', and had above it a large star or sun, which, from the description would seem to have been illuminated at night. Inside it was painted with a composition 'in the Chinese taste' representing 'Vulcan catching Mars and Venus in the historical net'.[28]

From this description it seems likely that the Temple was an extravagant literary conceit. The 'large star or sun' being a concrete expression of Comus's opening lines in Milton's masque:

> The Star that bids the Shepherd fold,
> Now the top of Heav'n doth hold.

The 'rays' which embellished the Temple could derive from this same speech four lines further on:

And the slope Sun his upward beam
Shoots against the dusky Pole

Certainly whoever conceived the idea of a Temple of Comus for Vauxhall Gardens should have been congratulated. In the atmosphere of night-time fairy-magic in which the visitor immersed himself at Vauxhall, after crossing the Thames by boat, he would surely be scarcely surprised to find Circe's son lurking behind the foliage, prepared for assault with his 'cordial Julep', or even Sabrina herself rising from the Thames.

The middle years of the eighteenth century were a very successful period for the London theatre. Hogarth engraved many representations of the theatre, the most famous of which was 'The Beggar's Opera'. Garrick was a friend of Hogarth and Hayman and a member of the Slaughter's group. In his opera *The Faeries* (1755) Garrick used parts of *L'Allegro* and *Arcades*. The theatrical adaptation of Milton's poetry was not unusual during the period. Milton's poetry has dramatic qualities which make it ideally suited to such adaptations. *Comus* with an abridged text and additional songs was one of the most popular entertainments of the century and many other musical works used libretti based on Milton's poetry.[29]

Francis Hayman (1708–76), like Hogarth, is known to have worked in a number of astonishingly different artistic fields. Easel painting, 'fancy' pictures, historical subjects, book illustrations,[30] ceiling paintings, sporting pictures and conversation pieces are all forms of art at which he tried his hand. However, the earliest record tells of his employment as a scene painter at Drury Lane.[31] The influence of these formative years was a lasting one and a certain predilection for theatrical settings seems to have remained with him for life. It can be easily recognized in two of the illustrations he designed (engraved by C. Grignion) for the edition of *Paradise Lost and Paradise Regained* published in 1749 by Thomas Newton. This edition, with its pleasing decorative plates, proved very popular and was reprinted many times with the same designs or with Hayman's designs reworked by the engraver J. S. Mueller (who himself designed the frontispiece for an edition of *Paradise Regained* published in 1760) until at least 1818. Hayman designed plates only for the 1749 edition and it is in this edition that all Hayman's Milton illustrations referred to in this chapter may be found.

Hayman's illustration to Book II of *Paradise Lost* (40), designed and executed at least fifteen years before Hogarth's 'Satan, Sin and Death' (53), shows a moment in the narrative after that chosen by Medina and Cheron, and by Hogarth, Fuseli and other subsequent artists. Hayman avoids the moment of extreme conflict and shows Satan looking like Mercury, having passed through the gates of Hell which Sin has opened, just setting off on his flight to Earth. Satan, with fluttering cloak and outspread wings, his finger pointing out to space whilst his head is turned back to Death and Sin, is one of Hayman's most successful figures. Death is seen only in the background and Sin is rendered more capable of movement than hitherto by reason of the two serpentine coils like legs on which she is able to kneel. Hayman thus finds a compromise which is not Miltonic but is artistically acceptable. The whole action takes place on a giant doorstep on the threshold of Hell and the effect thus created closely resembles the raised dais of a stage. The flames and clouds make a most effective back-cloth to this scene.

In view of the popularity of the stage version of *Comus*, it is not surprising to find that Hayman's illustration to the masque showing the moment when the brothers rush into Comus's palace to free their sister looks very much as though it were taking place on stage (41). The characters are all dressed in contemporary costume and, in the torchlight, the sombre classical background architecture provides a dramatic tonal contrast to the glimmering satin folds of the lady's fashionable dress. Comus is just endeavouring to escape from the raised platform on which the lady is seated. Like Satan in Hayman's illustration to Book II (40), he moves forward, arm outstretched, but looks back over his shoulder, a very theatrical pose. It is also an artistically successful pose, for the glance of Comus (and the same applies to Satan in Book II) relates him to the main group of the composition, whilst his movement indicates another world outside the picture and another episode in time. Hayman has chosen, for this one illustration to *Comus*, to portray the only moment, in a masque largely concerned with denial, which involves any real action on the part of the main characters. As in the illustration to Book II, one can almost imagine the front rows of the audience sitting a little below the level of the dais.

Hayman relied much less than Medina or Cheron upon the iconographic tradition of Genesis illustrations. However, two of Hayman's *Paradise Lost* illustrations show traces of derivation from Bible illustrations. 'Adam and Eve Admonished', the plate to Book X of *Paradise Lost* (42), is, according to C. H. Collins-Baker, 'taken from a picture by Coypel, engraved by Pierre Drevet, fils'.

40 After F. Hayman, 'Satan at the Gates of Hell'

41 After F. Hayman, 'The Brothers Attack Comus'

He also says: 'There is a title page with the same design (excluding the top part), belonging to the book of Genesis, in a bible of which I have not ascertained the date.'[32] The Bible referred to here is elusive. However, this rather awkward illustration in which a baroque cloud appears incongruously above a naturalistically drawn tree, and a rather ungainly Eve grovels before her admonisher, may well owe some of its clumsiness to the inclusion of foreign elements from the work of other artists. It is curious, in view of what C. H. Collins-Baker says about a title-page design in which the top part differs from Coypel and Hayman, that a Bible published by Goadby in London in 1759 has a title page of which the upper part very closely resembles in design the upper part of the Hayman illustration to Book X. This Bible frontispiece shows Christ and angels seated on the same baroque cloud. Below, in place of Hayman's Adam and Eve, beneath the cloud the artist has depicted a prophet. The upper part of this design may have been taken from

42 After F. Hayman, 'Adam and Eve Admonished'

43 After F. Hayman, 'Michael Foretells the Future'

the same print after Coypel on which Hayman based his 'Adam and Eve Admonished'. But since the only illustration to Genesis in this same 1759 Bible is a frank re-engraving of the Hayman design for *Paradise Lost*, Book IV, it would seem more likely that the upper part of the frontispiece was taken direct from Hayman. It is worth seeing how the engraver of the 1759 Bible changed Hayman's illustration. He reversed the design and made the central group of Adam and Eve smaller. Satan peering from behind the tree is excluded and only the dog and the sheep of Hayman's four animals appear at the feet of Adam and Eve. Apart from this the re-engraving is identical to Hayman's original design for Book IV.

The illustration to *Paradise Lost*, Book XI, by Hayman depicts Michael showing to Adam some of the events which will befall as a result of his and Eve's transgression (43). The two great birds flying in the sky are reminiscent of Medina's illustration to Book XI (10). The event to which Adam is witness in Hayman's illustration is the murder of Abel by Cain. It is interesting that Hayman should have chosen this of all the biblical events so vividly described by Milton in Book XI, as the first murder was one of the most popular scenes with Genesis illustrators, although it was rarely chosen as an illustration to *Paradise Lost*. In his design for Book IX (49) Hayman follows the tradition of biblical illustration, as well as the example set by Medina in his illustrations to *Paradise Lost*, by including a variety of animals: here a lion, a deer and a rabbit. This was a tradition which was rejected by many later artists as such detail was thought to detract from the grandeur and classical generality of the scene.

Hayman's illustration to *Paradise Lost*, Book I, a book which had great appeal for artists and writers during the Romantic Movement, is disappointing. His subject is Satan summoning his legions from the fiery lake (44). In accordance with theatrical practice of his day, Hayman's Satan and Beelzebub both appear in semi-contemporary costume. They are wearing armour and cloaks but have eighteenth-century knee-breeches. They are both about the same size and are very small in relation to the whole picture area. The foreground with its flaming craters and the background of smoke-laden clouds occupy most of the space. The sinuous lines of the flames, the flickering quality of light playing on Satan's and Beelzebub's clothing and the very varied tonal effects create an overall decorative pattern which distracts the eye from the drama and from the already rather insignificant-looking chief figure. The shimmering effect of half-light or candle-light on clothing occurs throughout Hayman's illustrations. Some of the finest rococo, decorative use of light in this way is to be seen in Watteau's torch-light scenes, for example in 'The Italian Comedy' (London, National Gallery). It is originally a feature of French painting and is found also in Hogarth's conversation pieces. Hayman's use of this effect probably derives from the work of Mercier and other French artists working during the 1720s in England.

G. Schiff thinks that the illustration by Hayman to *Paradise Lost*, Book I, is the first attempt made by any artist to give Satan and Beelzebub the grandeur of fallen angels.[33] It is impossible to agree with this as Hayman's puny figures completely lack the grandeur which Medina achieved through stark lines and violently dramatic chiaroscuro. Great pictorial emphasis is laid on the figure of Satan in Medina's illustration to Book I (9) and even the elongated warriors of Thornhill's illustration (16) have more of the stature of fallen angels than Hayman's Satan and Beelzebub.

Hayman's use of baroque clouds is persistently awkward. It is unfortunate that Hayman was unable to rid his work of this last

44 After F. Hayman, 'Satan Summons his Legions'

45 After F. Hayman, 'The Fall of the Rebel Angels'

survival of the grand, decorative art of the early eighteenth century. His baroque stylization seriously detracts from the design for Book VI of *Paradise Lost*, 'The Fall of the Rebel Angels' (45). The upper part of the design comprises Christ holding his gown up from around his ankles, perched on the edge of a column of cloud, whilst below the rebel angels fall towards Hell. All around Christ angels emerge most improbably from the clouds. The faces and torsos of these angels are treated in a realistic and pedantic fashion and the sight of them popping up from behind the cloud bank is very odd. The lower part of the design is more successful and the falling mass of tangled bodies has a degree of dynamism which anticipates the early work of Fuseli, and particularly a childhood pen-and-ink drawing of 'The Fall of the Titans' (46).[34] There is no attempt in the lower part of Hayman's illustration to create a pretty, decorative effect. The thrashing mass of limbs is a most effective portrayal of rebel confusion. Hayman's design bears some resemblance to Rubens's 'Last Judgement' and a definite similarity to Rubens's

46 J. H. Fuseli, 'The Fall of the Titans'

'Fall of the Rebel Angels' (c. 1620, Brussels). The falling figure who holds a staff in the lower left-hand corner of Hayman's design is a copy of the figure in the lower left-hand corner of Rubens's picture.

E. K. Waterhouse has written of Hayman's landscape backgrounds in general that the style '. . . is sometimes so curiously

similar to early Gainsborough that we may be permitted to wonder
whether Gainsborough did not in fact sometimes paint them for
him in the later 1740s'.[35] The writer is here referring primarily to
Hayman's canvases but, nevertheless, a distinct relationship between Gainsborough and Hayman in respect of their landscape
drawing can be seen from an examination of the landscape backgrounds in Hayman's series of Milton illustrations. It is possible
that Gainsborough actually assisted Hayman in his drawings, but
it is more likely that their friendship and association led to some
sort of reciprocation of ideas. Gainsborough was later to prove
himself the more forceful and talented artist of the two, but Hayman was the older and therefore more likely to have been an influence on Gainsborough than vice versa. As Gainsborough's senior he
might have introduced him to the work of Ruysdael, Hobbema,
Everdingen and Waterloo, whose work could have proved a source
of inspiration to Hayman as it did to Gainsborough. Either way,
the relationship between the two artists presents problems too

47 After F. Hayman, 'Delilah Visits
Samson'

48 After F. Hayman, 'Adam and Eve in
Paradise'

numerous to be pursued here. Gainsborough had a variety of different early landscape styles. The style which most closely approximates to Hayman's landscapes is that belonging to early portraits like 'Heneage Lloyd and his Sister' (c. 1750). Perhaps the only conclusion that one can safely draw is that the youthful Gainsborough was a very eclectic artist and that Hayman was one of his sources.

G. Schiff refers to the landscapes in Hayman's Milton illustrations as quasi-antique, pastoral idylls of the rococo.[36] But there is little in them that is reminiscent of the antique, and overtones of Claudian or Poussinesque landscape are quite absent. However, they can be related to rococo pastoral paintings chiefly because of Hayman's great delight in the minute depiction of very lush, fluttering foliage and gnarled tree-trunks and branches (47). The decorative surface quality in these landscapes is similar to Gainsborough's treatment of foliage in his early years. Hayman's illustration to Book V (48) with its wealth of leaf forms and its diversity of surface

49 After F. Hayman, 'Adam Tempted'

50 T. Gainsborough, copy of Ruisdael's 'La Forêt'

texture is a good illustration of this. Nevertheless, the more sombre
Dutch landscape style rather than the pastoral idyll of the rococo is
the dominant influence in Hayman's work. Wooded scenery with
secondary vistas, contorted tree-stumps, blasted trees and pools of
water are recurring features of Hayman's Eden (Gainsborough's
early portraits such as that of Heneage Lloyd and his sister contain
similar landscape elements). Six out of Hayman's seventeen Milton
illustrations contain a landscape background with a pool (see 37,
42, 48, 49, 51, and the illustrations to Book VII of *Paradise Lost*
and to *Paradise Regained*). The rhythmic grouping of the trees, the
stretches of water and the closely observed foliage as they appear,
for example, in Hayman's illustration to Book IX (49) are all features of Ruysdael's work. They appear also in Gainsborough's
drawings after Ruysdael (50).

  The only illustration to Milton where Hayman really emerges as
a precursor of the Romantic Movement is that to *Il Penseroso* (51).
It is especially interesting to see in this particular design evidence of

51 After F. Hayman, 'The Poet by the Pool'   52 After F. Hayman, 'The Expulsion'

the growing concept in the eighteenth century of poetic melancholy, of which one result was the 'grave-yard school' of poets. Milton's poem *Il Penseroso* is concerned with melancholy as a positive poetic mood. In writing *L'Allegro* and *Il Penseroso*, Milton relied on the familiar medieval idea of syncrisis, and his Melancholy in *Il Penseroso* has many of the traditional features specified by Cesare Ripa in his *Iconologia* (1603), a work Milton undoubtedly knew. But in *Il Penseroso* Melancholy has none of the nightmare, impoverished quality of the Italian *Afflitto*. Milton's Melancholy possesses positive spiritual and poetic value and is in essence not a medieval but a Renaissance concept.[37] The eighteenth century glorified Melancholy as a mood of poetic self-awareness and as a mood associated with death. This is most clearly exemplified in Gray's *Elegy* and Blair's *The Grave*. In Hayman's illustration to *Il Penseroso* the poet is seen seated, legs crossed and chin in hand in the traditional pose of Melancholy. All around are the requisite accoutrements of the romantic 'poetic' scene: the slightly shrouded moon, the owl, the still pool and the crumbling, moss-grown masonry. This creation of a pre-defined mood through the juxtaposing of various elements typifies the aesthetics of the eighteenth-century precursors of the Romantic Movement proper.

Hayman's illustrations were very popular. They were issued a great many times and therefore, it may be assumed, reached a wide audience. Hayman's work, as we have seen, was not entirely free from the influences of formal baroque and yet his original and lively treatment of Milton's poetry prepares the way for the increasingly liberal interpretation of it by nineteenth-century artists. Hayman's choice of scene established a pattern that was followed by many of his successors. More directly the influence of Hayman's frontal treatment of the 'Expulsion' scene (52), a break away from Raphael, is seen in the final *Paradise Lost* designs of Burney, Corbould and Blake. In spite of their defects Hayman's illustrations make an important and influential contribution to the history of Milton illustration.[38]

In about 1764, some forty years after his two baroque Milton illustrations, Hogarth executed his only other known Milton picture, 'Satan, Sin and Death' (53) (Tate Gallery), a work which is of prime importance as the prototype of the romantic rendering of this scene by later artists and the first attempt by an artist to create an historical painting based on Milton. G. Schiff claims that this is also the first uncommissioned Milton work.[39] However, in view of the fact that an engraving after the picture (British Museum),[40] dated 1764, is inscribed:

W. Hogarth pinx. J. Ogborne sculp. Satan, Sin and Death from Milton's
Paradise Lost. Book the 2nd. The original picture by Hogarth is in the
possession of Mrs. Garrick. This from a painting in chiaroscuro by R.
Livesey . . .

it seems most probable that the actor Garrick, a great lover of melodrama and one of Hogarth's circle, commissioned the painting.
'Satan, Sin and Death' was certainly intended as a serious grandiose
historical painting. It is the first really dramatic rendering of this
scene and Fuseli was sufficiently impressed by it to base his design
on Hogarth's. It is not, as G. Schiff suggests, a parody.[41] Satan,
whose conflicting passions are reflected in his face and who is depicted in Roman theatrical costume, appears for the first time in real
conflict with Death. Hogarth seems to have been indecisive about
the placing of Satan's right arm but the position in which he shows
the three protagonists is crucial and is almost invariably followed

53 W. Hogarth, 'Satan, Sin and Death'

by subsequent artists. Death still appears as the traditional skeleton, but his movements have dynamism and flames flare from his joints. His malignant leer suffices to suggest some, at least, of the terror invoked by Milton's description. Satan's feet still terminate in animal claws (a legacy from the medieval devil), but his shield really is of 'Ethereal temper, massy, large and round'[42] and his celestial curls stream from his head in the violence of his actions. Sin is rather less successful as she is placed much lower than the two combatants. Hogarth's mode of solving the problem of joining the upper and lower portions of her anatomy is responsible for her inferior position. The gestures of her hands are somewhat languid, but she occupies the crucial position between the two combatants and looks appealingly towards Satan. It is thus that Milton aptly describes her. The uncertain and shadowy quality of the background, shrouded in mists and clouds of smoke, the chain and the great portcullis all contribute towards the convincing re-creation of the menacing and gloomy atmosphere described by Milton in Book II.

Fuseli must either have known Hogarth's engraving of 'Satan, Sin and Death' or seen the original canvas at the house of his acquaintance, Garrick. When in 1776 he composed in Rome the first of the nine variations on this theme which he executed during his life,[43] he recalled Hogarth's composition (53). Fuseli's design has even greater vigour than Hogarth's but the placing of the figures is almost identical and the general conception of the scene is similar. This was not the only occasion on which Hogarth provided a model for Fuseli. Another Milton picture, 'The Lazar House' (103), reflects Hogarth's 'Rake in Bedlam'.

Notes to Chapter II

1. J. Warton, 'To Health'. Ode III in *Odes on Various Subjects* (1746).
2. A. Pope, 'Epistle to Mr. Jervas with Dryden's Translation of Fresnoy's *Art of Painting* c. 1720', lines 13–16. Alexander Pope, *Minor Poems* (1954).
3. J. Richardson, *The Theory of Painting* (1719) in *The Works* (ed. 1792).
4. M. Whinney, *Sculpture in Britain 1530–1830* (1964), pp. 87–8.
5. Good, App. J. W. Good does not give the source of his information concerning Benson and he refers to Rysbrack as Rysbeck.
6. Ibid., p. 275.
7. Lord Chesterfield, Letter 'To Mr. S. at Berlin', Oct. 4th, 1752. Quoted by Good, p. 183.

8. For an examination of this group and its activities, see M. Girouard, 'English Art and the Rococo', *Country Life* (Jan–Feb. 1966).
9. See L. Gowing, 'Hogarth, Hayman and the Vauxhall Decorations', *B. Mag.* (Jan. 1953), pp. 4–19.
10. Waterhouse, p. 113.
11. J. Nichols and G. Steevens, *The Genuine Works of William Hogarth* (1808), I, p. 143.
12. W. H. Pyne (pseudonym Ephraim Hardcastle), *Wine and Walnuts*, 2nd ed. 1824, reprinted in the *Somerset House Gazette* (1824), p. 280.
13. R. Paulson, *Hogarth's Graphic Works* (1965), App. I, pl. 337. J. F. Kerslake, 'The Richardsons and the Cult of Milton', *B. Mag.* (Jan. 1957), pp. 23–4, discusses Richardson's portrait of himself and his son in the presence of Milton (Collection, Lt.-Col. and Mrs. Bromley-Davenport, reproduced in this article).
14. J. Richardson, *Explanatory Notes and Remarks on Milton's 'Paradise Lost' with the Life of the Author, and a Discourse on the Poem* (1734). Reprinted in H. Darbishire, *The Early Lives of Milton* (1932).
15. Between 1780 and 1816 at least eight different engraved portraits of Milton were issued. See British Museum *Catalogue of Engraved British Portraits*, III (1912).
16. J. Richardson, op. cit., p. 201.
17. Ibid., p. 318.
18. F. Antal, *Hogarth and his Place in European Art* (1962), p. 31, has written: 'Taken all-in-all, Hogarth's art, so new and yet so deeply rooted in the tradition of English intellectual life, may be most simply summed up by recalling his three favourite writers and the qualities he esteemed in them: the baroque descriptions of Milton, the mocking satire of Swift, and above all the characters of Shakespeare, so vivid and three-dimensional . . .'
19. A. Pope, 'Epistle to Burlington' (1731) (Twickenham text 1963), lines 132–40:

> 'His study! With what Authors is it stor'd?
> In Books, not Authors, curious is my Lord;
> To all their dated Backs he turns you round,
> These Aldus printed those Du Sueil has bound
> Lo some are vellom, and the rest as good
> For all his Lordship knows, but they are Wood.
> For Locke or Milton 'tis in vain to look,
> These shelves admit not any modern book.'

20. W. Hogarth, *The Analysis of Beauty* (1753) (ed. J. Burke, Oxford, 1955).
21. R. Paulson, op. cit., cat. nos. 55, 56.
22. Op. cit., pp. 143–4.
23. See L. Gowing, op. cit.
24. Waterhouse, p. 137.

25. C. Mitchell, 'Benjamin West's "Death of General Wolfe" and the Popular History Piece', in *England and the Mediterranean Tradition* (Oxford, 1945), p. 187.
26. A. Dobson, 'Old Vauxhall Gardens', in *Eighteenth Century Vignettes* (1st series, 1892), p. 244. L. Gowing, op. cit., does not mention this piece of sculpture.
27. National Portrait Gallery, Scotland.
28. A. Dobson, op. cit., p. 241. L. Gowing (op. cit.) describes the Temple and reproduces a print by Müller after Wale showing the Temple exactly as Dobson describes it. However, Gowing makes no mention of the name 'Temple of Comus'. Havens, p. 28, describes 'the temple of Comus as one of the most prominent features of Vauxhall', and cites Pearch's *Collection* (1783), i, p. 329, as a source.
29. See introduction, p. xxxvi.
30. Besides his illustrations to Milton, Hayman also designed plates for Hanmer's edition of Shakespeare, for Congreve, Pope, *Don Quixote* and for Dodsley's 'Portraits'.
31. Waterhouse, p. 135.
32. Collins-Baker, *The Library* (June 1948), p. 14, n.
33. G. Schiff, *Johann Heinrich Füssli's Milton Galerie* (Zurich, 1963), p. 41.
34. Offentliche Kunstsammlung, Basel. Reproduced in F. Antal, *Fuseli Studies* (1956).
35. Waterhouse, p. 137.
36. Schiff, p. 41.
37. For a full discussion of literary and artistic concepts of Melancholy, see E. Panofsky (Klibansky and Saxl), *Saturn and Melancholy* (1964), Part III.
38. In addition to the illustrations by Hayman cited in this chapter, the 1749 edition of Milton's poems contains three illustrations I have not mentioned because they are not of particular artistic interest. They are 'Raphael Discoursing' (Book VII), 'Raphael Departing' (Book VIII) and an illustration to *Paradise Regained*, 'Christ Tempted to Change the Stone into Bread'.
39. Schiff, p. 41.
40. B.M. 1858–4–17–477.
41. Schiff, p. 50. G. Schiff writes: 'In Hogarth's unvollendetem Gemälde wirken der als ältlicher Provinzschauspieler wiedergegebene Satan, der kinderschreckartige Tod und die betulich schlichtende Sünde so offen rankaturistisch, dass man es nur als Parodie auffassen kann.'
42. *P.L.*, I.
43. Ashmolean Museum, Oxford. This drawing pre-dates Fuseli's 'David and Goliath' (c. 1786), so that the figure of Death is probably the prototype for Goliath rather than vice versa as P. A. Tomory suggests in *A Collection of Drawings by Henry Fuseli, R.A.*, Auckland City Art Gallery (Auckland, 1967), no. 6.

III   Milton & the
Precursors of
Romanticism

1784–1800

The period which opens only five years before the establishment of
the Royal Academy in 1769 and which closes with the conclusion
of the French Revolution in 1800 is one of the most interesting and
productive eras in the history of English painting. After the foundation of the Royal Academy in 1769 the work of English artists is
more easily traceable. But even taking into account the greater
availability of material, the sudden increase in illustrated editions
and the noticeably greater number of artists painting subjects from
Milton in the years around 1795 is very remarkable. The intensified
illustration of Milton is consistent until the latter years of the nineteenth century.

There are two distinctly perceptible and separate currents of interest shown by painters of this period in the poetry of Milton. The
first current originates in the gentle serpentine lines and decorative
prettiness of the rococo. A strictly neo-classical overtone is derived
probably from the Royal Academy life classes. This combines with
a predilection for the lyrical qualities of the Picturesque ideology
(qualities associated with artists like Claude and poets like Thomson
and Dyer) to produce a blend of classicism and sentiment which is
very typical of this period of English art.[1] It is most emphatically
seen in the work of Stothard with its mixture of academic preten-
sion and rustic sweetness. Elegance was the term used by the
eighteenth century to describe the quality inherent in paintings by
artists like Stothard. This quality was contrasted with that of the
sublime (the second current evident in the art of the period).
Reynolds was typical of his age in distinguishing between these two
qualities in painting. Reynolds—it is also interesting to note—
demands 'a poetical mind' in the landscape artist and implies that
Milton's *L'Allegro* and *Il Penseroso* are landscape poems. Discussing
the necessary conditions for the creation of a good landscape scene
Reynolds says:

All these circumstances contribute to the general character of the work,
whether it be of the elegant or of the more sublime kind . . . A landskip
thus conducted under the influence of a poetical mind, will have the same

superiority over the more ordinary and common views as Milton's Allegro and Penseroso have over a cold prosaik narration or description.[2]

The second current of interest in Milton among artists during this period is concerned with the tough, melodramatic qualities of the sublime as defined by Burke.[3] The resultant style, typified by the work of Fuseli, is still strictly allied to the neo-classical, heroic ideal. Yet in its adherence to any subject savouring of wildness, blackness, terror or any extremity of emotion it heralds the Romantic obsessions of nineteenth-century artists. Dr. Johnson was one of Milton's most severe critics and, for this reason, his testimony to the qualities of the sublime in *Paradise Lost* (as opposed to the inferior quality of elegance), which the period so much admired, is all the more forceful:

The characteristick quality of Milton's poem is sublimity. He sometimes descends to the elegant but his element is the great. He can occasionally invest himself with grace; but his natural port is gigantick loftiness. He can please when pleasure is required; but it is his peculiar power to astonish.[4]

The divergent characteristics of sentiment and sublimity are present simultaneously in much of the work of the period. However, for the sake of clarity, it is helpful to distinguish between, on the one hand, the large group of eclectic, fashionable artists whose work tends to lack originality and to be primarily concerned with tasteful sentiment and, on the other hand, artists of a more original frame of mind whose work is primarily concerned with the sublime and is more immediately recognizable as typical of an early phase of Romanticism. The work of this latter group of artists is usually related in some way to Fuseli's Milton Gallery. These two groups comprise two sections of this chapter. The work of Blake (which forms the third section) is treated separately, due to the size of his output of Milton illustrations and the individuality of his attitudes and style.

(i) Minor Painters of Sentiment

J. H. Mortimer (1741–79) is an enigmatic figure in the history of late eighteenth century English art. He was renowned for pictures of '*banditti*', 'frolics of monsters' and 'horrible imaginings'.[5] Much of his work is unlocated, but E. K. Waterhouse thinks that: 'It is probable that the historian would be correct in considering John Hamilton Mortimer more important than Wright or any other as the pioneer of romantic literary subjects . . .'[6] Mortimer was responsible for the first four illustrations to Milton that occur within the period 1764–1800. It would be reasonable to expect, from the references to monsters and horrors, to find Mortimer's work included with that of Fuseli's disciples in the section on the sublime. But Mortimer's four illustrations to Milton's poems, dated 1777 and engraved by C. Grignion and Hall for Bell's *Poets of Great Britain* (1776–82), are not at all of that character. 'Eve among her Fruits and Flowers' (54) is a scene of Arcadian simplicity and rural harmony and bears little relation to the darkly characterized heads from Shakespeare, which are among Mortimer's most distinguished and characteristic engravings (1775–61). The illustration to 'Ode on the Morning of Christ's Nativity' is no less surprising (55). This engraving, based on a line from 'The Passion':

My muse with angels did divide to sing . . .

shows Milton, seated with pen and paper, and an angelic figure, which is presumably his muse, playing a harp in a cloud above his head. The rather dishevelled appearance of Milton's clothing and the way he slouches casually in his seat is reminiscent of the informality of Roubiliac's statue of Handel (1738). This sense of familiarity, the untidy heap of papers and the classical props of masonry and muse combine to create a rather loose, rococo composition.

'Samson Agonistes' (56) and 'Satan Flying' (57) do bear some relation to the Salvatoresque *banditti* most immediately associated with Mortimer's work. The exquisite little ink and wash drawings for these subjects are to be found in the Victoria and Albert Museum (58, 59). In these the heavy chiaroscuro, the rocky background to Samson and the wild, raggedness of the figures can be related to the 'sublime' aspects of Mortimer's other work. In 1779 Mortimer is recorded as having exhibited a washed drawing of 'Satan and Death' at the Royal Academy. Graves says that this was among a series of pictures 'intended for exhibition before his decease'.[7] His death may, therefore, have caused a break in an intended group of Milton pictures.

Mortimer's name is connected with an amusing and, it is reasonable to assume, fairly typical case of Milton adulation. In 1775 Thomas Jones exhibited two pictures at the Society of Artists entitled 'Milton's House at Chalfont St. Giles' and 'Its Companion'.[8] T. Jones was a pupil of Richard Wilson and a friend of Mortimer and his journal creates a vivid picture of the travels and social engagements of a respectable but minor painter in the 1770s.[9] From this journal we learn that 'Milton's House' and its companion (both of which are lost) were produced in collaboration with Mortimer. Painted in the form of two ovals, they were intended as interpreta-

54 After J. H. Mortimer, 'Eve amongst her Flowers'

55 After J. H. Mortimer, 'Ode on the Morning of Christ's Nativity'

tions of *L'Allegro* and *Il Penseroso*. Evidently Mortimer painted the figures and Jones the landscape, a form of collaboration that was common. In the same year 1774, Francis Wheatley, who, like Jones, was taught by Wilson and worked with Mortimer,[10] exhibited at the Society of Artists a painting entitled 'A Study of the Coast of the Isle of Wight, the figures by Mr. Mortimer'.[11]

The circumstances surrounding the painting of Jones's Milton pictures give such a delightful picture of an eighteenth-century Milton pilgrimage that it is worth spending some space in following the artist's progress as recorded in his journal. On August 1st, 1774, Jones set off by coach with his friend Dr. Bates for Little Missenden in Buckinghamshire. Dr. Bates had commissioned Jones to paint a view of the house at Chalfont St. Giles, 'whither,

56 After J. H. Mortimer, 'Samson'   **57** After J. H. Mortimer, 'Satan Flying'

according to tradition the Poet Milton retired during the plague in London and where he wrote his "L'Allegro" and "Il Penseroso" '. They arrived at the house—now occupied by a wheelwright—and Jones set to work. Having taken provisions with them they 'sat down to dinner in the same room in which [they] fondly imagined that Mr. Milton had so often dined'. Jones then describes how they indulged themselves in 'the sweetest reveries, and contemplated every old Beam, rafter and Peg with the greatest Veneration and Pleasure—on those very boards', they thought, 'the great Milton trod—on that very ceiling (for he was not at that period blind) the Poet's eye in a fine frenzy rolled'. Jones then recounts how his patron's Milton enthusiasm really carried him away:

I had not long retired to my station again to proceed with my work but I heard the Doctor over the second bottle spouting with an elevated voice

58 J. H. Mortimer, 'Samson'   *59* J. H. Mortimer, 'Satan Flying'

the L'Allegro and Il Penseroso to an old woman who was spinning in one corner of the Parlour—I could not proceed—but shutting up my portfolio hurried into the house to join him, when we drank many a bumper to the immortal memory of that illustrious bard.

On October 4th Jones says that Mortimer is going to paint some figures from *L'Allegro* into the picture of Milton's house. It is interesting evidence of the clear distinction maintained at this period between the ideal and the actual in landscape painting that Jones, for his picture 'Il Penseroso', actually searched the 'most solitary places near Chalfont' for a suitable scene but was unable to find one. He was finally 'obliged to paint an ideal one—more sequestered and wild'.[12]

Alexander Runciman in 1773 was more fortunate in his search for a Miltonic landscape. He is known to have painted a picture entitled 'Il Pensoroso' which is lost, but its partner, 'A Landscape from Milton's *L'Allegro*' (signed and dated 1773), survives in the collection of Sir Steven Runciman. An engraving which renders the composition almost exactly in reverse (60) (perhaps by John Clerk, in the possession of the National Gallery of Scotland) indicates more clearly the descriptive intentions of the artist. It illustrates the lines from *L'Allegro* beginning, 'Streit mine eye . . .' and incorporating the celebrated pastoral description which Samuel Palmer found an unhappy combination of a 'mappy Buckinghamshire

60 After A. Runciman, 'Landscape from Milton's *L'Allegro*'

treatment' and a 'general poetic swoon'. Runciman has shown on a grassy knoll in the foreground the cottage 'betwixt two aged Okes' before which '*Corydon* and *Thyrsis* met' are being served with 'their savoury dinner' by the 'neat-handed *Phillis*'. Beyond, in a pleasant valley of 'Russet Lawns' the 'tanned haycock' and the 'nibbling flocks' are seen. Out of the 'tufted trees' the 'towers and battlements' of a castle rise, overlooking the wide river. In the far distance a church spire (the 'upland hamlet') points starkly against the mountain's 'barren brest'.

Milton's very formalized landscape passage tends to read like an inventory of features necessary for the fabrication of a seventeenth-century rustic scene. Despite this basically synthetic landscape and despite the essentially Claudian vista (articulated by horizontal lines of shadow and by the inevitable distant bridge) within which Runciman re-creates the scene, a degree of realism is achieved (except in the figures) which is surprising in the work of one of Fuseli's associates. The composition also conveys a mood of lyricism which would have delighted Samuel Palmer. Sir Steven Runciman recognizes in the distant view the tower of St. John's Church and the bridge of Perth. Since Runciman knew and clearly loved the Tay Valley (Sir Steven owns at least two other Runciman landscapes featuring the Tay Valley), it seems probable that he overcame the difficulties facing any illustration of *L'Allegro* or *Il Penseroso* and painted a real landscape which yet corresponds to the mood created by Milton's verse. The Tay Valley—far from Chalfont St. Giles—thus provides a setting which Palmer did not believe could exist in which 'meadows trim with daisies pied' lie snugly beneath 'the mountain's barren brest' and which Milton never surely envisaged but as ideal.

The latter years of the eighteenth century seem to have been the heyday of many minor illustrators. One such artist whose work has survived the vicissitudes of time is Robert Smirke (exhibiting at the Royal Academy 1786–1813) who, like many of his fellows, took advantage of the sudden increase during this period in the demand

61 R. Smirke, 'The Village Festival'   **62** R. Smirke, 'Walking in the Woods'

for illustrated books. Bryan refers to him as an 'excellent painter of humorous and sentimental subjects, taken from poets and novelists'.[13] His technique is adequately displayed in two drawings in the British Museum illustrating *L'Allegro* (61, 62). Both are executed in indian ink and wash and show, respectively, the village festival and a young man walking in the woods whilst in the background a milkmaid and a ploughman are seen at work. These drawings with their delicate prettiness and oval frames are much indebted to the rococo pastoral idylls of thirty years earlier. The contrast between the world of the cultivated aristocrat and that of the honest rural worker is particularly noticeable in the second of the drawings, where the impeccably dressed and rather foppish-looking young man is clearly enjoying Nature as Fashion has dictated in contrast to the real rustics. In addition to these drawings from Milton, Smirke exhibited 'The Lady and Sabrina, from Milton's *Comus*' at the Royal Academy in 1786. There is also in existence an engraving by Heath after Smirke entitled 'Eve Sees her own Reflection' (1780).[14]

In 1781 a toy edition of *Paradise Lost* was published for inclusion in *The Poetical Magazine* with three engravings by Birrell after a very minor artist named Dodd. In 1782, and again in 1791, subjects from Milton were exhibited at the Royal Academy by Robert Lucius West. These works have long been forgotten, but judging by their titles, 'The Battle between Michael and Satan', and 'Satan after his Fall', they probably attempted to portray the sublime in Milton. Likewise lost and forgotten are two canvases exhibited at the Royal Academy in 1784 by T. Freeman. These were 'Eve Administering to the Angel Raphael' and 'Satan at the Court of Chaos'. The disappearance of the latter is regrettable because it is the first example of the pictorial interpretation of a subject later chosen by Fuseli, Martin and other artists.

The year 1785 saw the exhibition by Joseph Wright of Derby of his picture, 'The Lady in *Comus*' (63), fortunately preserved in the Walker Art Gallery.[15] The picture comprises a very neo-classical female figure painted in the grand style, seated in a romantic moonlit landscape. Wright's special concern with the peculiar qualities of moonlight and artificial lighting is well known. (See, for example, 'Matlock High Tor, by Moonlight': Detroit Institute of Arts; 'Moonlight Landscape': R. C. A. Palmer-Morewood, Alfreton Hall; and 'An Experiment with the Air Pump': Tate Gallery.) 'The Lady in *Comus*' was painted as a companion picture to 'The Indian Widow' (Derby Museum and Art Gallery) and, from one of Wright's letters to William Hayley dated April 1784, one may con-

clude that it was the specified moonlight in the scene from *Comus*
which attracted Wright to this subject. He writes:

I have also nearly finished a companion to the Indian Widow, the burst
of light in wch picture suggested to Miss Beridge those lines from Comus,

'Was I deceived? Or did a sable cloud
Turn forth her silver lining on the Night etc.'[16]

The Indian widow is seated under a tree on which hang her dead
husband's arms and the full moonlight is much brighter than the
partial light of 'The Lady in *Comus*'. The two pictures thus comple-
ment each other. However, it seems that it was not only the theme
of moonlight which caused Wright to choose this subject from
Comus. The dramatic circumstances of the lady in the masque provide a full and complex parallel to those of the Indian widow. In
the words of B. Nicolson:

63 J. Wright of Derby, 'The Lady from *Comus*'

64 C. Metz, 'Satan meets Chaos'

Here again the theme is virtuous womanhood, done down by tragic circumstances over which the victims have no control . . . A fresh white girl and a Noble Savage, are seated under trees facing one another, the one on the soft old English hills, the other on the rugged new North American coast; the one waiting for her brothers . . . the other mourning the loss of her warrior husband . . . The Lady in Comus sits patiently 'in the blind mazes of the tangled wood;' the widow of the Indian chief 'perseveres in her mournful duty at the hazard of her own life from the inclemencies of the weather' . . . They are resigned to loneliness, fixed in position by their stylized gestures, their clear cut contours and pro-files—posed so artificially that they seem not to inhabit their landscapes at all but to have been damped down there like figures in relief on Wedgewood plaques.[17]

Mr. Nicolson has rightly emphasized the pathos and sentiment which, though not immediately evident in the *Comus* picture when considered on its own, can be clearly seen when it is considered alongside its partner. The pathos is particularly significant as it is exactly this quality which made the Lady in *Comus* one of the most popular Milton subjects of the mid-nineteenth century. It presumably appealed to the philanthropic conscience of the period.

Mr. Nicholson also notes the fact that the figures 'seem not to inhabit their landscapes'. We have seen the practice, adopted by Jones and Mortimer, of superimposing figures upon a ready-painted landscape. Not surprisingly, this was a convenient and common practice among minor artists, but 'The Lady in *Comus*' is ready evidence that, even with the fine landscapes of Gains-borough's later years readily at hand, an artist of Wright's skill and distinction still was not able to reconcile the demands of the real and the ideal. If the landscape is too ideal then the figures appear incongruous in their setting. If the figure—as in Wright's case—is ideal then it does not appear the natural inhabitant of its sur-roundings.

Thomas Macklin opened his Poets' Gallery in Fleet Street in 1788. In the catalogue of the following year two Milton subjects appear, both of which seem to have vanished with most of the rest of the contributions to the gallery.[18] 'Comus tempting the Lady' was exhibited by a Mr. Martin. This was probably Elias Martin who, in 1790, exhibited 'Our First Parents in their State of Inno-cence' at the Royal Academy. The Rev. Mr. Peters's offering to the Poets' Gallery was 'Adam's First Sight of Eve'. Two other artists painting Milton pictures during these latter years of the century were Conrad Metz and T. Braine. Braine was a miniature-painter who exhibited a picture of Satan in 1793. Metz (1749–1827) was a native of Bonn who worked in London, 'an eminent engraver in the chalk manner and aquatint'.[19] His master was Bartolozzi, who engraved Stothard's Milton illustrations. Metz's chief claim to fame seems to have been as a copyist of Holbein in London and of various artists in Rome, where he died. He exhibited three Milton works at the Royal Academy, 'The Lady in *Comus*' and 'Samson and Delilah' in 1791 and 'The Contest between Satan and Death' in the following year. No trace remains of these. However, some very competent, lively drawings of three subjects from *Paradise Lost* are in the collection of Mr. Walter Brandt. Two, signed and dated 'Roma 1814' and 'Roma 1816', depict Eve offering a handful of apples to Adam. The two figures are conventional and rather clumsy, but the background is full of wild-life and varied vegetation presented in fascinating detail reminiscent of the Flemish engraver tradition as it appears in Bernard Lens's illustration (12). The animals and birds portrayed most accurately are probably copied straight from a standard Natural History manual as the swan and the cow appear in almost identical form in another two drawings (similarly signed and dated), both of which represent the angelic guard expelling Satan from Eden at the end of Book IV. Here, the division of the page into areas of interest—Satan in the foreground, the angelic band, Adam and Eve asleep, the groups of birds and animals—recalls the traditional, episodic, pictorial treatment of *Paradise Lost* in the works of Lens and Medina. The heroic stance and classical dress of the angelic guard seem, if anything, to emphasize the contrast between the dramatic gestures of the figures and the crowded detail of the background.

While in Rome, where he executed the two drawings, Metz was engaged upon imitations of drawings by Parmigiano and copies of the Sistine ceiling. The highly mannerist style of drawing in a third, single Milton subject (owned by Mr. Brandt) is not, therefore, surprising. The subject, an extremely rare one in Milton iconography, is Satan's meeting with Chaos at the end of Book II of *Paradise Lost* (64). This drawing is more successful than the other two subjects and is designed as though for a ceiling panel. The disproportionately large figure of Satan, with his stereotyped profile and pompous, statuesque gestures, cannot but appear somewhat absurd. Metz was not evidently inspired by the enthusiasm for Satan shared by some of his contemporaries. However, Metz recreates this abstruse and complicated scene successfully—much more successfully than Fuseli in his Milton Gallery picture. The oval ceiling-panel type of composition used by Metz ensures a greater cohesion of all the disparate elements—Sable-vested *Night, Rumor, Chance, Con-*

fusion and the rest—than Fuseli achieves. Metz is surprisingly imaginative (for one who made his reputation as a copyist) in depicting '*Discord* with a thousand various mouths' where the monster forming the top part of the composition is endowed with types of human and bestial head including that of a lobster or crab. One is reminded of the statue of a lobster in the foreground of Gandy's 'Pandemonium' (174). The wildly unbalanced scales above Satan's head set the tone for this scene in which chaotic figures fight with each other and with the four elements. Peace with a Dove is being brutally battered in the bottom right-hand corner, while winged Rumour's many-headed bugle is blown above the head of the elderly bent figure of Chaos. Behind Satan's theatrical form we see the shadowy form of Mulciber, Pandemonium's architect, whom Metz has chosen to introduce into this episode (there is no mention of his presence in the poem) presumably as a reminder of the feverish building activities which preceded Satan's departure and the journey that brought him to Chaos. Altogether, this boldly executed drawing is an intelligent and imaginative interpretation of the scene as described by Milton.

Thomas Stothard designed at least twenty-three illustrations to Milton's poems. Most of them, engraved by Bartolozzi, were published by Jeffryes in 1792–3, and were augmented by a number of new plates in editions appearing in 1818 and 1826.[20] Stothard's biographer has said of his illustrations to *Paradise Lost*: 'There is little of Stothard's peculiar genius to be seen in these designs, many of which, did they not bear his name would be readily attributed

65 After T. Stothard, 'The Council in Pandemonium'

to one or other of his contemporaries.'[21] It is certainly true that
they are, by and large, a mediocre set of designs. They are, however, worth considering because, besides being typical of one type
of illustrative art of this period, they are related stylistically to some
unpublished illustrations by Flaxman for *Paradise Lost*.[22]

One fault of Stothard's designs is their lack of consistency in
style or conception. Some scenes like 'The Council in Pandemonium' (65) and 'Sin and Death' are formalized to such an extent
that they are nothing but page headings. The former is treated like
an architectonic fresco based on the theme of a 'Council of Elders'
or a 'Dispute of Ancient Philosophers'. Other illustrations like 'The
Gate of Heaven', 'Faery Elves' or the delicate pencil and wash
drawing in the British Museum depicting 'Eve and the Serpent'
(68) create an atmosphere of sweetness and sentiment. Stothard
normally uses the vignette form for this type of illustration as it
helps to suggest a sort of stylized intimacy. In the British Museum
drawing of Eve (and in the two full-scale, rather academic figures
of Adam and Eve in the illustrations to Books IV and V) we see for
the first time a real interest in the lush, natural vegetation of Eden
which, from now on, is one of the more attractive features of
Paradise Lost illustrations. Yet another style is used for the grand,
heroic scenes in which Satan figures, as, for example, the two illus-

66 After T. Stothard, 'Satan Summons his
Legions'

67 T. Stothard, 'Satan'

68 T. Stothard, 'Eve and the Serpent'   **69** After J. Flaxman, 'Milton'

trations to Book I showing 'Satan Rising from the Burning Lake' (16) and 'Satan Summoning his Legions' (66). In these designs, a certain debt to Fuseli, though not necessarily to the Milton Gallery, can be discerned. Fuseli was already working on his Milton Gallery pictures in 1792, but most of them were done between 1794 and 1799, after the publication of Stothard's illustrations. Nevertheless, Stothard was friendly with Fuseli and doubtless very familiar with his other work. Stothard's fine ink and wash drawing in the British Museum for 'Satan Summons his Legions' (67) is particularly close to some of Fuseli's work. The muscular tautness of Satan's physique, his curling locks and Michelangelesque stature, the linear style and the dramatic chiaroscuro are all characteristic of Fuseli's drawings. This artistically economic and dramatic design is scarcely recognizable when transferred to the engraving (66) in which the armour-clad Satan is set in an over-crowded background. One could wish for further knowledge of Stothard's preparatory drawings.

Flaxman's proper place is not alongside Mortimer and Stothard for two reasons. Firstly his work is more strictly neo-classical than

70 After J. Flaxman, illustrating *Elegy on the Death of the Bishop of Winchester*

theirs (or than that of any of the other artists we have to deal with in this period), and secondly his only published illustrations to Milton appeared in 1808, eight years after the chronological limit of this chapter. However, since the small collection of Milton drawings by Flaxman are undated and were probably executed before 1800, and since he was a close friend and associate of Blake, Fuseli and Stothard, it is convenient to discuss his work here.

Flaxman's three designs for Joseph Johnson's publication of Cowper's translation of Milton's *Latin and Italian Poems*, edited by

71 After J. Flaxman, illustrating *Elegy to his Tutor, Thomas Young*

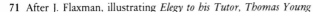

Hayley (1808), are in his strictest style of neo-classical line drawing. Engraved by A. Raimbach, they comprise a frontispiece showing Milton seated, surrounded by various references to his life and
work (69), the dream from 'Elegy III', 'On the Death of the Bishop
of Winchester' (70) and, finally, 'Doris and her Nymphs' from
'Elegy IV', 'To his Tutor, Thomas Young' (71). The frontispiece
is designed as though for a cenotaph, which is not surprising considering Flaxman's many commissions for tomb monuments.

The contrast is astonishing between the linear formality of these
designs and the exuberant and unleashed vigour of Flaxman's seven
Milton drawings in the British Museum and at the Slade. It seems
odd that Flaxman, so much in demand as an illustrator, a literary
man with strong religious convictions and particularly concerned
with man's constant battle against sin,[23] and, moreover, a friend of
several of the Milton illustrators of the period, should never have
published a set of illustrations to *Paradise Lost*. Flaxman's own lectures on sculpture delivered to the Royal Academy indicate that he
was aware that a great storehouse of subject-matter was to be
found in Milton's poetry and that he thought Milton a poet
neglected by artists. In Lecture X, prepared for delivery in 1826,
Flaxman says:

In the number of original subjects of the noblest class, derived from
revelation, we must remember the immortal poem of Paradise Lost by
our own countryman John Milton . . .

concluding the lecture Flaxman says:

And yet, it is to be believed that this poet, abounding in subjects and
characters of the most extraordinary kind, has been almost entirely
neglected in the arts of his own country, whilst his merits have been
vindicated and thus illustrated by the liberal mind and genius of a
foreigner![24]

This is something of an exaggeration of the state of affairs, but
Flaxman, understandably, felt chagrined by Fuseli's (the foreigner)
apparent exploitation of a part of the English cultural heritage.

Flaxman's drawings suggest that he was contemplating a full
series of illustrations to *Paradise Lost*. They are closely connected
in subject and style and may, therefore, be treated as a series. This
must date from the very early 1790s, firstly because of its relation
to Stothard's designs (issued in 1792), and secondly because of its
resemblance to a series of Romney drawings which date from the
1790s.

The drawings concerned depict the following: 'The Flight of

72 J. Flaxman, 'The Flight of Satan from Paradise'

73 J. Flaxman, 'Michael Seizing the Rebel Angels'

Satan from Paradise' (Slade 664), being a partial study for a rect-
angular relief, a plaster cast of which is in University College (72),
'Satan's First Words to Beelzebub' as they lie on the lake in *Paradise
Lost*, I (Slade 665), and five drawings (three of which are in the
British Museum, the other two being numbers 662 and 663 in the
Slade collection) concerned with the war in Heaven (73 and 74).
These are all well-established subjects in the iconographic pattern
of Milton illustration.

W. G. Constable has said in connection with Flaxman's Milton
drawings that 'Sophocles and Milton, like Homer and Aeschylus
called for a type of imagination he did not possess'.[25] This is certainly true, but the explanation for the absence of Milton illustrations among Flaxman's engravings cannot be so simple. Flaxman
was clearly fascinated by the confusion of fighting, falling bodies
and most of the drawings portray this sort of scene, of which there
are many fine descriptions in *Paradise Lost*. In some of these pencil
and ink drawings Flaxman approaches a degree of involvement in

74 J. Flaxman, 'Falling Angels'

75 After T. Stothard, 'Satan Rising from the Burning Lake'

the pure qualities of abstract design and reduces all to essential masses (73, 74). A similar thing occurs in some of Romney's drawings of this date. It may have happened that Flaxman was unable to transform these technical experiments into cohesive designs. It is not unreasonable to suppose that Flaxman's drawings from *Paradise Lost* were experimental as they show a certain violence which might

76 After T. Stothard, 'Satan Travels towards Earth'

77 After H. Richter, 'Adam and Eve Hear God's Voice'

78 After T. Kirk, 'Eve Confesses'

be associated with the 'sublime' and which is alien to most of his published work. He probably thought that this departure from the neo-classical fold was too much of a risk.[26]

The clearest evidence for Stothard's borrowing of certain motifs from Flaxman lies in Stothard's design for *Paradise Lost* I, 'Satan Rising from the Burning Lake' (76). Stothard's figure of Satan prone on the lake acquires much of its impact from the imitation of Satan in Flaxman's Slade drawing 665. The flatness of some of Stothard's backgrounds and the relief effect of figures against them is very reminiscent of Flaxman. In Stothard's depiction of Satan flying 'his oblique way' towards earth (75) (*Paradise Lost*, III), for example, in which the starry back-cloth, the decoratively fluttering drapery and the disposition of the long-limbed figure in space are

79 T. Kirk, 'Adam and Eve See Raphael'

close to many of Flaxman's tomb sculpture reliefs. 'Uriel Gliding through the Even' (*Paradise Lost*, IV) might almost—in gesture and in the fluid contours of body and drapery—be an angel from Flaxman's Monument to Mary Lushington (1799). A further drawing (illustrating Book IV, line 678, of *Paradise Lost*) by Flaxman in the collection of Mr. W. Brandt also depicts the softly floating female forms in which Stothard delights.

In 1794 a new edition of *Paradise Lost* was published by H. and J. Richter. It contains twenty-four engravings after designs by H. Richter, who was a pupil of Stothard, a member of the Old Water Colour Society, a popular artist of his day and a man whose very varied interests included metaphysics.[27] Richter's designs seem to be somewhat outside the mainstream of Milton illustrations. His primary concern was with landscape. 'Michael Describing the Future to Adam', a drawing in the British Museum, reinforces the impression of a rather poor draughtsman. Richter's figures are stiff and ungainly, but his landscapes of Eden, in which the closely observed details of nature are seen through a subtle softness of light and blurring of outline, have a certain charm (77).

The Poetical Works of Milton appeared in another new edition in 1796 published by C. Cooke with eleven engravings after Thomas

Kirk and one after W. H. Brown. Kirk died of consumption the year after the publication of this edition and a career 'of much promise'[28] was thus prematurely ended. According to Redgrave, Kirk was one '. . . of the painters to whom the new taste for book designs gave employment, while their works added a character into the publications of the time'.[29] Kirk's Milton illustrations show some proficiency in figure drawing and much superficial elegance (78). They are more dramatic than those of Richter, partly because the figures are more mobile and partly by reason of compositional devices such as the use of the low horizon of fashionable portraiture. The illustrations are designed in oval frames which are

80 After H. Singleton, 'Adam and Eve Admonished'

ornamented in a bizarre and sometimes macabre fashion by an artist named Satchwell.

A chalk drawing of 'Adam and Eve See Raphael' by a Thomas Kirk exists in the British Museum (79). The long-legged figure style of the drawing is exactly that of Kirk's Milton illustrations. This drawing must surely be by the same artist even though Binyon cites it as the work of a Thomas Kirk, sculptor (1777–1845), born in Ireland.[30]

Yet another new edition of *Paradise Lost* was published in this prolific year of 1796 by J. Parsons. The illustrations (twelve in all) were engraved after R. Corbould and H. Singleton and form quite a distinguished set. Singleton clearly had a taste for Milton because he frequently exhibited subjects from Milton at the Royal Academy: one in 1795, four in 1796, and one in 1818, 1820 and 1829 respectively. An album in the British Museum contains a number of Singleton's swift, experimental pencil sketches of subjects from

81 After H. Singleton, 'Satan and Uriel'

82 After R. Corbould, 'Satan Rises from the Burning Lake'

83 After E. F. Burney, 'Il Pensoroso'

84 After E. F. Burney, 'Adam Curses his Creation'

Paradise Lost (80). His two contributions to the 1796 edition are carefully considered compositions and were probably adapted from canvases exhibited at the Academy in the same year. It is interesting to note how 'Satan and Uriel' (81), a subject introduced by Hayman and used by Stothard, has now become a standard illustration for Book III of *Paradise Lost*. The choice of this scene is symptomatic of the growing tendency of illustrators to select scenes which involve only two main figures in order that they can more readily display their skill at academic figure drawing. In accordance with the artistic fashion of the time Singleton's Michael is attired in fully classical military costume and Uriel wears a sort of flowing Greek garment, draped over one shoulder.

Corbould's illustrations are firm and vigorous. While this is particularly true of his designs to Books I and II (82), when treating scenes involving Adam and Eve he tends to adopt the conventional gesture and composition. In the illustration to Book I, 'Satan Rears from off the Pool', the figure of Satan, seen frontally and wearing the type of dress in which Hogarth clothed him, occupies virtually the whole composition. The size and position of the figure and the fact that Satan possesses 'bat's' wings relate Corbould's design for Book I to that of the first illustrator, Medina (9). Corbould has tried, not too successfully, to give to Satan the expression of anguished determination with which Fuseli endows him. Despite the clumsiness of this heavy-limbed figure there is no doubt that the bold, frontal view, like Medina's, has great dramatic potential.

Most subsequent successful renderings of this scene follow the example of Corbould's composition.

In the same year, 1796, *Paradise Regained and the Minor Poems* was published by Longman, Law and associates. It contained four illustrations by E. F. Burney, who five years earlier had designed the frontispiece to *Comus* in Bell's British Theatre series. This very ornately rococo little piece of work portrayed Miss Storace as Euphrosyne. Although 'Samson' and 'The Baptism of Christ' in the 1796 edition show an endeavour on the part of the artist to achieve a greater degree of classical monumentality in his treatment of the figures, the other two illustrations ('L'Allegro' and 'Il Penseroso') are chiefly decorative. In 'Il Penseroso' (83) the figure, seated amidst a complexity of trees and foliage contrived mainly to create an attractive and symmetrical appearance on the page, has an unreal and artificial air. However, Burney's designs must have been admired in influential quarters, for in 1799 he was commissioned to design a complete set of illustrations for an edition of *Paradise Lost* which was published by C. Whittingham in 1800.

Some of Burney's designs for *Paradise Lost* provided the starting

85 After E. F. Burney, 'Eve Tempted'   86 After E. F. Burney, 'Satan, Sin and Death'

point for Blake's set of designs for the poem and will, therefore, be discussed later in connection with Blake. It will suffice here to establish that Burney himself was a highly eclectic artist who delighted primarily in complex surface pattern. His background is of some interest to the student of cultural history. E. F. Burney was born in 1760 into the distinguished family which included Dr. Burney the music-historian and Fanny, author of *Evelina*. In fact in 1778 Burney helped his cousin to get her novel published anonymously and in 1780 he exhibited designs for *Evelina* at the Royal Academy. He was a friend of Charles Lamb and has been considered '. . . certainly above the average illustrator of his time, but his talent was vitiated by a degenerate neo-classicism, the bane of eighteenth century artists'.[31]

The chief characteristic of Burney's 1799 *Paradise Lost* illustrations are figures which combine a certain exaggerated roundness of limb with great flamboyancy of gesture. The artist's feeling for natural detail and curving, serpentine lines helps to achieve this. The frontispiece to the edition is an astonishing mixture of sinuous and highly complex calligraphy and excessively decorative drawing.

87 After E. F. Burney, 'Satan Starts at the Touch of Ithuriel's Spear'

88 After J. H. Fuseli, 'Satan Starts at the Touch of Ithuriel's Spear'

It has a vignette showing 'Adam Cursing his Creation' from *Paradise Lost*, X (84). The whole page is a very appropriate introduction to the style of the subsequent illustrations in this edition. In 'Eve Tempted' (85) Burney's decorative impulse excels itself. There is surely no more richly ornamented illustration to Milton than this. Eve leans with elegantly curving body against the Tree of Life whilst the serpent in masses of 's' folds speaks to her. All around hollyhocks, roses and other English garden flowers grow in riotous profusion.

Burney's designs are closely based on those of earlier artists. In his illustration of 'Satan, Sin and Death' (86), whilst Death is related to Corbould's (and Hogarth's) figures of Death, Sin kneels in a position which is a compromise between limbs and serpentine coils as in Hayman's illustration of this scene (40). 'The Expulsion' by Burney in the 1800 edition is based directly on Hayman's frontal treatment of the subject with Michael leading, rather than driving, Adam and Eve from Paradise. The figure of Satan in 'Satan Starts at the Touch of Ithuriel's Spear' (87) is a copy in reverse of Fuseli's figure of Satan in his treatment of this scene (88). Similarly Burney's figure of Satan in 'The Expulsion of Satan and his Forces from Heaven' bears some relation to the illustration to the same lines in Du Rouveray's 1802 *Paradise Lost*. This edition was illustrated by Fuseli and, although Burney could not have seen it before designing his own illustrations, he may have seen sketches or similar works in the Milton Gallery (1799), or in Fuseli's studio. Certainly no illustrator of this generation could fail to know Fuseli's Milton work. Thus, with Burney, the most eclectic of this group of minor artists, we end this section and progress to a consideration of the work of an artist of considerable individuality, Henry Fuseli.

(ii) Artists of the Miltonic Sublime (1771–1800)

> Milton is like a Flood, whose Tide,
> Swell'd with tempestuous Deluge, roars,
> Which from some lofty Mountain's side
> Resistless foams, and knows no shores.
>
> Daniel Webb, *Remarks on the Beauties of Poetry*, 1762

There is no sudden change of artistic attitude or style in 1800, the chronological limit of this section. The gradual change in concepts from the 1750s onwards is a process of continuous evolution towards something recognizable as 'romantic', and the attitudes which are generally accepted as belonging to the Romantics are visible in the work of their precursors. It is important, therefore, to establish at the outset some of the most important landmarks in changing ideas during this period, and also to endeavour to define in exactly what form the romantic attitude is discernible in Milton illustrations.

The foothold of classical art in England has always been an uneasy one. England has never produced a writer as strictly classical as Corneille or Racine, or an artist as classical as Jacques Louis David. Shakespeare and Milton were unfailingly popular in this country throughout the eighteenth century and Pope, generally regarded as one of our more classical poets, in 1716 could write, in *Eloisa to Abelard*, of 'grots and caverns shagged with horrid thorn!'[32] Even Reynolds, the English bastion of neo-classicism, unleashed a surprising degree of sentiment in his child portraiture. It is, therefore, an artificial, process to contrast Romanticism with Classicism or with Realism. Nor is Romanticism a voluntary category. Byron, for example, wanted to be remembered as the successor of Pope, and Fuseli could not be induced to read the new romantic literature of his period. Burke in his *Enquiry* of 1757,[33] an essay which— more than any other single piece of writing of the period—was of prime importance for the early Romantics, bases his arguments on familiar neo-classical precepts, despite his novel interest in the emotions and passions as depicted in painting and poetry. Reynolds and Dr. Johnson both upheld the superiority of general truths, a generally accepted tenet of neo-classical art. Reynolds observed 'that perfect form is produced by leaving out particularities and retaining only general ideas', whilst Dr. Johnson believed that 'the business of a poet is to examine, not the individual but the species; to remark general properties and large appearances'.[34] Burke in Part II, Section IV, of his *Enquiry*, seeks to discover why the general effect rather than the individual detail is more powerful in art.

The proper manner of conveying the affections of the mind from one to another is by words; there is a great insufficiency in all other methods of communication . . . I do not know of any paintings, bad or good, that produce the same effect. *So that poetry with all its obscurity, has a more general as well as a more powerful dominion over the passions than the other art. And I think there are reasons in nature why the obscure idea, when properly conveyed, should be more affecting than the clear.* It is our ignorance of things that causes all our admiration, and chiefly excites our passions . . .[35]

Burke, despite the anti-classical nature of his subject, seeks—like the Augustans—to recognize absolute standards in Art and Nature.

During the latter years of the eighteenth century, the neo-classicists were looking for the salvation of art in a return to what they considered were its original principles. The new romantic impulse was towards an acceptance of progress as a natural law and the desire to extract artistic excitement from new sources. In the case of most artists there was a partial complicity between the two impulses.

Burke's *Enquiry* resulted from a number of combined factors: the growing eighteenth-century interest in Nature, the habit of travel in England rather than on the Continent as a result of the Seven Years War (1756–63) and the cult of the Gothic as the eighteenth century conceived of it. The essay defines the difference between the sublime and the beautiful. In short, the sublime is inspired by terror and fear and is characterized by obscurity, power, greatness of dimension, vastness of extent, infinity, magnificence. It involves also loudness of sound, darkness and gloominess of colour. The beautiful, however, entails smallness, smoothness, gradual variation, elegance, clearness and fairness in colour and softness and delicacy of sound. In 1792 Gilpin followed up Burke's *Enquiry* with his *Observations on Picturesque Beauty*.[36] Two years later Sir Uvedale Price published his *Essays on the Picturesque* and Richard Payne Knight published his poem *The Landscape*. By 1801 the dispute on the qualities of the sublime, the beautiful and the picturesque initiated by Burke was at its height.[37]

For our purposes, the significance of Burke's *Enquiry* lies in the fact that the author cites Milton as the English poet most capable of evoking the sublime. Just how rapidly and how thoroughly Burke's principles were assimilated into the general critical criteria of the period can be seen from the passage in which Dr. Johnson describes *Paradise Lost* in the sort of terms first used by Burke for purposes of literary assessment.

[Milton] seems to have been well acquainted with his own genius, and to know what it was that Nature had bestowed upon him more bountifully than upon others; the power of displaying the vast, illuminating the awful, darkening the gloomy, and aggravating the dreadful.[38]

The lines from Daniel Webb's *Remarks on the Beauties of Poetry*, quoted at the beginning of this section, further testify to Milton's unrivalled position as poet of the sublime.

The artists with whom we are concerned in this chapter were as conscious as the poets and men of letters of the qualities of the sublime established by Burke. For Fuseli, nurtured on the *Sturm und Drang* philosophy of art, the milieu was a natural one. Fuseli's delight in sublime excesses and melodramatic properties in art appears alongside his adherence to the classical belief in generalization and the grand style. Here is the complicity of the apparently opposed impulses of Classicism and Romanticism. Fuseli admires the terror and mystery of *Macbeth* but seeks to achieve this by means of grandiose generalities: 'All apparatus destroys terror as all ornament grandeur: the minute catalogue of the cauldron's ingredients in *Macbeth* destroys the terror attendant on mysterious darkness.'[39]

The delight of an artist like Fuseli in qualities of blackness and terror is also, in some measure, connected with the turmoil of an age which was breaking away from a strict code of universally held belief and which was in a state of political upheaval. G. Grigson has detected in the work of Barry, Mortimer and Fuseli qualities similar to those in Goya's painting. But, unlike Goya, the three English painters sought much of their subject-matter in literature:

It would be wrong to call any of the three [i.e. Barry, Mortimer and Fuseli] 'romantics' in the common use, but they share in the sense of the turmoil, of the black and red river, of the black and cavernous and jagged abyss within which we walk and fight, which was now felt again during the second half of the century, and which at this time was commensurately and fully expressed in painting only by Goya, and in a lesser way by Fuseli himself . . . Where Goya extracted visions out of himself and of the humanity around him, Fuseli, despising the temporal except as an aid, sought to record visions out of his own experience of life and out of the similar experience recorded by those whom he considered the deepest artists or deepest writers of the world.[40]

What could be more natural than for these English artists to express this sense of black turmoil through the Hell of Dante or, more probably, through the Hell of *Paradise Lost*.

The fact that the greatest creative figures of the Romantic era were poets gave an extra impetus to literary painting, which was already well established in this country. Nevertheless, it is important to remember that in England the Gothic Revival and the cult of the Picturesque inspired paintings the character of which is primarily romantic, some twenty years before the publication of Wordsworth's *Lyrical Ballads*. The romantic content of a work is not determined by its subject but by its treatment. *Paradise Lost* had been a subject in the repertoire of English artists for more than a century, but with the advent of Barry, Fuseli, Romney and Blake, a quite new concept of Milton's work is presented to the eye of the public. Up till the last quarter of the eighteenth century the pictorial treatment of Milton's poetry had been more or less purely illustrative. Romantic literary painting at its best is evocative rather than illustrative.

The two great themes of nineteenth-century art, themes which have their roots in the latter years of the eighteenth century, were the individual consciousness and landscape. The question of landscape does not, directly, concern us here. The only analogy for the concept of the Romantic man is that of the Renaissance man. We have already mentioned the sense of insecurity which must have been rife in an age that was breaking away from the pattern of belief accepted by the Augustans. The gap left by this estrangement from dominant eighteenth-century ideals was partially filled by the love of heroism and the worship of an individual or a group. Both Milton and his most famous creation, Satan, were seen by artists and writers of the period in this heroic light.

A further result (which can be seen in the reactions of a different group of artists and writers) was a new delight in revelation, scientific or religious. The two were frequently allied as in the work of that nonconformist most popular with artists of the period, Emanuel Swedenborg. The revelatory zeal was sometimes purely religious, as with Wesley, sometimes more a question of nature mysticism, as with Jacob Boehme. It usually involved a new consciousness of sin, and a search for primitive innocence outside orthodoxy. In either case, the subject-matter of *Paradise Lost* provided a relevant source.

E. R. Meijer has likened the art of the turbulent Romantic era to mannerist art, the art of an age engaged in similar upheaval.[41] Obviously the French Revolution was the cause of great ferment among artists and thinkers, and we shall see subsequently how the revolutionary atmosphere of Europe affected the cult of Milton and *Paradise Lost*. However, the revolution apart, why was the Romantic age so turbulent? The changes in belief and attitude exhibited by the Romantics originate in the different localization of various levels of reality. N. Frye has most clearly illustrated this by comparing the system of the cosmos accepted at the end of the Middle Ages, during the seventeenth century and at the end of the eighteenth century. Dante sees the cosmos in terms of the Ptolemaic system and places Eden in the centre, half-way up a mountain with Heaven above and Hell below. Milton was faced with a choice of possible systems and thus locates Heaven and Hell outside the cosmos. For the post-Newtonian poet the divinely ordered system is gone and he is faced with the realities of gravitation and the solar system.[42] To the pre-Romantic mind reality was something organized by God, but Rousseau, who more than any other writer completely expresses the 'philosophy' of the Romantics, works on the assumption that civilization is a purely human artifact. For him, arts are the centre of civilization and the basis of man's creative power. Fuseli was trained in youth to be a Zwinglian minister, yet in the pictures he painted for the Milton Gallery his rejection of God is total and complete. Not only is the Almighty never portrayed but the optimistic passages of the poem, those dealing with Divine Providence which were so popular with earlier illustrators, are largely ignored. Satan is the subject of the Milton Gallery, and not Milton's Satan inhabiting the ordered, meticulously described cosmos of *Paradise Lost*, but Fuseli's Satan, the independent, heroic, threatening symbol of the age, existing in a terrifying featureless void.

Now, to return to the question of the revolutionary ideal which the Romantics discovered in Milton. An increase in the publication of parts of Milton's prose during the rise of radicalism at the end of the eighteenth century suggests that writers and the literate populace perceived a direct parallel between Milton's own progressive political thinking and that of their own. Shelley in the preface to *Prometheus Unbound* (1820) writes: '. . . the sacred Milton was, let it ever be remembered, a republican, and a bold inquirer into morals and religion.'[43] There is no doubt that Milton was regarded as the prototype of the great English radical and nonconformist, a model for those who were to free Europe from tyranny. The disillusionment experienced by so many radicals towards the end of the French Revolution made even more tenable the parallel that artists drew between themselves and Milton. Having striven for *his* rebellion and failed, Milton then put all his energies into the creation of *Paradise Lost*, a work concerned with rebellion. Thus the disillusioned artists of the 1800s saw an example precisely applicable to their own condition. Wordsworth in his sonnet *London, 1802* expressed the feeling of many of his contemporaries:

Milton! thou should'st be living at this hour:
England hath need of thee: . . .

This vision of Milton as a great example for the time is expressed even more clearly by Godwin later in the century: 'The character of Milton is one of those which appears to gain by time . . . He is our poet . . . He is our patriot. No man of just discernment can read his political writings without being penetrated with the holy flame that animated him.'[44]

The popularity of *Paradise Lost* during the period of the French Revolution (1788–1801) exceeded even the popularity of its creator. Twenty-one editions of the poem were published during the period.[45] W. Gaunt has offered reasons for the way in which not only Blake and Shelley but numerous other artists and writers admired Milton's Satan:

Paradise Lost came from a Puritan century, in which the fall of man and the demand for unquestioning obedience to the will of God were fully and literally accepted. Yet in the demand for unquestioning obedience there was, if one chose to look at it in that light, an element of tyranny, that in merely human government would have been unbearable. Sympathy might well be directed to Satan who did rebel against the All-Powerful . . . Perhaps unconsciously they [i.e. the Romantics] associated him with the revolutionary struggle against the organized governments of Europe and as values became confused Satan was less a symbol of horror than of such hope as a hopeless defiance could contain. Good and bad were confused. The lofty and benevolent ideas with which the French revolution began had, in the eyes of other countries turned into bloodthirsty malignance, and the revolutionary himself in the age of Napoleon was confronted with the armed camp of absolutism planted on the foundations of liberty, equality and fraternity. Changing form, the thwarting tyranny that Blake represented by his Urizen was stronger than ever; the spirit of freedom, cut off from political and social aspirations, retained only the valour of opposition.[46]

Satan was completely humanized by the 1790s. Never again do we see the animal-like Satan of Medina and Cheron nor even the stiff, puppet-like actor of Hayman and R. Corbould. Satan appears in the work of Barry, Fuseli and nineteenth-century artists with athletic form, handsome features and determined but suffering visage. Adam and Eve, Uriel, Raphael and Michael are all now minor characters in the drama. Satan is the embodiment of all that is of primary interest in *Paradise Lost*.

It was not only in painting that Satan emerged as a hero. Schiller in *Der Räuber* (1781) bases his chief character, the robber Karl Moor, on Milton's Satan. In a scene which was later suppressed because it was considered heretical, Karl Moor says to Spiegelberg:

I do not know, Maurice, if you have read Milton. He who could not endure that another should be above him, and who dared to challenge the Almighty to a duel, was he not an extraordinary genius? He had encountered the Invincible One, and although in defeat he exhausted all his forces, he was not humiliated; eternally, even to the present day, he makes new efforts, and every blow falls back again on his own head, yet still he is not humiliated. . . .[47]

In fact Milton's Satan is humiliated. Milton pictures his gradual degradation from the heroic figure of the first two books (who retains traces of his 'original brightness') to a wolf leaping over the boundaries of paradise, to a crow, then to a toad at the ear of Eve and finally to a serpent. Karl Moor's speech is some degree of confirmation that, particularly abroad, the Romantics concentrated on the first two books of *Paradise Lost*. Shelley, in *A Defense of Poesy* (1822), sums up the attitude of the age in this matter: 'Nothing can exceed the energy and magnificence of the character of Satan as expressed in *Paradise Lost*. It is a mistake to suppose that he could ever have been intended for the popular personification of evil . . .'[48] Shelley could have drawn on a variety of Miltonic literary interpretations from the 1780s and 1790s to underline his statement. The evil hero of the Gothic novel was probably a descendant of Milton's Satan. Mario Praz has said that:

Rebels in the grand manner, grandsons of Milton's Satan and brothers of Schiller's Robber, begin to inhabit the picturesque, Gothicized backgrounds of the English 'tales of terror' towards the end of the eighteenth century. The little figures of banditti, which formed pleasing decorative details in the landscapes of the Salvator Rosa school then in fashion, came to life in the writings of Mrs. Anne Radcliffe, 'the Shakespeare of romance writers', and took on gigantic and Satanic proportions, becowled and sinister as Goya's bogeys.[49]

Joseph Farington's Diary gives us a fascinating glimpse of the way in which writers and artists at the turn of the eighteenth century discussed Milton's work and, on social occasions, argued vigorously about his merit as a poet. On January 6th, 1795, Farington mentions a conversation with a friend during which it emerges that Hayley's *Life of Milton* was written at first in such a strong spirit of republicanism that it could not be printed. It is not surprising that Fuseli, who opened his Milton Gallery in 1799, features in many of these recorded conversations. On March 10th, 1804, we hear that Fuseli had met Coleridge at Johnson's and 'thought little of him'. Northcote and Coleridge had disputed about Milton:

Coleridge sd. He was next to our Saviour in Humility. Northcote on the contrary thought that ambition was the prevailing quality of his mind. That He was arrogant and tyrannical—Opie sd. that Don Quixote was nearer to that pattern of humility than Milton . . . Fuseli sd. the speech of Adam to his Creator requiring a mate was equal to anything. Opie sd. throughout it abounded with the highest excellence.[50]

This passage in *Paradise Lost* was, evidently, a favourite with Fuseli because on July 5th, 1810, Farington tells us:

89 J. Barry, 'Adam Tempted by Eve'

Carlisle left us soon after tea, and the conversation from that period became better. The subject was poetry. Fuseli spoke with tears in his eyes
of a passage in Milton as excelling in beauty & sublimity, & feeling, all
that he had read. It was that where a conversation is held between the
Creator and Adam upon the subject of His having a mate, a companion.[51]

90 J. Barry, 'Adam's Detection'

This, then, was the vigorous cultural and social environment in which Fuseli and his contemporaries painted their pictures from Milton.

According to W. Whitley, James Barry returned from Italy in 1771 and in the same year exhibited for the first time at the Royal Academy. The work with which he made his début was 'Adam and Eve' and it 'occupied one of the best places at the academy where it was well received although its frank nudity shocked some of the critics'.[52] This picture was probably the same as or very similar to a canvas now in the National Gallery of Ireland showing 'The Temptation of Adam' ('I feel the link of nature draw me'). There is an engraving in the British Museum after this canvas (89) from which we may deduce that Barry's work in the 1770s was already fully mature. Adam and Eve are drawn on an enormous scale, occupying almost the whole canvas. Their figures are almost exaggeratedly athletic. Adam, for the first time in the history of Milton illustration, is given a deeply worried expression and Eve insinuates herself in gesture and expression into the mind of her partner. The pair lean against an outcrop of rock, as massive in its proportions as their limbs, and the whole is treated in violent chiaroscuro, creating a sombre, mysterious and threatening effect.

Barry seems to have been a very fiery character who made as many enemies as friends. Born in Ireland, he impressed Edmund Burke at an early age. Burke brought him to England and financed his stay in Italy from 1766 until 1771. 'No painter of his generation took the President's encouragement towards the "grand style" so close to the letter and with so small a grain of the salt of common sense.'[53] His figure style, like Fuseli's, betrays a close dependence on Michelangelo, but he has less feeling for linear pattern than Fuseli and more for monumentality. The influence of his patron Burke, author of *The Enquiry*,[54] is immediately evident in the subjects he painted from Milton, which are vast, sombre, grandiose and violent. One of his admirers, Francis Burroughs, in *A Poetical Epistle to James Barry, Esq* (1805) eulogizes the artist in appropriately lofty vocabulary:

> To you, was giv'n, those myst'ries to explore,
> Where truths divine, were veil'd, with heathen lore;
> Bid, glowing thoughts on glowing canvass rise,
> And mend our morals, while you charm'd our eyes,
> Nay more:—the mystick genesis to scan,
> And 'vindicate the ways of god to man'.

However, the work of this artist of the 'sublime' did not please everyone. Dr. Bryan very acrimoniously wrote of Barry:

Whatever may have been the singularities or infirmities of Mr. Barry, it is to be wished that the art of painting may never be more degraded by the productions of eccentric absurdity than it has been by this original and daring artist.[55]

Barry's Milton pictures are very numerous and all on the same monumental scale. In addition to the 'Adam and Eve' already mentioned, there is an engraving in the British Museum (most probably belonging to the 1770s) of 'Adam's Detection' which exactly follows a drawing in the Soane Museum (90) with the addition only of a few foreground plants and flowers. The work is a strange mixture of Mannerism and Romanticism. Barry, unlike Fuseli, does not hesitate to portray the Divine Presence. All three figures are seen from a low viewpoint which both emphasizes the elongated, muscular limbs of the standing Adam and serves to concentrate all attention upwards towards the figure of God. Eve is hiding under an overhang of rock and grass and the whole rather indistinct background indicates a rocky, violently lit landscape of the sort that De Loutherbourg or James Ward later painted.

'Satan Summoning his Legions' (an engraving and identical ink and wash drawing both in the British Museum) (98) shows Satan as a huge, heroic figure seen from the same mannerist angle as Adam in 'Adam's Detection'.[56] Myriads of devils are seen in ranks behind Satan, and neither Satan nor his troops retain any of the characteristics of the popular devil which, up till now, have usually coloured the artist's conception of this scene. 'The Fall of Satan', an engraving in the British Museum, dated 1777 (91) must have been a design intended for the interior of St. Paul's Cathedral, for it is inscribed:

The Royal Academy having in the year 1773 selected six of its members to paint each a picture for St. Paul's Cathedral, this sketch of the fall of Satan being one of the designs executed for that purpose is with the greatest respect dedicated to the right reverend father in God Thos. Lord Bishop of Bristol, Dean of St. Paul's. . . .

(A rough but vigorous pencil drawing by Barry in the Soane Museum (116) must be a study for this.) It is an impressive design conveying an atmosphere of the terrifying void of the abyss between high rock walls. The terror of the unknown was an aspect of *Paradise Lost* that no previous artist had really succeeded in recreating. James Barry's treatment of such scenes is quite different from that of Fuseli, despite the fact that there are so many similarities between the two artists. In Fuseli's Milton pictures the action almost invariably takes place in a great vacuity where no background is indicated. Barry skilfully creates a fantasy world of rocky landscapes inhabited by Romanoesque giants. These backgrounds provide a framework for the action and emphasize its violent nature.

'Satan, Sin and Death' (engraving in the British Museum) (92) is a less successful work. As in Hogarth's treatment of this scene (53) the kneeling figure of Sin loses all force by her squatness in comparison to the figures on her immediate left and right. Death has a skull for a head and is draped in a monkish cowl. This is an improvement on the usual skeleton as the garment suggests a threatening degree of substance and therefore strength in this character. The picture fails primarily because Barry seems to have been so intent on creating figures of gigantic stature that he omitted to remember that three such figures would jostle each other off the stage. Barry also did a version of 'Milton Dictating *Paradise Lost*' (drawing and engraving in the British Museum) and a version of 'Satan Starting at the Touch of Ithuriel's Spear' (drawing—Rockhill Nelson Gallery).

The wild, fantasy element in James Barry's backgrounds was fully exploited by Philip James de Loutherbourg, an artist of French origin working in this country at the same time as Barry. Originally employed as a scene painter to Garrick, De Loutherbourg's landscapes, which are mostly known to us only from contemporary descriptions, not surprisingly seem to have epitomized the popular and theatrical concept of the sublime. His 'Deluge' (c. 1790, Victoria and Albert Museum) and his 'Avalanche in the Alps' (1804, Petworth) show the extent of the difference between the treatment of such natural phenomena at this period and Turner's treatment of them only a little later. In De Loutherbourg's work the direct link with the theatre is manifest. It is as though stock requirements for a particular mood were assembled together beforehand and then composed into one fantastic composite scene. There is no question of observation or recollection or any real degree of naturalism. The work of artists of the 'sublime', like De Loutherbourg, did not pretend to naturalism, their aim was a preconceived mood achieved by a heightening and forcing of natural effects into an artificiality which created terror by the very fact that it was unnatural. It was the sort of terror created by Shakespeare in plays like *Macbeth* and *Julius Caesar*, the terror of the owl at midday, of earthquakes, lamentings in the air and 'strange screams of death', a terror originating in human horror of the unnatural.[57]

91 J. Barry, 'The Fall of Satan'

92 J. Barry, 'Satan, Sin and Death'

It is this sense of horror that De Loutherbourg exploited when in 1782 he added two new scenes to his Eidophusikon (opened the year before), one of which featured the Hell from *Paradise Lost*. The Eidophusikon was a precursor of the cinema and involved the use of coloured lights, coloured glass and varied sounds to create a theatrical and changing effect around a sequence of pictures presented to a seated audience. It was tremendously popular. Reynolds 'honoured the talents of the ingenious contriver by frequent attendance' and Gainsborough 'was so wrapped in delight with the Eidophusikon, that for a time he thought of nothing else, talked of nothing else and passed his evenings at that exhibition in long succession'.[58] 'Satan Arraying his Troops on the Bank of the Fiery Lake, with the Palace of Pandemonium: from Milton' was seen by the audience at the end of a sequence including a famous shipwreck and 'The Cataract of Niagara'.

The Eidophusikon, having toured the country and changed owners several times, was destroyed by fire at the beginning of the nineteenth century. A vivid picture of what the Miltonic scene was like is given by W. H. Pyne in *Wine and Walnuts*. He writes:

But the most impressive scene which formed the finale of the exhibition, was that representing the region of the fallen angels . . . De Loutherbourg had already displayed his graphic powers, in his scenes of fire, upon a great scale at the public theatre—scenes which had astonished and terrified the audience; but in this he astonished himself—for he had not conceived the power of light that might be thrown upon a scenic display, until he made the experiment on his own circumscribed stage. Here, in the foreground of a vista, stretching an immeasurable length between mountains, ignited from the bases to their lofty summits, with many-coloured flame, a chaotic mass arose in dark majesty, which gradually assumed form until it stood, the interior of a vast temple of gorgeous architecture, bright as molten brass, seemingly composed of unquenchable fire. In this tremendous scene, the effect of coloured glasses before the lamps was fully displayed; which being hidden from the audience threw their whole influence on the scene, as it rapidly changed, now to a sulphurous blue, then to a lurid red, and then again to a pale vivid light, and ultimately to a mysterious combination of the glasses, such as a bright furnace exhibits in fusing various metals. The sounds which accompanied the wondrous picture, struck the astonished ear of the spectator as no less preternatural; for to add a more awful character to peals of thunder and the accompaniments of all the hollow machinery that hurled balls and stones with indescribable rumbling and noise, an expert assistant swept his thumb over the surface of the tambourine which produced a variety of groans that struck the imagination as issuing from infernal spirits.[59]

Fuseli's Milton Gallery has been thoroughly explored by Dr. Schiff[60] and Appendix C comprises a list of the names and details of all the pictures exhibited there. Therefore instead of discussing the works of the Gallery in detail, we shall endeavour to gain a general view of the Milton Gallery and the circumstances leading to its foundation. But our particular interest in the following pages will be a number of questions which have hitherto been neglected and which are of special importance to a general survey of Milton and English art. For example, what was the peculiar affinity between Milton and Fuseli that led Fuseli to devote some nine years of his life almost exclusively to pictures based on Milton's poetry? Was this something stemming from Fuseli's individual artistic needs or was Fuseli much more within the mainstream of English art than is often assumed? Was his predilection for Milton not just one aspect of the general cult of Milton at this period? Why was the Milton Gallery such a failure with the general public? How far did Fuseli depend on earlier illustrators of Milton and how great an influence did he exert on his contemporaries and successors? All these are questions which we shall try to answer.

Fuseli's biographer, Knowles, gives us a thorough account of the origins of the Milton Gallery.[61] In 1790 the Boydell Shakespeare Gallery was almost complete and Fuseli, feeling the effect of a sudden decrease in commissions, was looking around for some new scheme which would provide, for a period, a stable source of income. Boydell's illustrated edition of Shakespeare had been very successful and the publisher, Johnson, taking this as his example, decided to produce a really superlative edition of Milton edited by Cowper and illustrated by Fuseli. Unfortunately Cowper became seriously mentally ill and the scheme had to be abandoned. However, Fuseli, who had already shown his considerable sympathy with the poet in a series of drawings executed over a span of some fifteen years, clung to the idea of a scheme involving pictures from Milton. In August 1790 Fuseli and Johnson were in Ramsgate whence Fuseli wrote to his friend Roscoe, the Liverpool banker, broaching the idea of a Milton Gallery for which Fuseli would be solely responsible. This letter makes it clear that his aims are twofold. Firstly, he felt that an artist who created a comprehensive but unified corpus of work had more chance of lasting fame. Secondly, he saw the Milton Gallery as a permanent source of income; presumably to be derived from entrance money and engravings after the pictures.

Fuseli, having some savings by him to compensate for the lack of the normal sale of pictures, and encouraged by Johnson and

Roscoe, set to work soon after this on the first of the Milton Gallery pictures. However, by 1797 he was in serious financial difficulties. Messrs. Coutts, Lock, Roscoe, G. Steevens, Seward and Johnson came to his rescue and lent him money. The opening took place in 1799 and Knowles comments that adverse press reports even before the Gallery had opened may have prejudiced the public. In 1800 the Gallery was re-opened with a special Royal Academy dinner to mark the occasion and several new pictures. But matters only became worse and the pictures had to be dispersed. The friends who had lent Fuseli money for the venture were paid in pictures in lieu of cash.

Fuseli's enthusiasm for Milton was not something he acquired only after years spent in this country. The seeds of it are perceptible during Fuseli's youth and early training. Fuseli's mentor was Bodmer, who caused a great stir with his translation of *Paradise Lost* finished in 1725 and published in 1732. In 1740 and 1741 Bodmer wrote two essays on the miraculous in poetry which were chiefly about Milton. Fuseli participated in these learned and anglophile activities when he illustrated Bodmer's epic *Noah*, an imitation of Milton in 1765.[62] As a young student in Rome he departed from the usual procedure by choosing to illustrate not only antique authors but, at least as frequently, scenes from Shakespeare, Milton and Gray.

Milton's political doctrines which were applicable to the situation in Europe in the 1790s probably had little effect on Fuseli, who by then was in his fifties. He associated with Johnson's circle during his time in England, but he could never have been very active in radical politics. In 1804 he was appointed Keeper of the Royal Academy in preference to Smirke, who was considered unsuitable because he was a democrat. It was the imaginative not the political possibilities in Milton which appealed to him in Rome, and long before he came to paint the Milton Gallery pictures he had made up his mind about the qualities that he liked in Milton's verse. His attitude to Milton can be seen in the following passage from a letter to Dalliker (12–15 Nov., 1765). The passage also offers some explanation for Fuseli's refusal to portray God in his Milton Gallery pictures:

That Homer degraded his Zeus to a king, Milton Jehovah to a pedagogue, Klopstock the Father to a prosecutor, inquisitor and judge is not what exasperates me. The imagination of the finite succumbs to Infinity, and what-ever a sinner like Warburton may snivel, it is neither from Homer, Virgil nor Milton that we have to learn morality, politics and religion. Delight the imagination, paint mankind as they are, and the Gods as best you can, seems to be the most universal law of epic poetry.[63]

It is difficult to learn anything more specific about Fuseli's attitude to Milton from his writings. It is clear that he admired Milton and that he was not interested in English poetry written after about 1790, but this is all. One eminently significant point, however, is revealed in Fuseli's letters to Roscoe. Time and time again Fuseli compares his own difficulties while painting the Milton Gallery pictures with the adverse circumstances in which Milton composed *Paradise Lost*. There are, upon examination, many similarities between the situations of Milton and Fuseli, as G. Schiff has pointed out.[64] Both came from Puritan backgrounds and were destined to be clergymen but later developed a contempt for dogma and official religion. Both studied extensively in the classics during their youth and retained throughout their lives a love of antiquity. Both, in their creative work, continually drew on the heritage of the classical world. Travel in Italy had developed in both a heightened awareness of the classical tradition. Both had unhappy love affairs which were the most probable cause of the misogynistic tendencies evident in their work. Milton wrote *The Doctrine and Discipline of Divorce* and gave literary permanence to the waywardness of womankind in Eve and Delilah. Fuseli constantly represented woman as vain, irresponsible and destructive, louring huge and implacable over the fates of men. It has been plausibly suggested that Fuseli's Satan is a hermaphrodite hero, 'a subtle equation of the heroic masculinity of Death and the erotic femininity of Sin'.[65] Milton saw God's purpose thwarted by the tragedy of human sin. Fuseli as an artist required, throughout his life, the stimulus of tragedy. Fuseli must have been greatly disillusioned in the early 1800s by the corruption and despotism which had emerged during the French Revolution. His native Switzerland was conquered by France in 1798 and his close friend Lavater died in 1801 after having been wounded by a French soldier. These disappointments and, especially, the failure of his Milton Gallery, on which he staked so much financially and spiritually, must have filled him with the sort of despair which Milton felt at the collapse of the commonwealth.

Dr. Schiff does not go to the extent of stating that the Milton Gallery is an isolated phenomenon in English art. Nevertheless, he does not take sufficiently into account firstly the tremendous popularity accorded to Milton in this country from the 1750s onwards, a popularity which should have made a Milton Gallery the natural sequence to the Shakespeare Gallery, and secondly the native tradition of literary painting and the debt which Fuseli owes to that tradition. Fuseli's originality must not, of course, be understated. But the Milton Gallery is not just the first comprehensive or effective collection of Milton pictures of the century but the logical culmination of the eighteenth-century cult of the Miltonic sublime.[66]

Fuseli's work, the Milton Gallery included, can be seen as part of the mainstream of English art. F. Antal has written:

The gamut of English painting ran from West through Reynolds and Fuseli to Blake. In some more conventional traits Fuseli does not seem far from certain historical compositions of Reynolds; in others he is exactly the opposite in character, not far from Blake.[67]

The truth of this statement can be seen in certain pictures from the Milton Gallery in which Fuseli, as the younger and more eclectic artist, is clearly the debtor to Reynolds. In the case of Blake the

93 J. H. Fuseli, 'L'Allegro'   94 J. H. Fuseli, 'Silence'

matter is a little different as these two artists avowedly borrowed ideas from each other.

Ignoring its more overt eroticism, Fuseli's 'L'Allegro' (Heidelberg) (93) is stylistically very close to Reynolds's grand female portraits. 'The Night Hag' (95) (British Museum), a tempera study most probably for 'Lapland Orgies', the lost no. VIII of the Milton Gallery, could easily be mistaken for one of Blake's hovering mythical or religious figures. The 'consciously unrealistic reduction of classicism to contours without light and shadow as it appears (after 1793) in Flaxman's illustrations of antique authors'[68] is discernible in a drawing by Fuseli, the study of a pensive, seated woman (94) (probably connected with the Milton Gallery 'Silence. Il Penseroso') which, in its total rejection of narrative and its reduction of all parts to the statement of mood, looks forward to expressionist art.

It would seem that Fuseli not only thought and worked in terms familiar to his contemporaries but also made use of the existing tradition of Milton illustrations. Fuseli's most popular Milton Gallery pictures—the ones which he painted in more than one version or which were engraved or appeared as book plates—are

95 J. H. Fuseli, 'The Night Hag'

frequently scenes which we have seen gradually established in the illustrator's repertoire. 'Satan Risen from the Flood' (105), 'Satan Summoning his Legions', 'Satan, Sin and Death' (107), 'Eve Tempted' (96), 'The Expulsion' and so on are all standard scenes. It is in these scenes that the dramatic concreteness of Fuseli's figure style has most scope. But in the treatment of entirely novel and abstruse subjects like 'The Birth of Sin', 'Sin pursued by Death' (127) and 'Ulysses between Scylla and Charybdis' (97) the abstract and the ephemeral force Fuseli out of his familiar, polished and heroic style into a grotesque confusion of the material and the immaterial.

Most of Barry's Milton pictures seem to belong to the 1770s (at least one is dated 1777 and he died in 1806) and therefore predate Fuseli's Milton Gallery works to which they appear to be related. Whereas the customary figure style in Fuseli's drawings is linear, tense and highly economical, when working in oil in the Milton Gallery pictures his figures attain a ponderous monumentality very similar to that seen in Barry's work. Compare, for example, Barry's 'Adam Tempted' (89) and Fuseli's 'The Flood' (Kunst-verein, Winterthur) (99). Moreover, the indeterminate rocky

96 After J. H. Fuseli, 'Eve Tempted'

97 J. H. Fuseli, 'Ulysses between Scylla and Charybdis'

98 J. Barry, 'Satan Summons his Legions'

99 J. H. Fuseli, 'The Flood'   **100** After J. H. Fuseli, 'Creation of Eve'

confines and the violent chiaroscuro of Barry's 'Satan Summoning his Legions' (98) and 'The Fall of Satan' (91) can also be seen in many of Fuseli's Milton pictures, for example, 'The Flood' (99), 'Satan Risen from the Flood' (105), 'The Creation of Eve' (100) and 'The Expulsion' (179).

In October 1776, Fuseli, then in Rome, drew 'Satan Starting at the Touch of Ithuriel's Spear' (101), a subject which he exhibited at the Royal Academy in 1780 and which he later included in the Milton Gallery. The drawing is signed 'Roma Oct. 76' (National-museum, Stockholm). Alexander Runciman, who was acquainted with Fuseli in Rome, exhibited a painting of this same subject at the Royal Academy in 1773 (collection of Sir Steven Runciman), three years before the date of Fuseli's drawing. A washed drawing by Runciman of the same subject (102) which the exhibited picture closely follows must be pre-1773. Admittedly Runciman left Rome in 1771, but he could have done the preparatory drawing before this date, in which case Fuseli could have seen it in Rome. The marked similarity of the intertwining bodies of the two angels and the prostrate forms of Adam and Eve, not to mention the general effects of light, is such as to make it almost certain that Fuseli must somehow have seen Runciman's drawing.

101 J. H. Fuseli, 'Satan Starts at the Touch of Ithuriel's Spear'

Fuseli's indebtedness to Hogarth for his composition of 'Satan, Sin and Death' (53) has already been mentioned (p. 59). A drawing of 'The Vision of the Lazar House' (Kunsthaus, Zurich) (103), which in a later version became one of the most popular subjects of the Milton Gallery, owes much to Hogarth's 'Rake in Bedlam'. The mad woman with raised arm in the left-hand corner of Fuseli's drawing resembles Hogarth's central figure of the squatting tailor. An earlier drawing of the same subject was executed by Fuseli in Rome as an illustration to Lavater's *Essays on Physiognomy* (1792). The text is inscribed with the words 'Hospital San Spirito' which indicates that, despite the expressionist-mannerist treatment of the subject, Fuseli, like Hogarth, had observed it from life. Fuseli's interest in documentary realism was not just a whim, for in 1804 he gave Farington figures on the types of lunatic in Bedlam.[69] Fuseli could never in any real sense be termed a realist, yet it is surely significant that he shares the concern for madmen, prisoners and slaves (he illustrated a topical poem by Cowper, 'The Negro's Complaint', directed against the slave trade)[70] with so many of his contemporaries. Fuseli can be seen in this as a man of his age and 'The Vision of the Mad House' can be related not only to Hogarth,

102 A. Runciman, 'Satan Starts at the Touch of Ithuriel's Spear'

but also to Goya's 'The Madhouse' (1794), Blake's 'The House of Death' (1795, Tate Gallery) (124) and Francis Wheatley's pictures of the philanthropist Howard visiting prisons. The period also produced many pictures in which negroes are depicted.

The influence of the Milton Gallery upon the work of other artists was evident even before its opening. David Scott's undated drawing of 'Satan Starting at the Touch of Ithuriel's Spear' (collection of Mr. Walter Brandt, London) is closely dependent on Fuseli and Runciman, and probably therefore belongs to the 1770s. A work which is so close to Fuseli as to be almost a copy is Lawrence's Royal Academy Diploma exhibit, 'Satan Summoning his Legions' (R.A. 1797). The drawing for this work (collection of Mr. W. Brandt) shows a splendidly heroic Satan, glaring commandingly from beneath a helmet wrought in the shape of a hawk (104). According to Whitley, Pasquin, the art critic, said of this work that Satan resembled 'a mad German sugar-baker dancing naked in a conflagration of his own treacle'.[71] The stance of Satan, the low viewpoint and the vast size of the figure all derive from Fuseli's 'Satan Risen from the Flood', a canvas in the possession of the Duke of Wellington. This canvas is in such a ruined condition that

103 J. H. Fuseli, 'The Vision of the Lazar House'

the similarity can best be observed from a comparison of Lawrence's picture with Bromley's engraving after Fuseli's picture for
Du Rouveray's *Paradise Lost* (1802) (105). The only difference between the Lawrence and the Fuseli is that in the former Satan is
seen from in front. A drawing showing 'Satan as a Fallen Angel
with Beelzebub' (collection of Colonel Michael Barne) is probably
a preparatory study for the diploma picture.

On June 9th, 1792, Gillray published an engraving entitled 'Sin,
Death and the Devil' (British Museum) (106). The engraving is inscribed as follows:

Sin, Death and the Devil, vide Milton.
    'So frown'd the mighty combatants . . .
    With hideous outcry rushed between . . .'
pubd. June 9. 1792 by H. Humphrey, no. 18 Old Bond St. N.B. The

above performance containing Portraits of the Devil and his relatives drawn from the life is recommended to Messrs. Boydell, Fuseli and the rest of the Proprietors of the 385 editions of Milton, now publishing.

The great influx of editions of Milton and the fascination of Milton's poetry for artists had not passed unnoticed by Gillray. His engraving also shows that 'Satan, Sin and Death', already popularized by Hogarth and Barry and now painted by Fuseli (107), was familiar to the London public to such a degree that Gillray could rely on his public to recognize the much abbreviated quotation.[72]

Gillray's 'Sin, Death and the Devil' could have been based on Hogarth or Barry but, in fact, circumstances indicate that Gillray's source was Fuseli. The two artists were probably acquainted and it is likely that Gillray was influenced by Fuseli's mannerist style of drawing. According to D. Hill, Gillray produced during a period of insanity a series of bizarre drawings which have been mistaken for Fuseli's work and which were probably based on engravings after Fuseli, who was fifteen years Gillray's senior:

104 Sir T. Lawrence, 'Satan Summons his Legions'

105 After J. H. Fuseli, 'Satan Risen from the Flood'

106 J. Gillray, 'Sin, Death and the Devil'

107 J. H. Fuseli, 'Satan, Sin and Death'

108 After R. Westall, 'Satan Alarmed'   **109** After R. Westall, 'The Birth of Sin'

The possibility of personal acquaintance between them is a fascinating topic for speculation . . . In a discussion with Sneyd about the illustrations for the *Poetry of the Anti-Jacobin*, Gillray referred to Fuseli and to 'ye use to be made of him'. Over a ten year period commencing in 1789, Gillray made use of him, most specifically on at least six occasions. In addition to a concentration of travesties and burlesques between 1789 and 1792, there are other circumstantial factors which point to an association between the two men during the early nineties. Most significantly Gillray contributed one meticulous engraving after a Fuseli drawing to the English translation of Lavater's *Essays on Physiognomy*, published in 1792. As Fuseli directed the preparation of this edition, it seems probable that he commissioned this plate himself. The likelihood of contact between the two is also suggested by the speed with which Fuseli's 'Satan encount'ring Death, Sin interposing', completed on the 28th May, 1792, was followed by Gillray's 'Sin, Death and the Devil' on the 9th of June.[73]

Richard Westall, Fuseli's partner in the 1802 Du Rouveray edition of *Paradise Lost*, is to be admired for the degree to which he succeeded in preserving his independence from the very forceful influence of Fuseli's work. He was first employed on illustrating Milton in 1794 for Boydell's edition of Milton's *Poetical Works*. A

110 After R. Westall, 'Sabrina Frees the Lady'   111 After R. Westall, 'L'Allegro'

few new plates after Westall were also included in *The Works of the British Poets*, published by J. Sharpe (1805–8).

Westall adopts Barry's and Fuseli's practice of concentrating on one or at most two giant-sized figures to create the required sense of awe-inspiring grandeur. Westall's Satan has the characteristic Fuselian expression of heroic defiance. Westall comes closest to Fuseli in his illustration to Book IV of *Paradise Lost*, 'Satan Alarmed—Dilated Stood' (108). The athletic structure of the figure, the expression of the face, the characteristically oratorical stance and the low horizon are very Fuselian. Compare Westall's figure with the expression of Satan in the engraving after 'Satan Starts at the Touch of Ithuriel's Spear' by Fuseli (88), and with the general stature of Satan in 'Satan Summons his Host' (engraved by P. W. Tomkins for Park's edition, 1808) (119). If anything, the softer lines of Westall's illustrations and the gently flowing drapery which mitigates the linear harshness of Fuseli's muscular figures create a more pleasing and less severe—if less strictly appropriate—general effect. See for example the more subtle contrast of light and texture and the greater fluidity of line in Westall's 'Birth of Sin' (109).

112 After R. Westall, 'Eve amongst her
Flowers'

Westall's Milton illustrations are more conventional and more
academic than Fuseli's and more emphasis is laid on narrative, particularly in scenes which Fuseli has never seriously treated, as for example that to *Comus* (110). In illustrations such as that to *L'Allegro*
(111) Westall ignores the vocabulary of the sublime and instead
adheres to the formula used in the portraiture of sentiment by
artists like Angelica Kauffmann.

Westall was famed for his emotive illustration and Payne Knight,
we are told, 'found in his oil painting the embodiment of his personal conception of "beauty", in that its rustic types illustrated
"those tender feelings which we call pathetic", while at the same
time it contained rich, clear colour'.[74] It is likely that Payne Knight
was attracted to the leisurely, rural scenes from among Westall's
Milton illustrations. 'Eve among her Fruits and Flowers' (112), for
example, exudes a rococo sweetness which relates Westall to
Stothard and Burney. The profusion of English flowers in the illustration of Eve might almost have served as a model for Burney's
'Eve Tempted' (85).

George Romney was another artist whose period of study in
Italy (1773–5) coincided with Fuseli's. Romney must have come

113 G. Romney, 'L'Allegro and Il Pensoroso'

114 G. Romney, 'The Expulsion'

early under Fuseli's spell, but he seldom allowed this influence to show in any of his exhibited works. There is, however, a vast number of drawings by Romney which must have been almost unknown to his contemporaries and which show Romney to have been one of the group comprising Fuseli, Barry and other artists of the Miltonic sublime. Romney's painting of 'L'Allegro and Il Pensoroso' (113) is typical of his public style and bears no suggestion of the fervour of Romney's innumerable Milton drawings. The canvas was exhibited at the Society of Artists in 1770, before Romney's visit to Italy. The classical dress, the fashionable faces, the generalized Italianate background, the touching reference to time in the hour-glass in the left-hand corner all relate this to the grand style of modish, Reynoldsian portraiture.

It seems to have been about the year 1788 that Romney, suffering from depression and ill health, first turned to subjects from Milton.[75] His intention was to produce a small series of historical pictures, none of which ever fully materialized. Romney's son is our most reliable authority for Romney's activities during this period. He writes of his father:

He had studied Milton with much attention, and selected a series of subjects from Paradise Lost, for great pictures, both of a sublime and a beautiful character. He had also formed a scheme of painting a number of pictures, representing the most important periods in human life . . . The first subject of this series representing the Birth of Man, was considerably advanced. Another great work, which he commenced about 1796 was The Temptation of Christ. Had he finished this picture, it would have ranked him with Michelangelo . . .[76]

Cunningham quotes a letter from Romney to Hayley, dated February 1794, in which Romney says:

I had formed a plan of painting the Seven Ages, and also the Vision of Adam with the Angel—to bring in the flood and the opening of the Ark, which would make six large pictures. Indeed, to tell you the truth, I have made designs for all the pictures; and very grand subjects they are. My plan is, if I live and retain my senses and sight, to paint six other subjects from Milton—three where Satan is the hero, and three from Adam and Eve; perhaps six of each. I have ideas of them all, and, I may say, sketched, but, alas! I cannot begin them for a year or two.[77]

From Romney's sketches it is clear that the three subjects 'where Satan is the hero' were to be, 'Satan Summoning his Legions', 'Satan, Sin and Death', and 'Satan Starting at the Touch of

115 G. Romney, 'The Expulsion'   116 J. Barry, 'Falling Angels'

Ithuriel's Spear', though Romney also seems to have paid much attention to the fall of the rebel angels. There are many sketches for 'The Flood' and for 'The Temptation of Christ' (*Paradise Regained*), but which were to be the scenes involving Adam and Eve is not clear. Many of the sketches are indecipherable scribbles, but several which might relate to these scenes with Adam and Eve show an expulsion scene in which Michael is literally flogging Adam and Eve out of Paradise, an interpretation quite alien to Milton (114, 115).[78]

Romney's studies for 'The Fall of the Rebel Angels' (117) are very rough and approach a greater degree of abstraction even than Flaxman's (p. 81) (73, 74). But whereas Flaxman seems most fascinated by the irregular density of bodies in a falling mass, Romney seems more concerned with speed and the pattern of chiaroscuro. Romney's many drawings of this subject invariably show a mass of inflexible bodies falling diagonally across the page. The angularity and fleeting quality of these drawings relate them most closely to Barry's study in the Soane Museum (116).

Out of the chaotic and repetitive confusion of Romney's in-

numerable drawings from Milton a number of significant characteristics are discernible. One is the quality of overwhelming violence
evident even in the slightest drawing. Not only do many figures
brandish sharp weapons but every drawing seems to be full of
threatening gestures. 'Satan, Sin and Death', a subject from the epic
which was most popular with Romney's contemporaries, is interpreted in a personal manner. Satan resembles a powerful but beatific
guardian angel and in at least one drawing (118) there is no visible
sign of Death, only a writhing Sin and two human shapes cowering
under the shadow of Satan's mighty wings. In the top left-hand
corner of the drawing Romney has frenetically blobbed in a dark
planet (a feature not confined to this drawing). Even in the slightest
sketch the sense of helpless struggle as human bodies writhe in
great masses is strangely disturbing. Many of the drawings (see, for
example, those for 'Satan Summoning his Legions' (121), 'The
Flood' (123) and 'The Temptation of Christ') depict one or two
dominant figures who stand or sit on a rocky promontory while the
mass—threatening or appealing—founder in great confusion below. There seems little doubt that Romney was suffering from
severe depression at the time. It would not be extravagant to say
that the turbulence and violence in all these drawings—frequently
far greater than could ever be justified by the text—shows evidence
of manic depression or some form of paranoia.

117 G. Romney, 'The Fall of the Rebel Angels'

118 G. Romney, 'Satan and Sin'

119 After J. H. Fuseli, 'Satan Summoning his Host'

120 G. Romney, 'Satan Starts at the Touch of Ithuriel's Spear'

The drawings for 'The Temptation of Christ' suggest that Romney's sickness may have taken the form of some sort of persecution complex. The drawings for this subject all show, with slight variations, a large white-clad, seated figure—usually in the lower left-hand corner—which is being attacked by myriads of creatures all converging upon it. These drawings are more reminiscent of sixteenth-century representations of the 'Temptation of St. Anthony' than of the 'Temptation of Christ'. In his description of his father's preparations for his 'Seven Ages' John Romney refers to '. . . the arch-fiend, the Miltonic Satan, grand as the human mind can conceive him, [who] viewed from the upper corner of the picture, with malignant satisfaction, the ready obedience of his imps'.[79] There are many experimental studies among the Romney drawings for the head of Satan. The picture, as John Romney saw it in preparation, was to have been given 'a sombre hue' and 'a certain degree of obscurity'.

The drawings for 'Satan Summoning his Host' show Romney's debt to Barry and Fuseli. Satan stands with feet firmly set apart and arms raised, hands holding shield and spear, the characteristic pose of Barry's and Fuseli's Satan. Compare, for example, the Fitzwilliam drawing (124) with Barry's and Fuseli's treatment of the

121 G. Romney, 'Satan Summons his Legions'

122 J. Barry, 'Satans Starts at the Touch of Ithuriel's Spear'

same scene (98, 122). 'Satan Starting at the Touch of Ithuriel's Spear' (120) is, likewise, a combination of Barry's and Fuseli's concepts of this subject (122, 88, 101). The two angels in Romney's drawing are closest to Barry's in the Rockhill Nelson Gallery picture, but the figure of Satan sharply ascending in a sort of arrow shape is much closer to Fuseli's Rome drawing. The drawings for 'The Flood' mostly show a series of mourning, sorrowing people climbing slopes and heights (123). However, in the Fitzwilliam

123 G. Romney, 'The Flood'

124 W. Blake, 'The House of Death'

Museum sketch book (no. 3688) there are also a number of nude studies, and one drawing on f. 3 shows a kneeling male figure supporting over his shoulder a nude female figure. This is very close to Fuseli's painting of 'The Flood' (Winterthur) (99) and even closer to a drawing for this subject in a private collection in Winterthur.[80]

The Fitzwilliam Museum also owns the famous 'Providence Brooding over Chaos' drawn in ink by Romney in Rome in 1773. The similarity of the long-bearded figure of Providence to some of Blake's figures—for example, the Tate Gallery colour print or the two British Museum drawings of 'Pity'—has frequently been observed. It is possible that this drawing is based on an image occurring twice in *Paradise Lost* (I, 19–20, and VII, 234–5). It is also possible that it represents a verse from Isaiah (ch. XXIV, v. 2).[81] The work was sold as 'Jupiter and Pluvius', probably because John Romney was appalled that his father should have presumed to represent the Divinity.[82] There is certainly a resemblance to the Jupiter Pluvius from the column of Marcus Aurelius which, as it appeared in Montfaucon's *L'Antiquité Expliquée* (1719, I, pl. xiii), was used by Fuseli in his drawing of the 'Fertilization of Egypt'. This in turn was copied and engraved by Blake for Erasmus Darwin's *Botanic Garden* (1791). Blake used the same hovering figure

125 After J. H. Fuseli, 'Friar Puck'

126 After J. H. Fuseli, 'The Lubbar Fiend'

again in his drawing of Milton's 'The House of Death' (1795) (124). Moreover, Flaxman used it either direct from Montfaucon via Fuseli in plate xv of his designs for the *Inferno* (1793)[83] (a work which has always provided a point of comparison for the Hell of Milton's *Paradise Lost*). Therefore, although Romney's drawing is based on an image connected with Milton's *Paradise Lost* it seems doubtful whether it was intended as an illustration to this work.

It is evident from the various works by Gillray, Westall, Barry, Romney and others we have just examined that the influence of the Milton Gallery on contemporary and subsequent illustrators was considerable, especially between 1770 and 1800. However, the Gallery was not to any extent influential on the work of major English artists after 1800 as G. Schiff would have us believe. For example, it seems a great over-simplification to suggest, as Schiff does, that Fuseli's 'Ulysses between Scylla and Charybdis' with its slightly misty atmosphere and sea spray anticipates Turner.[84] It is an isolated example in the work of Fuseli and, as far as we know, Turner was never particularly interested in the work of Fuseli. Nor does it seem any more likely that Haydon always remained a prisoner of the Fuselian imagination or that William Etty step by step repeats Fuseli's grouping of figures.[85] If there is a similarity between Etty and Fuseli it is far more likely to be the result of a common classical source. In the sense that any illustrator of Milton after Fuseli was bound to take the Milton Gallery into account, John Martin can be said to be in some degree dependent on Fuseli. But his concept of *Paradise Lost* and his pictorial treatment of the poem differ so radically from Fuseli's that one cannot talk in terms of 'influence'. Fuseli's Milton Gallery, despite its considerable influence between 1770 and 1800, was a part of the general movement of English late eighteenth-century art and it would be absurd to focus on Fuseli as the pivot and guiding force of such a wide variety of English artists. The similarity between the work of any one such artist and Fuseli's Milton Gallery only occurs in a fraction of a complex œuvre.

There is no doubt that Fuseli's Milton pictures (as an important part of his total output) formed the central core of Milton illustration in the last quarter of the eighteenth century. Since these works impressed artists as widely different as Westall and Romney, why was the Milton Gallery such a fiasco with the general public which had flocked to see Boydell's Shakespeare Gallery? Certainly this was a bad time economically and politically for England. The war in the West Indies (1793–6) had drastically weakened England's military power, which was to be so soon called forth again in 1803 for battle against Napoleon and his armies. Pitt introduced income tax in an endeavour to increase revenue to cover the costs of the war. The economic suffering was greatest among the poor and the merchant classes. It was in the latter group that Boydell and Fuseli hoped to find a sale for popular engravings after the works in their galleries. These external factors may account for Fuseli's financial difficulties but they do not explain the lack of popularity of the Milton Gallery with critics and with the general public.

In many ways the Milton Gallery was an improvement on the Shakespeare Gallery. Fuseli relinquishes the attempt to achieve historical accuracy of costume—those of his figures which are clothed simply wear drapery 'all' antica'. Fuseli often selects the moments of highest tension in the poem, whereas in the Shakespeare Gallery very minor scenes were often selected to represent one play simply because they were subjects congenial to the artist. Fuseli clearly makes a determined attempt to achieve variety in his choice of subject by mingling episodes taken from folkloric epic similes like 'A Gryphon Pursuing an Arimaspian', 'Faery Mab', 'Friar Puck' (125) and 'The Lubbar Fiend' (126) with those concerning Satan, Adam and Eve. However, the fact remains that forty-seven works by the same artist all based on the verse of one poet must become tedious to the average viewer. Fuseli achieved a certain unity of concept which Boydell sacrificed to the more immediate attraction of the variety of interpretations and treatment of many different artists.

G. Schiff considers that the public was not ready to receive a body of work like the Milton Gallery.[86] Admittedly some of Fuseli's Milton pictures are more unreservedly sensational, more extravagantly indicative of passion and more romantic than most of popular English art at that time, but, nevertheless, we have seen that Milton's popularity was widespread and general and there was a firmly established, thriving tradition of Miltonic painting.

A certain degree of unity—absent in Boydell's Gallery—cannot be denied to the Milton Gallery, but it is the superficial unity that inevitably results from one artist painting from one poet. The more significant unity which would result from a progressive and coherent series of pictures of Milton's poems dealing with each stage of idea and imagery as presented in the verse is almost totally lacking. G. Schiff believes that Fuseli did coherently reproduce the pattern of Milton's thought as presented by him in *Paradise Lost.* This writer believes that Fuseli selected a series of epic similes for illustration, specifically because they show the results of the Fall through the various aspects of man's alienation from God. 'The

Sleeping Shepherd', says Schiff, embodies lust, 'The Lapland Orgies' indicates witchcraft and sorcery, 'The Gryphon' scene stands for the striving after mammon and 'Ulysses' is seen facing the powers of evil which lie in wait for man on his journey through life.[87] Certainly Milton uses these vivid similes for their associative value. Ulysses, for example, has frequently been seen as the proto-type of post-lapsarian man. But the predilection that Fuseli showed throughout his life (and long before he even thought of the Milton Gallery) for the more tense moments from the classical authors and for anything savouring of Nordic folklore makes it far more likely that Fuseli picked out such scenes at random from *Paradise Lost* because they offered scope to his talents and inclinations.

In the Milton Gallery the pictures based on epic similes often alternate with pictures representing the progress of Satan towards Earth, the Fall, and the results of the Fall. It must have been very difficult for anyone not extremely familiar with every detail of *Paradise Lost* to follow the narrative at all from Fuseli's pictures, even with the help of selected extracts in the catalogue. Fuseli had ransacked Milton for any odd line or image that fired his imagina-tion. Cunningham sums up public feeling when he says:

When the doors of the Milton Gallery were opened to the world, it was seen that the genius of Fuseli was of a different order from that of Milton. To the severe serene majesty of the poet the intractable fancy of the painter had refused to bow.[88]

Fuseli rejected entirely the unwritten laws of the illustrator. He refused to make the sort of compromise with his imagination and with the text which John Martin managed to make in the following century. The allegorical character of his choice of material resulted in poetical but not completely comprehensible pictures. Writing of West's 'Death on a Pale Horse' in the *Analytical Review*, Fuseli says:

The Sin and Death of Milton are real actors, and have nothing allegorical but their names. The poet unskilfully gave to positive beings names adopted by theology and common language to convey notions of mental qualities, ideas of privation. The portress and guardian of the infernal gates are no more allegoric than Force and Labour, when they chain Prometheus . . .[89]

To a certain extent Fuseli is correct. Sin and Death in *Paradise Lost* are very substantial figures, but a certain freedom or looseness is possible in literary allegory which, if carried into pictorial allegory, may result in incongruity or confusion. This shows itself most clearly in some of the more abstract scenes which Fuseli chose

127 After J. H. Fuseli, 'Sin Pursued by Death'

to illustrate. The attempt to portray the seduction of the very
fleshy Sin by the iron-visored, insubstantially bodied Death in
'Sin Pursued by Death' (127) is odd to say the least.

Finally the Milton Gallery was not all that its creator had hoped
because Fuseli's skill as an artist did not lie primarily in painting.
The spontaneous and momentary impulse which gives birth to a
drawing but never achieves a finished painting is a typical feature
of the Romantic Movement. His best works are drawings in which
his superb skill as a draughtsman is evident. Even allowing for the
terrible deterioration of the large canvases, most of them are no
more than blown-up drawings. The fact that many of them could
be reduced to book-plate size without substantial reduction of
effect bears this out. Furthermore, the financial difficulties and the
lack of variety in his work must have affected Fuseli whilst he was
working on the Milton Gallery. Many of the works, especially
those which show Satan, are schematized, stylized and repetitive.

The same familiar poses tend to recur throughout Fuseli's work. For example, the figure of Satan risen from the Flood (105) closely resembles that of the Bard (Kunsthaus, Zurich) and of Achilles (Auckland City Art Gallery, New Zealand). F. Antal, writing of Fuseli's work in the nineties, has made a statement to this effect:

Unrealistic artists necessarily schematise in their compositions more than those whose art is continually fed and rejuvenated by studies after nature. Fuseli's anti-realism is apt to lend too great a facility, a certain conventionality to his contours.[90]

(iii) William Blake and Milton (1801–1825)

William Hayley's reputation has never recovered from the unfortunate picture which Blake drew of him as a bigoted tyrant and persecutor. Undoubtedly the two men were incompatible and Hayley's plans for Blake were not ideally suited to an artist of Blake's unusual temperament. However, despite our regret for the real and imagined indignities and hardships suffered by Blake during the three years (1800–3) that Hayley employed him at Felpham, it cannot be doubted that it was Hayley's commission for a library frieze which initiated the extraordinary amount of painting and poetry related to Milton which Blake produced during the last years of his life, between 1801 and 1825.

Although almost all Blake's Milton illustrations are post-1800, his work is included in this chapter because he was very much one of the group comprising Fuseli, Romney, Flaxman and Stothard. Blake illustrated 'The Lazar House' (124) from *Paradise Lost* in 1795 (Tate Gallery) and, although Blake's concept of the subject differs radically from Fuseli's, it is most likely that Blake was inspired by Fuseli's rendering completed in 1793. Blake may have known an engraving (1791, Thomas Holloway) after an earlier Fuseli drawing of the same subject. Blake's real output of Milton subjects begins in 1801 and, since this was between five and ten years after most of his associates executed their Milton illustrations, it is reasonable to assume that Blake had been assimilating the Milton illustrations of the 1790s, culminating with Fuseli's Milton Gallery in 1799. Blake's exile in Felpham away from the familiar artistic environment and his interest in Milton as a subject whose portrait he was painting probably provided the necessary extra incentive to precipitate Blake's imagination into the realm of Milton's poetic creation.

Hayley had written a *Life of Milton* and Blake was to have contributed with Romney and Flaxman to his edition of Milton's poetry. In fact Westall provided the illustrations to all the volumes except Cowper's translation of the Latin poems which Flaxman illustrated. However, Blake, expecting to provide illustrations, had already made preparatory sketches and must, therefore, have been reading Milton at this time.[91] The portraiture on which Blake was engaged at Felpham involved a series of heads of poets, among which were Ercilla, Dante and Milton, that were to be incorporated into a frieze for the library.[92] An artist of Blake's intellectual curiosity would be unlikely to paint a portrait of Milton without first finding out as much as possible about his subject. Writing to Hayley about the frieze on November 26th, 1800, immediately after commencing the project, Blake's enthusiasm, even allowing for flattery of his patron, is very evident: 'Absorbed by the poets Milton, Homer, Camoens, Ercilla, Ariosto and Spenser whose physiognomies have been my delightful study, Little Tom has been of late unattended to.'[93]

The enthusiasm for Milton engendered by the political climate of the time probably affected Blake even more than other writers and artists of the period. Some time after the disappointing culmination of the French Revolution Blake wrote to Hayley thanking him for a book on contemporary heroes which Hayley had sent him. Blake concludes: 'In the meantime I have the happiness of seeing the Divine countenance in such men as Cowper and Milton more distinctly than in any prince or hero.'[94] Indeed Blake did not see the 'Divine countenance' in Milton, and his prophetic poem *Milton* begun about 1804 and completed about 1808 makes it evident that Blake saw in the poet a more than human power. Blake's poem takes up Wordsworth's cry:

Milton thou should'st be living at this hour[95]

and actually resurrects Milton. His attitude to Milton was always tinged with disapproval for the puritanical, moralistic side of Milton's work, but this disapproval was far outweighed by admiration for the creator of Lucifer and for the hedonist who described Adam and Eve in the Garden of Eden.

In his symbolic poem which Blake said he had written 'From immediate dictation, twelve sometimes thirty lines at a time, without premeditation & even against my will',[96] Blake sees Milton as a saviour who will deliver his people from a Satanic figure who may be identified as Hayley and whom Blake sees as the prototype of passive conformity, that semblance of moral virtue which is dangerous in proportion to the protection with which it is provided by society.[97]

The first of Blake's series of illustrations to Milton are two sets of eight illustrations to *Comus* (1801, Huntington Library and Museum of Fine Arts, Boston).[98] Blake followed on with two sets of illustrations to *Paradise Lost*. Twelve illustrations plus one larger duplicate are in the Huntington Library and can be dated about 1807, the other set of nine designs (Boston) about a year later. There are also several drawings in the Victoria and Albert Museum which must relate to these sets. For *Ode on the Morning of Christ's Nativity* Blake again executed two sets of illustrations (1808–9, Huntington Library and Whitworth Art Gallery). A set of illustrations to *L'Allegro* and *Il Penseroso* (Pierpont Morgan Library) were drawn about 1817 and a set of designs for *Paradise Regained* (Fitzwilliam Museum) were executed about 1825.[99] There are also a number of odd pencil drawings of subjects from Milton in the British Museum.[100]

Blake was a forceful member of the group of artists centred around Fuseli during the 1790s and he owed a considerable number of ideas in his designs for Milton's poems to his contemporaries as well as to other sources. But, unlike any other illustrator of Milton, Blake incorporated into his designs his own interpretations of the poem. Various artists ranging from Medina to John Martin embroidered on the text in order to portray more convincingly the

128 W. Blake, 'Satan in Council'

129 W. Blake, 'The Baptism of Christ'

scene described, but Blake actually contributes to the symbolic content of the poem through his own very personal interpretation. Nevertheless, no illustrator more closely follows Milton's pattern of idea and image and few are so precise in following details of the text. The reason for Blake's success, particularly with *Paradise Lost*, is that his illustrative method is symbolic rather than representational. He is concerned with idea rather than with narrative.

The disadvantages of this method are immediately recognizable in all Blake's Milton illustrations. The rejection of most of the narrative interest, Blake's eclecticism in the matter of figure drawing and his tendency towards a kind of abstract pattern-making result in the repetition of basic types of composition. (A similar stylization is also a feature of Fuseli's late work, pp. 134–5)[101] For example, there is the pattern centred around the heroic figure on a raised dais with arms held above his head as in 'The Shrine of Apollo' (*Ode on the Morning of Christ's Nativity*) (151), 'Satan in Council' (128) and 'Christ on the Pinnacle of the Temple' (*Paradise Regained*) and 'Satan Summons his Legions' (*Paradise Lost*) (135). Another familiar type is the figure flying away from the central group as in 'The Sullen Moloch' (*Ode*) (152) and 'The Baptism' (*Paradise Regained*) (129). Blake frequently uses a large frontally

130 W. Blake, 'The Brothers Lingering under the Vine'

131 W. Blake, 'The Brothers Overcome Comus'

viewed figure, flanked on one or both sides by figures seen from behind. See, for example, 'Satan's and Raphael's Entries into Paradise' (*Paradise Lost*) (138), 'The Attendant Spirit with the Two Brothers' (*Comus*) (132) and 'Christ Tempted to make Bread from Stones' (*Paradise Regained*).

Blake's illustrations to *Comus* comprise two sets of six water colours. Those in the Boston Museum, from which all subsequent examples are taken, all measure about 12·2 × 15 cm., are smaller than those in the Huntington Library and probably a little later. They are nearly all literal illustrations of the masque, the best being 'The Brothers under the Vine' (130) and 'The Brothers Overcome Comus' (131). In these the somewhat mannerist elongation of the figures with their small heads contributes to the generally stylized pattern of movement in the design. Elsewhere, particularly in 'Comus with his Revellers' and 'Sabrina Freeing the Lady', unity of design is spoilt by the artist's contradictory tendencies towards on the one hand a statuesque tableau and on the other an essentially mobile composition.

It is interesting that even in the *Comus* illustrations which are literal representations of the narrative and which create an atmosphere of rustic simplicity and naiveté (a quality which the academic artists were incapable of achieving and which enhances the more cultivated rusticity of *Comus*), Blake brings his own imagination to bear upon the text. Plate four (132) represents the two brothers and the Attendant Spirit. The latter is telling the brothers (who have just concluded a long dispute on whether the power of Chastity will be strong enough to protect their sister) about the plant haemony with which they can overcome Comus. The flower can be seen in the hand of the Attendant Spirit, dressed as Thyrsis, in the centre of the group. Above the trees rides the moon-goddess in her serpent-drawn carriage, a figure which does not feature in Milton's poem.[102] Diana, goddess of the moon, is also goddess of Chastity. In portraying her above this scene Blake is giving symbolic pictorial form to what is in fact happening whilst the brothers converse, and what is in fact the whole subject of the poem. Chastity is ruling the hour: 'Vertue may be assail'd, but never hurt' (*Comus*). Again, in the illustration of 'The Brothers Driving out Comus', Blake shows in a cloud above the head of Comus the visible embodiment of the sorcerer's evil magic.

Blake's designs for *Paradise Lost* are among his most impressive book illustrations and the best of all his Milton illustrations. They are far more carefully composed and executed than any of his other designs for Milton's poetry and they all (particularly the Boston

132 W. Blake, 'The Attendant Spirit and the Brothers'

series) show a great richness of detail and finish. This quality is most striking in the scenes showing Adam and Eve in Eden in which Blake, by exploiting a stylized but highly effective technique of surface decoration, creates a most convincing impression of natural beauty and sensuous pleasure. In the words of Sir Anthony Blunt:

The artist has evolved a quite new technique to give full value in visual form to the descriptions by Milton, whose text he follows scrupulously. The relatively loose forms of the Bible illustrations are replaced by a jewelled precision of detail and an intensity of colour by which Blake contrives to render with the utmost vividness such passages as the description of Eden . . . All the illustrations to these scenes from the fourth book of the poem reveal a sensuousness which is quite new in Blake. It is the expression of his new realization that the senses are not evil, as he had previously felt, but can be used as a means to further the spiritual life, a doctrine towards which he had been led largely by the reading of Milton.[103]

It is in his *Paradise Lost* illustrations that Blake's transformation of Milton's poetic imagery (and the philosophy inherent in that imagery) into pictorial symbolism is most complete and most successful. Occasionally, it must be admitted, Blake's own esoteric mythology becomes intrusive. One such case is 'So Judged he Man' (133). God with a benign and merciful visage stands in the centre with Adam and Eve on either side whilst the serpent, now on his belly, stretches on the ground the width of the page. This is one result of the Fall. The most important result of the Fall, the bridge built by Sin and Death, is seen above the figures. Blake's idea of showing the bridge actually composed by the bodies of Sin and Death is ingenious even if it constitutes an infidelity to the text. But neither Sin nor Death looks wicked or triumphant and both are engaged in puzzling activities. It has been suggested that the arrows which Death showers down are the traditional weapons of Death

133 W. Blake, 'So Judged He Man'

134 W. Blake, 'The Creation of Eve'

and that Sin is pouring out vials of disease.[104] But the gentle face of Death belies his fatal activity and Sin bears such a close resemblance to an antique river goddess (carrying associations with bounty and fruition) that it is difficult to see Blake's Sin as pouring forth poison onto the earth.

In Blake's 'Expulsion' (147) four horsemen ride above the black cloud which hangs over Adam, Eve and Michael. There is no mention of any such horsemen in Milton, though their presence in Blake's illustration, summoning recollections of the Apocalypse and the Last Judgement, is not inappropriate. However, in the wider context of Blake's work as a whole it seems very likely that the artist intended the horsemen to represent the four Zoas, that is, the four different aspects of man's nature (the rational, the feeling, the imaginative and the body with its sense organs) which must pull in harmony and which accompany man out of Eden.[105] If this interpretation is correct, Blake—despite his incomparable skill in the difficult craft of the illustrator in the absolute sense of the word—must in this scene be regarded as having gone beyond the limits of illustration into the company of those artists like Fuseli and John Martin who used Milton's poetry as a starting point for an essay in imagination.

However, allowing for the occasional intrusion of Blake's private symbolism, his *Paradise Lost* illustrations are remarkable primarily for their sensitivity and fidelity not only to the major patterns of idea in the poem but to the slightest change in tone or emphasis. The scenes of Eden are rich and decorative. Other illustrations in the series are complex in their reference to the poem yet Blake, when the text demanded, was capable of reducing detail to absolute essentials and allowing the scene to speak for itself. Note, for example, the simplicity of 'The Creation of Eve' (134). (The Huntington version is not as good as the Boston drawing, which has more solidity of form.) God is seen in profile, Adam lies asleep on the leafy ground and Eve—with the expression of a quattrocento madonna, daughter of Eve who would bear the second Adam— hovers between Adam's heart and the sickle moon, symbolic of purity and new growth.

'The Creation of Eve' is a subject which (apart from Fuseli's example) was not popular with eighteenth-century illustrators, who presumably found it too biblical. Yet in general Blake's designs follow the iconographical pattern of earlier illustrators very closely. The episodes he chooses are almost invariably well established in the tradition of Milton illustration, but his concept and treatment are usually entirely novel. Blake tends to prefer the scenes from

135 W. Blake, 'Satan Summons his Legions'   136 W. Blake, 'Satan, Sin and Death'

Paradise Lost which portray the positive goodness of God towards man, and his choice of 'The Creation of Eve' is, therefore, typical. 'The Creation', 'Christ Offering to Redeem Man' (137) and 'The Crucifixion' (146) are subjects which emphasize the optimistic aspects of the expulsion and which contribute to the creation of a set of designs in which, for the first time since Medina and Cheron, we see a poem which sets out to justify the ways of God to man.[106]

Blake's first design for the *Paradise Lost* series represents 'Satan Summoning his Legions' (135), an extremely popular scene. Blake's treatment is not only literal—he shows the fallen angels actually chained to the rocks—but quite different from that of other artists. His concept of the scene is formal rather than dramatic. Satan stands, a central figure with arms raised in a dramatic gesture, but the distribution of figures in the space makes for a formal pattern rather than a depiction of dramatic action. This finished design with its reminiscences of Michelangelo's 'Last Judgement' in the Sistine Chapel is less successful than a rough drawing by Blake on a similar theme, 'The Warring Angels'. It does, however, reflect Blake's poetic description of the horrors of the Hell on earth in the wine-press of life in *Milton*:

But in the Wine-presses the Human grapes sing not nor dance:
They howl & writhe in shoals of torment, in fierce flames consuming,

137 W. Blake, 'Christ Offering to Redeem Man'

In chains of iron & in dungeons circled with ceaseless fires,
In pits & dens & shades of death, in shapes of torment & woe.

'Satan, Sin and Death' (136) is not much more successful than
'Satan Summons his Legions'. This may be due to the existence of
so many pictorial versions of the scene which Burke singled out as
the purest example of the sublime. Blake bases his design on that of
Fuseli (107), but he gives Death a transparent though athletic body
as a compromise between the heroic Death of Fuseli and the in-
substantial medieval skeleton Death of Hogarth. Sin's torso is still
simply superimposed onto her snaky coils, but it is typical of
Blake's delight in pattern-making that he has greatly enlarged Sin's
coils which now, instead of simply fading into the background as
in Fuseli's and Barry's drawings, are arrayed in symmetrical folds
along the foot of the page, terminating (in the larger Huntington
version (136)) in venomous snake-heads like the biting heads seen
in the borders of English thirteenth-century manuscripts. Sin's hair
is likewise highly stylized and suggestive of Medusa. In comparison
with Blake's other illustrations this design lacks the artist's peculiar
originality nor does it possess the ease of movement demanded by
the narrative and achieved by Fuseli.[107]

'The Promise of the Redemption' (137) was a subject rejected by

138 W. Blake, 'Satan's and Raphael's Entries
into Paradise'

139 W. Blake, 'Christ's Troubled Dreams'

many eighteenth-century artists as it was incompatible with the concept of Satan as a hero. Blake's view of *Paradise Lost* was more balanced in this respect. Moreover, Blake (unlike Fuseli) did not hesitate to represent God in the act of creation on earth, but in 'The Promise of the Redemption' Blake's portrayal of the deity has all the more mystery and grandeur because Blake has not shown his face. Christ hovers with his arms in the attitude of the cross, another example of Blake's pictorial interpretation. The true crucifixion is Christ's voluntary adoption of flesh, not his enforced release from it. C. H. Collins-Baker suggests that the enthroned figure embracing the Son is 'Blake's inspired adaptation of a classical "Zeus and Ganymede" or the "Education of Olympus"'.[108] However, one only has to read the relevant passage in *Paradise Lost* to realize that the only source which Blake needed is there vividly in print.[109]

In 'Satan's and Raphael's Entries into Paradise' (138) the same hovering figure with arms outstretched that Blake uses in 'The House of Death' (124) and in 'Christ's Troubled Dreams' (*Paradise Regained*) (139) appears this time in the guise of the Almighty. The sources of this motif which Blake also used in his 'Pity' and which was used by Romney and Fuseli (from whom Blake probably borrowed it) are discussed on pp. 130–1 in connection with Romney's Milton illustrations. Despite Blake's non-realistic figure drawing, this design is highly successful. Blake makes Raphael, descending in cloud, the arrow-head or the executor of the divine will represented by the all-embracing gesture of the Almighty. Moreover, Raphael's position—separating Satan and the human pair—symbolizes his function. He has been sent to earth to warn Adam and Eve against the forbidden fruit. Satan, in anticipation of the next illustration in the series ('Satan with Adam and Eve' (140)), looks jealously at the loving glances exchanged between the human pair.

From the very beginning of the poem, and particularly after Satan's speech on Mount Niphates early in the fourth book, Milton makes it clear that Satan is imprisoned in his own guilt and obstinacy. Blake represents him in 'Satan with Adam and Eve' (140) imprisoned in the coils of the serpent to which it will be his fate to be forever tied. Satan's stiff body and restricted gesture make a formal and significant contrast to God's and Raphael's free and open movements.

Satan watching the endearments of Adam and Eve is a rare subject in the iconography of Milton illustration. W. H. Brown's illustration in the 1796 edition of *Paradise Lost* is the only real precedent

for Blake's design. Blake follows Milton in his frank description of
the lovers in Eden, and his treatment of the subject contrasts with
the conventional approach of W. H. Brown. Milton openly describes the couple:

> . . . He in delight
> Both of her Beauty and submissive Charms
> Smil'd with superior Love, as *Jupiter*
> On *Juno* smiles, when he impregns the Clouds
> That shed *May* Flowers; and press'd her Matron lip
> With kisses pure: aside the Devil turn'd
> For envie . . .
>
> *(Paradise Lost, IV)*

The jewelled effect of sensuous richness here almost dominates the
overall design. Although in Milton's poem this episode does not
take place in Adam's and Eve's bower, in Blake's design fronds of
foliage meet over the heads of the lovers, creating an atmosphere
of intimacy from which Satan is excluded. The placing of Adam
and Eve in an almost circular frame with the sun rising on the right
and the moon seen on the left creates a sense of universality. Eden,
we are told by Milton, is in the centre of the earth and the focal
point of Eden is Adam and Eve, our first parents. The scene is certainly one of universal significance. The endearments of Adam and
Eve are watched by Satan, whose great fault is self-love. Blake
therefore depicts Satan (in a pose reflecting that of Adam) caressing
the serpent which is but an aspect of himself. Satan's endearments
of the serpent are thus a counterpoise to Adam's endearments of
Eve. The image of the serpent coiled around the body recurs
throughout Blake's art.[110]

The next illustration, which also belongs to Book IV, shows
Satan as a toad at the ear of Eve while the human couple are
sleeping ('Adam and Eve Sleeping') (141). Above hover the angels
Ithuriel and Zephon, who have just discovered Satan. This too is
a rare subject in Milton iconography, although the episode immediately following this ('Satan Starting at the Touch of Ithuriel's
Spear') was one of the most popular of all the *Paradise Lost* illustrations with eighteenth-century artists. It was treated by Burney,
Scott, Runciman, Fuseli, Barry, Westall and Romney as well as by
many other lesser-known artists. For a precedent we have to go
right back to 1688 to Lens's illustration (12) to Book IV in which
this scene with the toad is one of many episodes represented on
the one page. In choosing to portray this scene Blake intentionally
and calculatedly lays the emphasis of *Paradise Lost* where Milton

140 W. Blake, 'Satan with Adam and Eve'

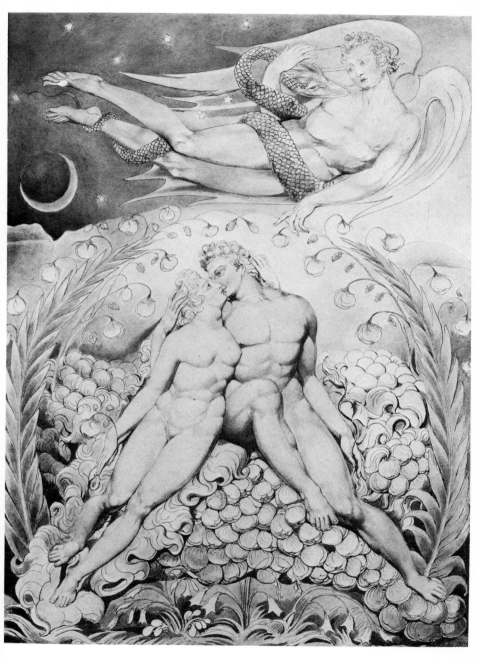

141 W. Blake, 'Adam and Eve Sleeping'

intended it, on the human pair. Fuseli, Barry, Westall and company chose to illustrate a moment later in the narrative when Satan appears in his own form because they could then make Satan the focal point of the illustration. In Blake's illustration all attention is centred on the prone figures of Adam and Eve.[111]

'Raphael Conversing with Adam and Eve' is one of the rare examples in Blake's *Paradise Lost* illustrations in which there is any substantial difference between the Huntington Library version and the Boston Museum version (142). The former is the earlier and this shows Raphael seated on the right and Adam and Eve on the left with the Tree of Knowledge seen in the middle distance. In the later version Blake has moved Eve to a position of greater symbolic value for the poem as a whole. Eve now appears directly beneath the tree, her body and the vertical of the tree forming a complete division of the page with Adam on one side and Raphael on the other. The natural pointed archway of Adam's and Eve's bower and Raphael's gesture towards the tree emphasize this.

It is clear that Blake had a very good understanding of all the nuances and allusions of Milton's poetry. Milton does not describe the positions of Adam, Eve and Raphael. Such details in the poem would become distracting and tedious. But Blake exploits the power of the pictorial image to refer to events in the past or the future whilst continuing to portray the narrative. The literary equivalent of this would be the use of words or images which call up associations in the reader's mind. In the case of Raphael conversing with Adam the composition forecasts what is to come. Adam will be separated from Heaven (Raphael is Heaven's ambassador) by his uxoriousness, which will not permit him to relinquish Eve who has sinned in eating the fruit via the agency of Satan. The latter is seen coiled round the tree. Blake's designs for *Paradise Lost* are in every way a complete set, for the presence of Satan here in the tree looks forward to the illustration of the crucifixion (146) in which Satan is seen crushed under the cross (the antitype of the Tree of Knowledge) on which hangs Christ, the second Adam.

'The Fall of the Rebel Angels' (144) was a popular subject with eighteenth-century artists, but Blake's treatment of it is quite novel. As in 'Satan Summons his Legions' (135) a certain impulse towards symmetrical pattern-making is discernible but here it is put to much better use. By employing the device of a circle from which the avenging angel shoots arrows onto the rebels Blake is able to distinguish clearly between the heavenly company and the falling angels, without having to make all his figures small (as in Hayman's version (45)) or exclude Heaven altogether (as in Barry's version

142 W. Blake, 'Raphael Conversing with Adam and Eve'

143 After E. F. Burney, 'Adam and Eve See Raphael'

(116)), and without having to have a great space between the two groups (as in Fuseli's version). The circle also gives one the sense of a tremendous degree of force pent up within the circumscribed area, and the rebels seem to be shot out of heaven at all points. The idea of a figure inscribed in a circle probably derives originally from Vitruvius's well-known image, but in this case Blake's kneeling figure also has associations with Urizen. Blake seems to have felt that the bow conveyed a particular sense of righteous punishment. A drawing in the collection of Sir Geoffrey Keynes could well be a study for this illustration.[112] Blake's source for the falling figures was probably the same as that used by other Milton illustrators for this subject, Michelangelo's 'Last Judgement' in the Sistine Chapel or Rubens's 'Fall of the Damned' at Munich. C. H. Collins-Baker suggests that the falling figures derive from Flaxman's *Purgatorio* illustration and that the circle of seraphim owe their origin to Flaxman's 'Christ'.[113] As Blake had an incredible facility for collecting and remembering motifs from diverse sources it is quite possible that all these works played their part in the creation of 'The Fall of the Rebel Angels'.

Blake's illustration of 'The Temptation of Eve' is one of his most

144 W. Blake, 'The Fall of the Rebel Angels'

145 W. Blake, 'The Temptation of Eve'

146 W. Blake, 'Michael Foretells the Crucifixion'

dramatic, particularly in the Boston version (145), in which the sky is darkened and the trunk of the tree is covered with thorns. This latter feature, entirely a creation of Blake's imagination, is peculiarly poignant when we recall that in Eden are:

> Flours of all hue, and without Thorn the Rose:
> (*Paradise Lost*, IV)

and that Christ, hanging on the tree to rescue mankind from the effects of Eve having eaten the fruits of this tree of Eden, wears a crown of thorns.

Readers of *Paradise Lost* are frequently unable to agree whether or not Milton intended to lay some blame on Adam for allowing Eve to wander off alone, thus laying her open to the guile of the serpent. Blake seems to have considered that Adam was to some extent guilty, for he portrays Adam with his back turned though still very much a part of the picture. Blake probably used a drawing in Brown's *Ars Pictoria* (p. 23) as a model for Adam in this design.[114] Eve at the moment of her fall is seen as essentially feminine, a most sensitive touch on the part of the artist for the serpent achieves his aim by flattery of Eve's womanhood:

> But all that fair and good in thy Divine
> Semblance, and in thy Beauties heav'nly Ray
> United I beheld; no Fair to thine
> Equivalent or second, which compelld
> Mee thus, though importune perhaps, to come
> And gaze, and worship thee of right declar'd
> Sovran of Creatures, universal Dame.
> (*Paradise Lost*, IX)

This is what Satan says to Eve and she accepts the flattery. Blake shows the serpent coiled around her body, thus indicating the intimate relationship that Satan builds between himself and Eve. She accepts the apple from the serpent's mouth while supporting his head with her hand.

'Michael Foretells the Crucifixion' (146) as a scene on its own is an entirely new feature in the iconography of Milton illustration. It is typical of Blake's optimistic reading of *Paradise Lost* that he chooses to represent this great promise of redemption rather than any of the horrific images of flood, disease and disaster which Michael also shows to Adam and which had hitherto invariably been chosen by artists illustrating Book XI or XII. 'The Mad House' or 'The Lazar House' and 'The Flood' were favourite subjects with Fuseli, Romney and others. Blake had earlier executed a drawing of the House of Death (124), but his choice for inclusion with his *Paradise Lost* designs was symptomatic of his balanced view of the poem and his own personal belief in salvation.

No doubt remains in Blake's interpretation of Satan's complete defeat. The serpent is seen coiled around the cross (a feature reminiscent of 'Raphael Converses with Adam') and his head is nailed under Christ's foot. Prone at the foot of the cross are Death and Sin which Christ, by his voluntary death, has overcome on behalf of mankind. In the foreground, the female form of Nature which Blake was to use so successfully in a later Milton illustration (p. 162) begins to stir with new life.[115] Here, as is so frequently the case, Blake shows his thorough familiarity with the text. In Book XII of *Paradise Lost* Michael, explaining the crucifixion to Adam, speaks of the destruction of Sin and the law of death by the crucifixion:

> But to the Cross he nailes thy Enemies
> The Law that is against thee, and the sins
> Of all mankind . . .
> (*Paradise Lost*, XII)

147 W. Blake, 'The Expulsion'   148 After E. F. Burney, 'The Expulsion'

Blake's positive attitude to the theme of *Paradise Lost* again emerges in his 'Expulsion' in which Michael wears an expression of sorrowing forbearance and Adam and Eve look hopeful. There is one slight difference of emphasis between the Huntington version (147) and the Boston version. In the former Adam and Eve gaze upwards at the horsemen, in the latter they look down at the serpent and thorns and thistles (a sharp contrast to the luxurious vegetation of Paradise).

The ambivalence of Milton's expulsion scene is here ideally expressed. The staring eyes of the horses, the great sheet of flame above the heads of Adam and Eve, and the lightning are very threatening, but Michael—in accordance with Milton's description—does not chase Adam and Eve from Paradise but leads them gently by the hand. The scene lacks the melodrama provided by the armed and vindictive Michael in Fuseli's and Romney's renderings of the scene (114, 115). It lacks also the sensual atmosphere of post-lapsarian sex which Fuseli manages to create in his swooning, half embracing, expelled lovers. The vision of the world that lies before Adam and Eve which John Martin laboured to create (159) is absent also in Blake's 'Expulsion'. But for all the absence of sensational effects, Blake's illustration—like most of his designs—is most faithful to Milton's last lines of *Paradise Lost*:

> In either hand the hastning Angel caught
> Our lingring Parents, and to th'Eastern Gate
> Led them direct . . .
> They looking back, all th'Eastern side beheld
> Of Paradise, so late thir happie seat,
> Wav'd over by that flaming Brand . . .
> Som natural tears they drop'd, but wip'd them soon;
> The World was all before them, where to choose
> Thir place of rest, and Providence thir guide.
> (*Paradise Lost*, XII)

M. Peckham has traced a distinct relationship between Blake's illustrations to *Paradise Lost* and Burney's illustrations to the 1799 edition of the poem.[116] Blake's 'Adam and Eve Conversing with Raphael' (142) is close in design to Burney's treatment of this subject (143). The resemblance is particularly noticeable in thirteen watercolour studies by Burney for the 1799 edition now bound into a volume in Princeton Library. Blake would almost certainly have seen the 1799 edition, as a Milton enthusiast like Hayley would have had a copy. He may also have seen Burney's drawings, as the 1799 edition was published by a group of London booksellers among whom were Dodsley, the Robinsons, the Rivingtons, Johnson and several others for whom Blake had worked. Moreover, Blake began studying drawing at the Royal Academy in 1778 at about the same time as Burney must have been there.

The argument for Blake's indebtedness to Burney is dependent on the view that a relationship between the two sets of illustrations exists on three levels: subject, general design and detail. As we have seen, Blake's choice of subject generally follows that of most other Milton illustrators, Burney included. However, the rest of M. Peckham's discussion is most interesting. The Burney drawings consist of twelve illustrations for *Paradise Lost* and a frontispiece vignette. Blake's drawings in the Huntington Library number twelve. If one adds to the nine Boston drawings the extra Huntington version of 'Satan, Sin and Death', a large drawing of 'Satan Summons his Legions' (Victoria and Albert Museum) which corresponds in size to the Boston drawings, and the lost drawing of 'God Judging Adam and Eve' mentioned in the Rossetti catalogue, the Boston set also comprises twelve drawings. Therefore the Burney and the Blake illustrations are numerically parallel.

M. Peckham has noticed that the closer in subject the Blake illustration is to the Burney illustration, the less symbolic and more illustrative is Blake's treatment of the subject. For example, Burney's general design in 'Satan Starting at the Touch of Ithuriel's Spear' (87) can be seen with adaptations in the supine positions of Adam and Eve and Satan in Blake's 'Satan with Adam and Eve' (140).

On the question of detail, M. Peckham is a little too precipitate in finding points of comparison between the work of the two artists. Similarities between Sin's key in the two artists' illustrations of 'Satan, Sin and Death' (86, 136) he cites as evidence of derivation. In fact the two illustrations are so totally different in concept that such minor detail can be discounted. However, the way in which Burney arranges the trees in 'Satan Starts at the Touch of Ithuriel's Spear' into the shape of a rough arch (87) may have given Blake the idea of the arch in 'Adam and Eve Conversing with Raphael' (142). Similarly, Eve's table and dish in Burney's illustration of 'Adam and Eve See Raphael Approaching' (143) may have provided the inspiration for all his astonishingly natural kitchen equipment and furniture in 'Adam and Eve Conversing with Raphael' (142). In the 'Expulsion' scene, Burney's frontal design (148) may have influenced Blake's treatment of the subject (147). The sinuous movement of Adam and Eve may be a reflection of the rollicking gait of Burney's figures.

The most that illustrators of *Ode on the Morning of Christ's Nativity* have generally achieved is a fairly conventional Nativity scene. Blake is the only artist within the period 1685 to 1860 who designed a comprehensive set of illustrations to this poem. Like his *Paradise Lost* illustrations, Blake's designs for this poem are often symbolic. He seldom depicts simple set scenes and most of his drawings either recall past verses or anticipate subsequent descriptive matter. All the designs are individually interesting, but as a set they tend to be a little repetitive. For example, there are two scenes in which the crib features as a major part of the design (149, 152) and another in which it appears in the background (150). The poem consists of variations on a theme, the idea of the light of Christ which subdues a pagan deity, and this, naturally, limits the possibilities open to the illustrator.

One of Blake's most successful designs for Milton's *Ode* is the first in the series (149). It illustrates stanzas 1 and 2[117] and demonstrates Blake's skill in combining into one coherent pattern many distant elements and details. For example, we see Peace, a particularly difficult abstraction to portray, descending:

149 W. Blake, 'The Descent of Peace'

150 W. Blake, 'The Old Dragon Underground'

> . . . Through the turning sphear . . .
> . . . Waving wide her mirtle wand.

Blake even manages to suggest by means of concentric circles the idea of the turning 'sphear'. The all-embracing gesture of Peace indicates what may be achieved on earth by Peace through the birth of Christ which is pictured below. Nature, Milton tells us:

> Had doff't her gawdy trim . . .
> Onely with speeches fair
> She woo's the gentle Air
> To hide her guilty front with innocent Snow.

Blake shows Nature, subdued by Christ's birth, lying obeisant in the snow below the crib. But her position at the base of the pyramidal-shaped composition is an indication that, though in bondage, she is still the foundation of the earth. The pyramid which encloses the birth of Christ was in Blake's mind from the very conception of the design and appears in a preparatory drawing (Rosenwald Collection, National Gallery of Art, Washington).

The second design in the series is a purely narrative illustration of the shepherds in the fields and the heavenly choir. The third design, however, is more complicated. This depicts the old dragon underground who, soon to be destroyed by the crucifixion and already discomfited by Christ's birth, 'Swindges the scaly Horrour of his foulded tail' in fear and disgust (150). Blake's grotesque dragon possesses six heads, rather like Typhon, each head looking in a different direction.

'The shrine of Apollo' (illustrating stanzas 19–21 of the poem) is the most complex design of the set and in it Blake strikes the death blow at classical values (151). At the centre of the design is the Apollo Belvedere and from this statue, before which the oracles are struck dumb, the spirit of Apollo is seen plunging towards the sea. In a cave sits an enigmatic figure which has been identified as the mad priestess raving,[118] but which could equally well be intended to represent the Lars or Lemures who 'moan with midnight plaint'. In the background we see 'the Flamins at their service quaint' and in the sky the flight of various mythological deities can be seen. Blake tried to include rather too much detail into this representation of the overthrow of the whole of the classical world, and the design consequently lacks the clarity of 'The Descent of Peace'. It is, nevertheless, a brave and unprecedented attempt at interpreting Milton's complex imagery.

'The Sullen Moloch' (152) illustrating stanza 23 is very much

151 W. Blake, 'The Shrine of Apollo'

more successful. Moloch was a Canaanite idol to whom children
were sacrificed. The Christ child is understood to be the cause of
all the various disruptions described in the poem. Blake very ingeni-
ously shows Jesus walking forth from the flaming tabernacle under-
neath the idol and overpowering the worshippers. Blake thus makes
explicit the antithesis, which is inherent in the verse, between the
power of the tiny child and the powerlessness of the great, satur-
nine, child-eating idol. The bat-winged spirit of Moloch, like that

152 W. Blake, 'The Sullen Moloch'

152 W. Blake, 'The Sullen Moloch'   153 W. Blake, 'The Virgin Blest'

of Apollo in an earlier illustration, flees from the shrine. The white-
ness and purity of the child contrast with the blackness and evil of
Moloch. From this turbulent scene we move on to the serenity of
the final design, which is a simple depiction of the nativity, illustrating stanza 27 (153).

Blake's designs for *Paradise Regained* were executed between
1817 and 1825, at least eight years after the illustrations to the
Ode. In style they differ considerably from all the earlier Milton
illustrations; the figures are depicted in a much less linear manner
and there is virtually a complete lack of detail. The method, as
always with Blake, is symbolic, but the designs to *Paradise Regained*
have a more iconic quality than any of the earlier ones. *Paradise
Regained*, unlike *Paradise Lost*, has as its constant poetic centre the
figure of Christ. This may be responsible for the iconic quality of
Blake's designs. The difference in artistic style between these
designs and Blake's earlier work is the result of gradual changes in
technique.

'The Baptism of Christ' (129) continues the theme of the *Ode*
series. In addition to the familiar figures of the Baptism, Blake
shows Satan fleeing away into the sky like Apollo and Moloch.
This unusual piece of iconography is amply justified by the passage
in which Milton describes the Adversary:

> Who roving still
> About the World, at that assembly fam'd
> Would not be last . . .
> With wonder, then with envy fraught and rage
> Flies to his place.
>
> (*Paradise Regained*)

There is some inconsistency about 'The Council in Hell' (*Paradise Regained*, I) because although he has flown away without the help of wings he now appears with bat's wings. This design is remarkable for the way in which Blake has attempted to portray the agony and passion in Satan's face.

In 'Christ's Troubled Dreams' (*Paradise Regained*, IV) (139) we see once again the familiar, hovering figure of 'The Lazar House', but here the figure seems to represent some kind of spirit of thunder or the storm, as it is from its hands that:

Fierce rain with lightning mixt, water with fire

is pouring forth. The pose of Christ, stretched diagonally across the page, is reminiscent of sleeping figures in medieval manuscripts. Blake chooses, also, to illustrate the great feast which miraculously appears to tempt Christ in the desert. Milton invented this scene, which does not appear in the Bible, and J. Beer points out that Blake 'grasps the very evident relationship between Comus's temptation of the Lady by means of a banquet and the preparation of a miraculous feast for Christ by Satan. . . . In both cases he shows the visionary human being refusing delights offered by figures in whom an apparent attractiveness barely covers the lineaments of distorted energy.'[119]

Blake's illustrations to *L'Allegro* and *Il Penseroso* can be dated around 1817, as his well-known stipple engraving of 'Mirth', the first of the *L'Allegro* designs, belongs to that date.[120] This engraving is further evidence of the relationship between Blake and Fuseli as (despite the more ethereal, fleeting quality of Blake's design) the general concept is quite close to that of Fuseli's 'Euphrosyne' (93).

In all the twelve designs to *L'Allegro* and *Il Penseroso* (Pierpont Morgan Library) the tendency of the artist away from philosophically based designs (such as most of those of *Paradise Lost*) towards a much more freely imaginative technique is very noticeable. Blake no longer directs all his fanciful and intellectual powers towards faithfully depicting Milton's poetry in comprehensible pictorial terms. Instead he translates the poetry into the terms of his own imaginative world. (He must have realized that the pictures might seem obscure, for he appended notes on each drawing.) For example, in the second illustration to *L'Allegro*, 'The Lark', the subject of the picture is no longer a bird but an angel on the wing.

All the scenes illustrated take place in the open air. Blake rejects the Elizabethan theatre of *L'Allegro* and the studious cloister of *Il Penseroso*, subjects popular with later illustrators. (See, for example, the 1848 Art Union and the 1849 Etching Club editions of the poems.) Instead, for *Il Penseroso* he chooses, in addition to the personification of 'Melancholy' as a partner for 'Mirth', 'The Wandering Moon', 'The Spirit of Plato', 'The Sun in his Wrath', 'Mysterious Dream' and 'Milton, Old Age'.

For Blake, illustrating the happy rural mood of *L'Allegro* towards the end of his life, there is no strict distinction between reality and the world of the fancy, the poetic or the mythical. He reduces human beings to very small figures, all but invisible as in 'The Sun at his Eastern Gate' (third illustration to *L'Allegro*). The sun, potent force and life-giving god, completely obsesses the painter. The limitations imposed by natural laws do not exist for Blake and, whilst human creatures are reduced in size, the beings of the fairy world take on human form in 'The Sunshine Holiday' and 'The Goblin' (fourth and fifth designs to *L'Allegro*).

The final illustration to *L'Allegro*, 'The Youthful Poet's Dream', is Blake's most imaginative. His design is used to express his continuing concern with Milton the man. He shows the youthful poet, the boy Milton, sleeping in the setting sun. But this setting sun is hardly noticeable beside the great symbolic sun of the imagination. Shakespeare and Ben Jonson are in attendance to inspire and direct the young poet.

It has been said that Blake's words are visual and that his paintings are literary and conceptual.[121] The unified approach which Blake was able to bring to Milton's verse must to some extent account for the success of the main body of his illustrations. Furthermore, Blake recognized Milton's poetry as symbolic, not simply as the ultimate in sublimity, nor as a poetic expansion of biblical history.[122] It is an astonishing phenomenon that an artist of Blake's individuality and vividness of imagination *and* a poet in his own right should have been one of the greatest illustrators of Milton's verse.

Notes to Chapter III

1. I use the word 'sentiment' in the eighteenth-century sense of refined feelings involving regard for some ideal consideration.
2. Sir Joshua Reynolds, *Discourse XIII*, delivered to the Royal Academy Dec. 11th, 1786. *Discourses*, ed. R. R. Wark (Huntington Library Publications, 1959).
3. Edmund Burke, op. cit.
4. Dr. Samuel Johnson, *The Lives of the English Poets* (1783), 'John Milton'. *Dr. Johnson, Prose and Poetry*, ed. M. Wilson (1963), p. 836.
5. Waterhouse, p. 200.
6. Ibid., p. 200.
7. A. Graves, *The Royal Academy of Arts. A Complete Dictionary* (1906). All subsequent references to works exhibited at the Royal Academy are cited from Graves.
8. A. Graves, *The Society of Artists of Great Britain. A Dictionary* (1907).
9. The journal is the property of Mr. D. E. T. Lindsay of Drumconreath, Co. Meath. It is reproduced in the *The Walpole Society*, XXXII, 1946–8 (pub. 1951).
10. C. Hussey, *The Picturesque: Studies in a Point of View* (1927), Index.
11. A. Graves, *S.A.* Two years later (in 1776) Wheatley is recorded as having exhibited 'Mr. Webster in the Character of Comus' at the Society of Artists.
12. *The Walpole Society*, XXXII (1946–8).
13. Bryan.
14. This engraving is one of a great many after different artists showing Adam and Eve. They are mounted in a volume compiled by F. Bosanquet now in the Victoria and Albert Museum. As this engraving does not appear in any edition of *Paradise Lost*—as far as I know—it must have been issued independently or else used in an edition of Genesis.
15. The canvas is 101 × 127 cm. and the design was engraved by J. R. Smith in 1789. Wright's account book in the National Portrait Gallery cites this picture as 'A moonlight from Comus—£84 – 0 – 0'. It was sold to Josiah Wedgwood after having been exhibited in Robin's Rooms, Covent Garden, in Spring 1785.
16. B. Nicolson, 'Two Companion Pieces by Wright of Derby', *B. Mag.* (March 1962), p. 113.
17. Ibid.
18. The 1788 catalogue seems to have been published in a very limited edition.
19. Bryan.
20. A. C. Coxhead, *Thomas Stothard, R.A.* (1906), p. 103.
21. Ibid., p. 103.
22. In the British Museum and the Slade College of Art.

23. See, for example, Flaxman's own poem, *The Knight of the Blazing Cross*, written and illustrated for his wife. Published in facsimile in H. N. Morris, *Flaxman, Blake, Coleridge and Other Men of Genius Influenced by Swedenborg* (1915).

24. John Flaxman, *Lectures on Sculpture* (1829).

25. W. G. Constable, *John Flaxman* (1927), p. 52.

26. There is evidence that Flaxman executed a bust of Milton. His account book has an entry for Aug. 25th, 1800, referring to 'Two Busts of Shakespeare and Milton' (not identified). See 'An Account Book of John Flaxman, R.A.', *Walpole Society*, XXVIII (1940).

27. See L. Binyon, *A Catalogue of Drawings by British Artists in the British Museum* (1898), p. 229.

28. R. and S. Redgrave, *A Century of British Painters* (1947), p. 187 (1st ed. 1866).

29. Ibid., p. 187.

30. L. Binyon, op. cit.

31. M. Peckham, 'Blake, Milton and Edward Burney', *The Princeton University Library Chronicle*, XI (Spring 1950), p. 109.

32. Pope, 'Eloisa to Abelard', l. 20. *The Poems of Alexander Pope* (Twickenham Text, 1963).

33. E. Burke, op. cit.

34. *Discourse IV* (Dec. 10th, 1771); *Discourses*, ed. R. R. Wark (1959); Dr. S. Johnson, *The History of Rasselas* (1759), ch. X; Dr. S. Johnson, *Prose and Poetry* (1963).

35. E. Burke, op. cit., Part II, Section IV. Author's italics.

36. W. Gilpin, *Three Essays*: On Picturesque Beauty; On Picturesque Travel; and On Sketching Landscape; with a poem on Landscape Painting (1792) (3rd edition 1800).

37. For details of this dispute, see C. Hussey, op. cit., ch. III.

38. Dr. S. Johnson, *The Lives of the Poets* (1779–81), 'John Milton'. *Johnson. Prose and Poetry* (1963), p. 836.

39. Aphorism 58 (1788–1818). Reprinted in E. C. Mason, *The Mind of Henry Fuseli* (1951), p. 218.

40. G. Grigson, 'Painters of the Abyss', *The Architectural Review*, 107 (Oct. 1950), pp. 215–20.

41. E. R. Meijer, 'The Romantics and their Time', *The Romantic Movement*, Arts Council Catalogue (1959), p. 41.

42. See N. Frye, 'Romanticism Reconsidered', *English Institute Essays* (1962), pp. 3–6.

43. Percy Bysshe Shelley, *The Complete Works* (1965).

44. W. Godwin, *The Life of Edward and John Philips* (1875), pp. 5, 6. Quoted by Dr. A. Von Gertsch, *Der Steigende ruhm Miltons* (Leipzig, 1927), p. 48.

45. J. W. Good, 'Studies in the Milton Tradition', *University of Illinois Studies in Language and Literature*, I, pp. 229–300.

46. W. Gaunt, *Arrows of Desire* (1956), pp. 117–18.

47. See M. Praz, op. cit., p. 77.

48. Shelley, 'A Defense of Poesy', *The Complete Works*, VII (1965).
49. M. Praz, op. cit., p. 78.
50. *The Farington Diary*, ed. J. Greig (1923).
51. Ibid.
52. W. Whitley, *Artists and their Friends in England 1700–1799* (1928), I, p. 284.
53. Waterhouse, p. 189.
54. E. Burke, op. cit.
55. Bryan.
56. There is also an ink and wash drawing of this subject by Barry in the William Rockhill Nelson Gallery, Kansas City. The figure of Satan is like that in the B.M. versions, but he has wings and does not hold his own spear and shield. These are held by the figure to be seen on Satan's right in the B.M. versions, who is seen full length instead of half length.
57. See Lennox's speech to Macbeth. *Macbeth*, Act II, Scene III.
58. W. H. Pyne, op. cit., pp. 265–6.
59. Ibid., p. 267.
60. Schiff, op. cit.
61. J. Knowles, F.R.S., *The Life and Writings of Henry Fuseli* (1831), ch. VIII. See also D. Irwin, 'Fuseli's Milton Gallery' (unpublished letters of Fuseli to Roscoe), *B. Mag.* (Dec. 1959), pp. 436–40.
62. F. Antal, *Fuseli Studies* (1956), p. 22 (n. 7).
63. Quoted in E. C. Mason, op. cit., p. 91.
64. Schiff, pp. 29–30.
65. P. A. Tomory, *A Collection of Drawings by Henry Fuseli*, Auckland City Art Gallery (Auckland, 1967).
66. Schiff endeavours to dismiss the Milton illustrations of other artists such as Hayman and Hogarth as unimportant in comparison with Fuseli's achievement (op. cit., p. 42).
67. F. Antal, op. cit., p. 87.
68. Ibid., pp. 83–4.
69. J. Farington, op. cit., II.
70. F. Antal, op. cit., p. 124.
71. W. Whitley, op. cit., II, pp. 213–14. It is a political caricature concerning allegations about the queen's influence over the king in the choice of Pitt or Thurlow.
72. See *James Gillray. Drawings and Caricatures* (catalogue). The Arts Council (1967).
73. D. Hill, *Mr. Gillray the Caricaturist. A Biography* (1965), pp. 147–8. For an interesting discussion on Gillray's caricatures in relation to the Romantic Movement in art, see E. H. Gombrich, *Meditations on a Hobby Horse and Other Essays* (1963), pp. 120–22.
74. C. Hussey, op. cit., Index.
75. A. Crookshank, 'The Drawings of George Romney', *B. Mag.* (Feb. 1957).

76. J. Romney, *Memoirs of the Life and Works of George Romney* (1830), pp. 244–5.
77. A. Cunningham, *The Lives of the Most Eminent British Painters, Sculptors and Architects* (1829–33) (2nd ed. 1837), V, pp. 122–3.
78. According to A. Crookshank (op. cit.), the bulk of Romney's sketches is to be found in a number of books. The largest collection, which probably contains many Milton sketches, is that of a private owner in Paris, acquired at the 1894 sale after the death of Romney's grand-daughter. Three sketch books dated November 1783, March 1790 and March 1794 which were in the possession of the Royal Institute of Cornwall at Truro were sold at Christie's in 1966. These certainly contained Milton drawings. The British Museum has a sketch book inscribed 'Milton/July 1792', the Barber Institute has one inscribed 'August 1792/Flood/Arke', and the Fitzwilliam Museum has one inscribed 'August 92/Milton/ flood'. The latter three are, for our purpose, most important. The drawings in all three books are very similar and very repetitive. Because of this it seems best to take one or two examples of Romney's treatment of each subject as fairly typical and see in what way—if at all—they can be related to the work of Fuseli and other artists.
79. J. Romney, op. cit., p. 244.
80. Reproduced in F. Antal, op. cit.
81. A. Crookshank, op. cit., p. 44.
82. A. Cunningham, op. cit., V, pp. 88–9.
83. A. Blunt, 'Blake's Pictorial Imagination', *J.W.C.I.*, VI (1943), p. 212.
84. Schiff, p. 60.
85. Ibid., p. 121.
86. Ibid., p. 40.
87. Ibid., p. 38.
88. A. Cunningham, op. cit., II, p. 310.
89. From a review (attributed to Fuseli) of Cumberland's *Calvary. The Analytical Review* (June 1792). Quoted in E. C. Mason, op. cit., p. 345.
90. F. Antal, op. cit., p. 91.
91. On Jan. 30th, 1803, Blake wrote to James Blake of 'labouring in my thoughts Designs for "Cowper's Milton" '. On April 2nd, 1804, he wrote to Hayley sending impressions of the plates he was engraving after Romney for the edition. See *The Letters of William Blake*, ed. Sir Geoffrey Keynes (1956).
92. Some of the series of portraits including that of Milton are in the possession of the Manchester City Art Gallery. They are a lugubrious collection executed in stagnant-looking greens and browns. A catalogue concerning the history of the Felpham portrait heads compiled by Mr. W. Wells has recently been published by Manchester City Art Gallery.

93. *The Letters of William Blake*, op. cit. *Little Tom* is an illustrated poem by Blake.
94. Ibid. Letter dated May 28th, 1804.
95. Wordsworth, *London*, 1802.
96. Letter to Thomas Butts, April 25th, 1803 (*The Letters of William Blake*).
97. N. Frye, *Fearful Symmetry. A Study of William Blake* (Princeton, 1947), p. 331.
98. Blake refers to his designs for *Comus* in a letter written to Flaxman on Oct. 19th, 1801 (*The Letters of William Blake*).
99. For a discussion of the dating of the various sets of Milton illustrations, see C. H. Collins-Baker, *A Catalogue of William Blake Drawings and Paintings in the Huntington Library* (San Marino, 1938). As there are frequently several versions of each drawing it has seemed most helpful to provide, in Appendix E, a catalogue of all Blake's illustrations to *Paradise Lost* rather than to be continually referring in the text to other versions.
100. See L. Binyon, op. cit.
101. A. Blunt in 'Blake's Pictorial Imagination', *J.W.C.I.*, VI (1943), p. 195, speaks of an exaggeration and uncontrolled quality in Blake's work which he attributes to the fact that Blake 'was a lonely figure, dependent for his inspiration, if not always for his methods, on his own imagination, and there is for that reason an exaggeration in his work, an uncontrolled quality which makes it reasonable that he should have been considered as a madman not only in his own day but throughout most of the nineteenth century. Circumstances compelled him to solitude, and to a reliance on his own judgement that must destroy balance. But he was not the only one who suffered in this way. In the circles with which he was most closely connected, Fuseli was notoriously eccentric, and Cowper and Romney died insane.'
102. This figure also features in Blake's 'Morning Stars' in *Job*.
103. A. Blunt, *The Art of William Blake* (New York, 1959), pp. 74–5.
104. S. F. Damon, *William Blake. His Philosophy and Symbols* (1924), p. 212.
105. G. W. Digby, *Symbol and Image in William Blake* (1957), p. 68. The writer refers to: '. . . the universality of this symbol of the "Four Living Creatures", as it has been extensively studied in Jungian literature, in connection with the psychological functions. It can be traced in the four sons of Horus, the vision of Ezekiel, the four beasts of the Evangelists; also in the fixed signs of the Zodiac; and in Hindu and Buddhist mythology in the Caryatid kings, the regents of the four quarters.'
106. J. Beer, who remarks on the significance of Blake's illustrations to Milton in relation to the development of the artist's humanist philosophy, writes: 'In his revolutionary days, he was most attracted by the figure of Satan and repelled by the Urizenic necessity of God

the Father. He does not now abandon his view that when Satan is thrown out of Heaven both he and the inhabitants of Heaven are deprived, but he shows a greater sympathy for the Father and the angels. If Satan remains the protagonist of human energy, God is now more clearly the protagonist of vision.' J. Beer, *Blake's Humanism* (Manchester, 1968), pp. 194–5.

107. C. H. Collins-Baker makes various suggestions as to sources for the figures in Blake's 'Satan, Sin and Death'. As many artists, who were Blake's friends and whose work he admired, interpreted this scene it seems contrived to search further afield. In his Huntington Library Catalogue (1938, p. 5) C. H. Collins-Baker thinks that Sin was based on 'Flaxman's invention of Scylla'. In an article in the *Huntington Library Quarterly* (Oct. 1940) ('The Sources of Blake's Pictorial Expression', p. 366) he suggests that the representation of the combat between Satan and Death is an adaptation of the well-known classic rendering of 'Archemorus'. He traces the back view of Death to one of Dalton's engravings of an Amazonian battle frieze. This seems to be carrying the treasure hunt beyond reasonable limits.

108. C. H. Collins-Baker, 'The Sources of Blake's Pictorial Expression', *Huntington Library Quarterly*, IV (Oct. 1940), pp. 365–6.

109.   Thee Father first they sung Omnipotent,
         Immutable, Immortal, Infinite,
         Eternal King, thee Author of all being,
         Fountain of Light, thy self invisible
         Amidst the glorious brightness where thou sit'st
         Thron'd inaccessible, but when thou shad'st
         The full blaze of thy beams . . .
                                        (*Paradise Lost*, III)

110. J. Beer sees it as an emblem of 'energy rising into selfhood', op. cit., p. 195.

111. The pose of Eve may derive from a drawing by or after Daniele da Volterra. See A. Blunt, *The Art of William Blake* (New York, 1959), p. 10.

112. It shows a male figure roughly drawn in pencil about to shoot an arrow from a large bow like the one in 'The Fall of the Rebel Angels', whilst above a vague figure hovers with arms outstretched. Reproduced in Sir G. Keynes, *Blake's Pencil Drawings* (2nd series 1956), pl. 22. J. Beer sees God the Son in this illustration 'in the midst of a sun-disk', indicative of God's vision.

113. C. H. Collins-Baker, 'The Sources of Blake's Pictorial Expression', *Huntington Library Quarterly*, IV (Oct. 1940), p. 366.

114. Ibid., p. 360.

115. J. Beer calls this figure 'Earth', op. cit., p. 196.

116. M. Peckham, op. cit.

117. This discussion of Blake's designs for *Ode on the Morning of Christ's*

Nativity refers only to the set of designs in the Whitworth Art Gallery.
118. J. Hagstrum, *William Blake: Poet and Painter* (Chicago, 1964), p. 27.
119. J. Beer, op. cit., p. 196.
120. This is illustrated in F. Antal, op. cit., p. 86. Antal traces similarities between Blake's 'Mirth' and the 'Morning' (1803–8) of Runge of which there are several versions, one in the Kunsthalle, Hamburg. For illustrations of some of the other pictures in this series by Blake, see C. B. Tinker, 'Blake: Dreams of Milton', *Art News* (1950).
121. J. Hagstrum, op. cit., p. 9.
122. For an assessment of Blake's feeling for and understanding of Milton, see J. Beer, op. cit. (especially ch. II).

IV   The Nineteenth Century

1800–1860

During the nineteenth century, the early academic neo-classical style exemplified by the work of Thomas Kirke, R. Corbould and Stothard at the end of the previous century grew to full maturity. The culmination of this style as applied in illustrations to Milton is seen in the grand productions of Haydon, Etty and other artists whose aim was to achieve in England under the auspices of the Royal Academy a school of history painting equal to that of the Continent. Inevitably the status conferred by the Academy attracted a great many very minor artists. It is necessary, therefore, to concentrate on artists who adapted the universal style of the academy life class to their own needs and purposes as individuals, and mention only in passing those who succumbed to a facile and fashionable cliché.

The style of the sublime, as exemplified by Barry and Fuseli, acquired new dimensions during the nineteenth century in the work of John Martin, an exponent of Romanticism in a more absolute sense than had hitherto been seen in England. The nineteenth century became the great age of English landscape painting. It is not surprising, therefore, that besides the styles of neo-classicism and the sublime a third approach to Milton's verse can be discerned during this century. This new style is exemplified most clearly in the work of Samuel Palmer and other artists who, towards the end of the period chose particularly to illustrate Milton's pastoral verse.

(i) The Landscape of Eden and the Architecture of Hell

John Martin must have been one of the most unusual and individualistic men of his generation. Born in 1789, the son of a Northumberland farm labourer, he was—throughout his life—a tireless worker and a great innovator. He not only submitted a *Plan for Working and Ventilating Coal Mines* to the Select Committee on Accidents in Mines (1835) but later in life he also devised an ingenious plan for better sewage disposal in London. Martin was clearly very conscious of the needs of his own time. In painting he is one of the last exponents of the Burkeian sublime, but his work bears few of the vestiges of neo-classicism which clung to the work of the eighteenth-century artists of the sublime. He looks back to Fuseli and forward to the naturalistic landscape painters of the century.

The commission which gave Martin the opportunity to design and execute his twenty-four illustrations to *Paradise Lost* must be one of the most astonishing episodes in the history of book illustration. In 1817 Martin had executed seven etchings for a volume entitled *The Characters of Trees*, published by Ackermann. A year later he completed his seven aquatints of Sezincote House which were bound in a presentation volume. Apart from these books, two odd etchings, and two Miltonic canvases ('The Expulsion of Adam and Eve from Paradise' and 'Adam's First Sight of Eve', Glasgow City Art Gallery) exhibited in 1813, Septimus Prowett—said to have been an American—can have seen little on which to assess Martin's ability as an illustrator of *Paradise Lost*. Nevertheless, probably in the early months of.1823, he gave Martin a commission of two thousand pounds for twenty-four mezzotints of *Paradise Lost*. Long before these were finished Martin was promised a further fifteen hundred pounds for a smaller set of plates. With these two sets of plates Martin may be said to have introduced into common usage the practice of designing specifically for mezzotint. Previously the medium had been used almost exclusively for reproductions of pictures.[1] It would appear that Martin's method of working was to paint an oil sketch and then transfer the design direct to the plate.[2]

Where, then, does Martin stand in relation to his predecessors and his contemporaries? The terms in which Martin couches his hopes and aspirations in the prospectus to his *Paradise Lost* leave little doubt that Martin saw himself as a painter of the sublime. Discussing the twenty-four engravings which are 'the chief object and distinctive charm of this publication', Martin (or whoever is his mouthpiece) writes:

Those only who have seen the grand Scriptural Paintings of this artist . . . can be duly impressed by the peculiar adaptation of his powers to the lofty undertaking of embodying the stupendous and preternatural imagery of the Paradise Lost; in which the sublime genius of Milton has given these wonderful descriptions of Heaven, and Hell, and Paradise, and Chaos, and Creation; these, it may be said, without wishing to derogate from the merits of the eminent Artists who have already employed their pencils to illustrate this Poem, have not yet been treated with a boldness and grandeur kindred to the mighty imagination which created them . . .[3]

Martin was evidently well aware of the tradition of Milton illustration within which he was working. The words 'stupendous', 'preternatural', 'grandeur' and 'mighty imagination' are all those used by eighteenth-century followers of Burke to describe not only Milton but such Miltonic productions as De Loutherbourg's 'Eidophusikon' (p. 105).

The possibility of a continuing tradition from De Loutherbourg to Martin becomes even more acceptable when one takes into account the way in which such journals as the *Literary Gazette* spoke of Martin's Milton pictures: 'There is a wildness, a grandeur, a mystery about his designs which are indescribably fine . . .'[4] J. Seznec has described the nineteenth-century quality of increasingly spectacular theatricality which was associated with works by artists like Martin and which originates with De Loutherbourg:

> Sa tradition véritable, il faut la chercher dans les dioramas. Charles Lamb avait malicieusement qualifié le 'Festin de Balthazar' de 'phantasmagoric trick', et il imaginait un commentateur expliquant au public populaire . . . Constable de son côté, appelait le Festin 'Martin's pantomime'. Or, des 1823, a l'heure même ou Martin remportait ses premiers succès, l'invention de Daguerre et Bouton commençait à subjuguer les foules par des moyens analogues aux siens: décors fantastiques, illusions de perspective, et, bien entendu, sujets bibliques tels que 'Le Deluge', ou 'L'Inauguration du Temple de Salomon'.[5]

Martin had followers and associates among his contemporaries. Artists like Gandy, Papworth and Danby were all painting in a similar vein and, among writers, Maturin and Beckford exhibit the same predilection for the sepulchral, the extraordinary and the vast.[6] The sociological causes of this continuation of the cult of the sublime have been discussed by F. D. Klingender:

> The mood of despondency which sprang from the unexpected frustration of the hopes placed in science and political reform led to a revival of the eighteenth century taste for the sublime. Horror assumed a new and startlingly topical meaning when Mary Shelley created the symbol of 'Frankenstein' (1917) . . . The stresses and contradictions arising from the conflict of classes in a rapidly changing economy were projected onto an ideal plane and dramatized as a struggle between 'man' and 'nature' or between rival forces in nature. Milton's Satan was readily accepted as the symbol of the new scientific forces in society, because he embodied intelligence, ingenuity and science in the cosmic struggle and was at the same time a symbol of man's self-destruction and inevitable doom.[7]

Despite the affinity between Martin's *Paradise Lost* illustrations and those of the eighteenth-century advocates of Burke's sublime,

Martin's work creates an entirely novel effect in the history of Milton illustrations. The landscape of Eden is Martin's primary concern. His figure drawing is very bad and the only two illustrations involving large-scale figures, 'Satan at the Gates of Hell' and 'Satan Starting from the Touch of Ithuriel's Spear' (154), are noticeably inferior to the rest of his plates. The figures are stiff and conventional and their expressions of fierce anger and pride appear ludicrously misplaced.

The novelty of Martin's designs and to some extent the degree of his achievement is best seen by comparing his work with that of previous artists. For Fuseli, nothing but the figures enacting the drama are important. One is given—in Fuseli's illustration—no sense either of the horrific physical surroundings in Hell, so clearly pictured in Milton, or of the delightful landscape of Eden. Artists like Burney (and, to some extent, Blake) endeavour to indicate Adam's and Eve's surroundings and to suggest something of the profusion of nature in Eden. But these are generalized or highly stylized portrayals of Eden. In Martin's illustrations, for the first time, a sense of real place is created by the detailed painting of trees and shrubs with particular attention paid to the variety of texture in the natural scene: rock, moss, bark and smooth lawn. All these things appeal to the viewer's tactile sense. By the use of Claudian vistas and false horizons Martin creates an amazing sense of the

154 J. Martin, 'Satan Starting from the Touch of Ithuriel's Spear'

vastness of the universe. By the use of strangely shaped trees and rocks and especially by the dramatic use of light Martin is able to change the mood of these landscapes and, avoiding repetitiveness, create variety in an imaginary world in which the artist constantly aspires to the same anti-naturalistic, fantastic ultimate.

These landscapes of Eden are interspersed with two other types of illustration, the rocky, semi-abstract composition usually used for scenes in Hell and the illustrations in which architecture plays the most important part. As the landscapes of Eden predominate these will be discussed first.

John Martin, like Fuseli, seems to have lived Milton's poetry and this helps to endow not only his Milton illustrations but his work as a whole with a certain unity. He exhibited canvases portraying *Paradise Lost* at the Royal Academy and the British Institute both before and after the Prowett commission.[8] He was steeped in the Old Testament and even pictures, the sources of which have nothing to do with biblical history, like 'The Bard' and 'Sadak in Search of the Waters of Oblivion' have a prophetic, elemental aura about them which is found in *Paradise Lost* and the Old Testament. Martin's choice of subject was almost invariably literary and nearly always involved the struggle of humanity in all its insufficiency against the natural powers of the universe or against the rule of some supernatural being.

155 J. Martin, 'Adam and Eve See Raphael Approaching'

Martin's Eden is a lush mixture of tropical and European fruits and plants growing, not without the sort of order which one would find desirable in a country park, but also with a more than natural fertility and profusion and the vague impression of unkempt wildness that would have delighted the Rousseauesque taste of the time. See, for example, 'The Morning Prayer' and 'Eve Sees Herself in the Lake'. Enormous trees, all in full leaf, tower one above the other, dwarfing Adam and Eve into insignificance in comparison with the grandeur of nature.[9] As in Milton's poem, the unrestricted profusion of natural growth is a reflection of the untrammelled nature of pre-lapsarian sex:

> Here Love his golden shafts imploies, here lights
> His constant Lamp, and waves his purple wings,
> Reigns here and revels.
>   (*Paradise Lost*, IV)

It is an important part of Martin's concept of Eden, however, that behind the lush vegetation, the hard relentless outlines of rocks and mountains are always visible. In 'Adam and Eve See Raphael Approaching' (155) the human pair stand on a firm plateau and look down into a thickly wooded valley. Beyond the far side of the valley outcrops of rock and cliff can be seen among the trees as the land rises to rocky mountain summits partially concealed by cloud. This is Paradise but, as Martin makes evident from the start, the benign and pleasant face of Paradise could quickly change and, outside Eden, in the distance, there is a world of barren mountains. K. Svendsen has pointed out that: 'In nearly every landscape a deep center or recession makes Adam and Eve seem perilously near the edge of a pit or of slopes falling away from them.'[10] This is especially noticeable in scenes like 'Adam Tempted' or 'Adam Repelling Eve' in which it really does seem as though Adam and Eve are on the edge of the abyss literally as well as figuratively speaking.

Martin is the only artist to portray Adam and Eve fully in the context within which Milton presents them in *Paradise Lost*. He does not attempt to indicate the dramatic or spiritual conflict by facial expression, in the way that Fuseli, Blake and others do. Satan, as in *Paradise Lost*, would really have to search for Adam and Eve in Martin's Eden, and the success of Satan in avoiding the angelic guard for the first time becomes a reality. Svendsen considers that Martin's failure to indicate the expressions of Adam and Eve renders his temptation scenes invalid, for 'these episodes by their very nature require[d] the human gesture in crisis'.[11] However, Martin had subtle means that were more in accordance with

156 J. Martin, 'Adam and Eve Entertain Raphael'

his style to denote the tensions of these situations. Compare, for example, the gentle, even quality of light in 'Eve Sees Herself in the Pool' and 'Adam and Eve Entertain Raphael' (156)—both happy scenes in Paradise—with the livid flush which lightens the distant

157 J. Martin, 'Eve Tempted'

158 J. Martin, 'Adam Repelling Eve'

hills in 'Eve Tempted' (157), the dark clouds through which a strange glow breaks in 'Adam Repelling Eve' (158), the eerie glimmer in 'Adam and Eve Mourning the Loss of Paradise' and, above all, the extraordinary lighting effects in 'The Expulsion'

159 J. Martin, 'The Expulsion'

160 J. Martin, 'Eve Sees her Reflection'

(159). In this last illustration Martin, by means of the enormous granite cliffs, the prehistoric creature silhouetted on the plain and the great glow illuminating the sky above the lightning, manages to achieve an unprecedented combination of terror and hope.

161 J. Martin, 'Adam and Eve Mourn the Loss of Paradise'

162 J. Martin, 'Sin and Death Build a Path from Hell'

Terror lies in the gloomy cliffs, beast and storm, hope lies in the
winding river and the glorious sky.

In addition to the varied use of lighting, Martin contrasts the
earlier, peaceful scenes of Eden with the later scenes by his treatment of tree forms and the general lay-out of the landscape. See,
for example, the classically tranquil 'Eve Sees her Reflection' (160)
and 'Adam and Eve Entertain Raphael' (156), built up of receding
horizontals stabilized by a heavy mass at the left and a repoussoir
tree at the right. The trees in these two pictures are gently rounded
and the bower of Adam and Eve, though a cave, looks pleasant and
inviting. In 'Eve Tempted' the figure of Eve is overshadowed completely by the tree of Knowledge of Good and Evil. She stands
under its shade, looking up at the serpent wound round a lower
bough. This tree is not smooth and rounded but rough-textured,
gnarled and every branch seems like another reptile coil. In 'Adam
Repelling Eve' (158) a similarly gnarled tree with sadly drooping
branches stands to the left of the figures. 'Adam and Eve Mourn
the Loss of Paradise' in a glade where they are quite shadowed
from the light by a great canopy of leaves. It looks a dank, dark
place (161).

Martin is one of the few artists who is able to portray Milton's
Hell as successfully as his Paradise. His fault perhaps lies in the fact
that he envisages Hell so convincingly that its chief occupant is

forgotten. Macaulay says that: 'Mr. Martin has succeeded perfectly in representing the pillars and candelabra of Pandemonium. But he has forgotten that Milton's Pandemonium is merely the background to Satan.'[12] But on the other hand, Martin is the only illustrator of *Paradise Lost* to convey a sense of the vastness of the universe (including Hell) and the infinite power of God, even over Satan.

Let us consider Martin's illustration to Book X of *Paradise Lost* showing Sin and Death building their bridge from Hell to Earth after the fall (162). Fuseli and Westall both illustrated this scene, but they concentrated on the figures of Sin and Death and avoided having to give any clear indication of what such an intangible object as a bridge through Chaos might look like. Fuseli's drawing in Auckland City Art Gallery, New Zealand, is a beautifully executed, vigorous work in which Satan hovers, God-like between the dark clouds of Hell and the brightness of the Earth, directing operations on the single archway over which Sin and Death appear to be creeping. Milton devotes fifty-three lines to his description of the actual building of the bridge. By constantly mentioning 'polar winds', 'Mountains of Ice' and many exotic-sounding cities and lands, Milton creates an impression of the immensity of the task which Sin and Death have undertaken. Their job is not easy and they, like Satan on his journey to the Earth, are prey to the powers of the Universe:

> Then Both from out Hell Gates into the waste
> Wide Anarchie of *Chaos* damp and dark
> Flew divers, and with power (thir power was great)
> Hovering upon the Waters; what they met
> Solid or slimie, as in raging Sea
> Tost up and down, together crowded drove
> From each side shoaling towards the mouth of Hell.
> As when two Polar Winds blowing adverse
> Upon the *Cronian* Sea, together drive
> Mountains of Ice, that stop th'imagin'd way
> Beyond *Petsora* Eastward, to the rich
> *Cathanian* Coast.
>
> (*Paradise Lost*, X)

In Martin's illustration, Sin and Death appear as tiny, hardly discernible figures perched high on the bridge, the base of which is somewhere far below lost in obscurity. Sin and Death built, we are told: 'Over the foaming Deep high Archt, a Bridge'. Over it from 'this now fenceless World' was made: 'a passage broad, / Smooth, easie, inoffensive down to Hell'. Only Martin with terrifying conviction really shows this bridge which is to make Hell so near to

163 J. Martin, 'Satan Enthroned'

Earth. The arches seem hewn from solid rock and resemble the
new railway viaducts of his time. The impression of a bottomless
pit opening up below the bridge is created by a vagueness and
mistiness in the lower area of the supporting arches. The exaggerated perspective and the fact that Martin, embroidering on Milton's
text, shows the bridge as being built through a tunnel also contribute to this effect. F. Klingender suggests that Martin, in depicting
this tunnel, was remembering Brunel's scheme for a tunnel under
the Thames. Brunel's company was formed in 1824, operations
started in 1825 and by the time Martin's illustrations appeared the
public were being admitted to view the first three hundred feet.
Klingender also points out the association between the tunnels and
caves which feature in Martin's scenes of Hell and contemporary
descriptions and prints of coal-mines and of places like the underground sections of the Caledonian Canal (described by Southey).[13]
Martin's prose works and pamphlets indicate that he, like so many
artists and writers of his time, was well aware of the fascinations
and the horror of industrial innovations. In his illustration of
'Satan Enthroned' (*Paradise Lost*, II) (163), Martin depicts the hall
of Pandemonium (it has been suggested) on the lines of the Albert
Hall:

164 After J. M. W. Turner, 'The Fall of the
Rebel Angels'

165 After J. M. W. Turner, 'The Temptation
on the Mountain'

The wheel-shaped flares by which it is lit illustrate the gas-fittings then recently introduced, while the throne on which Satan presumably rises from the ground and sinks back again at will anticipates the mobile consoles of modern cinema organs.[14]

In 1835 J. M. W. Turner provided seven vignette illustrations to Sir Egerton Brydges's edition of *The Poetical Works of John Milton.* Like Martin, Turner was not a skilful painter of figures and in all these illustrations the awkwardness of the figures detracts from the total effect. Although most of Turner's plates are inferior to Martin's a close relationship exists between the two sets of illustrations. W. G. Rawlinson believes that in the poetry of *Paradise Lost*: 'Turner's imagination had full scope, and his "Mustering of the Warrior Angels" and "The Fall of the Rebel Angels" are magnificent in conception.'[15] However, what Rawlinson does not point out is that the 'magnificent conception' of 'The Fall of the Rebel Angels' (164) is reduced to a vignette, approximately 8 × 11 cm. Into this space are crammed all the cosmic effects and myriads of figures demanded by Milton's description. In the vignette to *Paradise Regained* Turner succumbs to a sickly and conventional religious sentiment. 'The Temptation on the Mountain' (165) and 'The

Temptation on the Pinnacle' (166), like 'The Expulsion' (167), are not treated as dramatic episodes in Milton's narrative but as sorts of generalized, iconic glorifications of the subjects found in the Bible, rather than in Milton. According to Rawlinson, the drawings for this series are very 'unnatural and exaggerated in colour'.[16] At least in engraved form we are spared this.

We know that Turner, from 1798, was exhibiting landscapes to which he attached descriptive passages from Milton's poetry (see p. xxxi), and Martin would certainly have known these. They are more to Turner's credit than the series of vignettes, with which they bear little relation. The tendency to dissolve solid forms and the establishment of the vortex pattern is most evident in Turner's work after 1825, the date when Martin would have been working on his *Paradise Lost* series. But the Claudian landscape pattern that we have already mentioned in connection with Martin's 'Eve Sees

166 After J. M. W. Turner, 'The Temptation on the Pinnacle'

167 After J. M. W. Turner, 'The Expulsion'

her Reflection' (160), Martin could have already observed applied most effectively in such works by Turner as 'Crossing the Brook' (1815).

In 'Snowstorm: Hannibal Crossing the Alps' (1812) (168) and in several drawings of this period showing alpine scenes and avalanches, Turner has already introduced an element of the whirling, vortex form which he carried to an extensive degree of abstraction in his later work. Martin could have seen 'Hannibal', which in its violence, tumult and exploitation of atmospheric effects must surely have appealed to him. Martin must have liked Turner's work; an edition of *The Poetical Works of Milton* with Turner's illustrations belonged to Martin and was sold, along with other possessions from Lindsey House, in 1854.[17]

The use that Martin makes of rocks and boulders in 'Satan Hurled from the Sky', 'The Fallen Angels in Pandemonium' (Tate Gallery) (169) and 'The Fiery Gulf' (170) is very reminiscent of Turner's 'Hannibal'. The whipping of the waves into almost vertically directed spray in 'The Fiery Gulf' is a device that Turner had already used in his early sea-pieces, although he made greater use of it later, for example in 'Staffa, Fingal's Cave' (1831). The same device is seen in 'Satan Summoning his Legions' (171), where

168 J. M. W. Turner, 'Snowstorm: Hannibal Crossing the Alps'

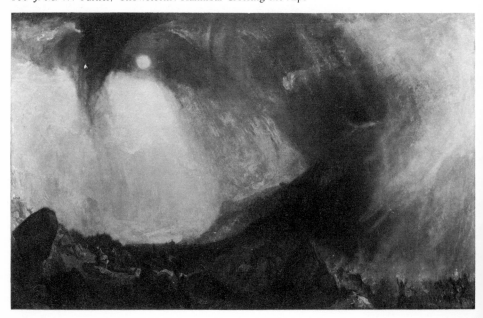

169 J. Martin, 'The Fallen Angels in Pandemonium'

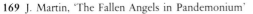

Martin also makes use of Turner's vortex pattern although, unlike Turner, he concentrates light at the edges rather than at the centre. 'The Fourth Day of the Creation' (172) with its central splash of light is even more Turnerian.

There must have been a lot that was compatible in the temperament and artistic inclinations of Turner and Martin. In the case of the Milton illustrations Turner designed and published his plates some ten years after Martin and one cannot, therefore, be sure that Martin did not have some influence on Turner. Both artists delighted in the use of dramatic lighting effects and both, from the early stages of their careers onwards, delighted in subjects concerned with the fall of Empires and with events of cosmic destruction: 'The Fall of Carthage', 'The Deluge', 'Sodom and Gomorrah' and so on. Certainly such subjects had a peculiar fascination for this

170 J. Martin, 'The Fiery Gulf'

age in which they were associated with ideas of revolution and radicalism. Volney's *Les Ruines, ou Méditations sur les Révolutions des Empires* (1791) was one of the most popular works of the day. But Martin and Turner showed a more than usual obsession with such subjects.

In making any comparison between Martin and Turner one must eventually come up against the question of naturalism. At first sight one would say that Martin's landscapes were pure fantasy, and that Turner differs from him in being a naturalistic painter. However, Turner's contemporaries did not consider that he realistically portrayed the natural scene, and he seldom or never painted from nature. Moreover, although Martin's landscapes are generally entirely imaginary, in his *Paradise Lost* illustrations he depicts an extraordinary variety of closely observed trees. His studies for *The Characters of Trees* (1817) must have supplied him with a good training in the depiction of natural plant and tree forms.

It seems clear that Martin was to some extent influenced by Turner in his *Paradise Lost* illustrations. What evidence, if any, is there that might indicate that Turner—in illustrating Milton ten years after Martin—turned for ideas to Martin's plates to *Paradise Lost*? The myriads of tiny figures in Turner's 'Fall of the Rebel Angels' (164) could derive from any of Martin's works which teem with tiny figures. However, a particular similarity is discernible between Turner's 'Temptation on the Mountain' (165) from *Paradise Regained* and Martin's series of Eden before the Fall. Notice how in 'The Morning Hymn' (173) or 'Adam and Eve Entertain Raphael' (156) Martin defines his composition by the basin-like formation created by the use of dark masses of rock and trees to the right- and left-hand sides of the picture, the central pool of light, the placing of the group of tiny figures in the foreground to one side, and the great expanse of plains and mountains spreading out from the high viewpoint of the foreground. This pattern is closely observed by Turner in 'The Temptation on the Mountain' (165), with some slight exaggeration in order to accommodate it within the vignette form.

The cult of ruins, which has already been mentioned in connection with Turner, Martin and Volney, was to some extent the nineteenth-century inheritance from Piranesi. It is seen in such works as Turner's 'The Destruction of Sodom' (1802) and in the fantasy

171 J. Martin, 'Satan Summons his Legions'

172 J. Martin, 'The Fourth Day of Creation'

architecture which Martin creates as a part of Milton's Hell, in which the contemporary taste for the oriental is also seen. Martin was certainly familiar with the Brighton Pavilion, and in 1818 he did a series of drawings of the Indian-styled Sezincote House. We know that De Loutherbourg's Eidophusikon included as one of its

173 J. Martin, 'The Morning Hymn'

scenes 'The Palace of Pandemonium' (p. 105), but apart from this
there is little precedent for Martin's large-scale treatment of this
architectural, Miltonic theme. However, between Piranesi and
Martin there is one essential link; an eighteenth-century architect
named J. M. Gandy. Gandy's architectural fantasies are more classical than Martin's, but he must nevertheless be considered a precursor of Martin.

Gandy was an assistant of Sir John Soane (who also enjoyed
architectural fantasies) and tutor to his son. Periods of his life were
spent in great poverty and he was clearly a man of a somewhat
introspective character.[18] Gandy was younger than Martin and
some of his work was exhibited after Martin's *Paradise Lost* series.
'The Hall of Pandemonium', for example, was exhibited in 1831
and 'The Gates of Heaven' in 1832.[19] However, Gandy's first
known Miltonic architectural fantasy, 'Pandemonium: or Part of
the High Capital of Satan and his Peers' (175), was exhibited as
early as 1805, twenty years before Martin's *Paradise Lost* illustrations, and a long time before his canvas, 'Pandemonium' (1841.
Collection of Mr. Hugo Huntington-Whitely) (175). It would
seem that such architectural-literary pictures were popular during
the early years of the nineteenth century. Subjects like 'The Hall
of Hela, the Regions of Eternal Punishment (Vide the Scandinavian
Mythology)' exhibited by John Papworth in 1807 recur fairly frequently in the Academy catalogues at this time.

Milton describes the Palace of Pandemonium in detail at the end
of *Paradise Lost*, Book I:

Anon out of the earth a Fabrick huge
Rose like an Exhalation, with the sound
Of Dulcet Symphonies and voices sweet,
Built like a Temple, where *Pilasters* round
Were set, and Doric pillars overlaid
With Gold'n Architrave; nor did there want
Cornice or Freeze, with bossy Sculptures grav'n,
The Roof was fretted Gold.

Milton then goes on to say that it was better than 'Babilon' or
'Alcairo' which might reasonably be assumed to be the source of
Martin's design. Gandy follows Milton's description almost word
for word. Both the pilasters and the Doric pillars can easily be discerned and the 'bossy sculpture' comprising devils' heads, balus-
trades of twining serpents, skulls and sphinxes must surely exceed
in Hellish imagination anything that Milton might have envisaged.
Gandy's 'Pandemonium' (ink and wash, Soane Museum) is badly

rubbed. It would seem, though, that the artist envisaged the high capital of Satan as a hall full of all kinds of astonishing pieces of sculpture, most of which refer in some way to *Paradise Lost*. There are Adam and Eve by the tree, and Satan, Sin and Death. But there is also a collection of symbolic items such as an enormous lobster on a pedestal at the turn of the stairs on the left, a toad and a pair of compasses in the foreground. The hall descends in stages in a way which is reminiscent of some of Piranesi's 'Carceri' scenes (1745). An Eastern atmosphere which would have delighted Martin is created by the presence of sphinxes and idols. The toad is present in Gandy's picture as it was this poisonous creature's form which Satan adopted when whispering into the ear of Eve in *Paradise Lost*, Book IV. The compasses belong to Mulciber, the architect of Pandemonium. Metz, nine years later, gives *Discord* a lobster head and it is just possible that he knew Gandy's drawing, although a mannerist artist like Metz might well find a source for this predatory sea-creature in some still-life scene. The most likely explanation for the presence of the lobster in Gandy's drawing is that the artist was familiar with the tradition by which soldiers, and especially soldiers taking part in the great rebellion of 1643, were des-

174 J. M. Gandy, 'Pandemonium'

cribed as lobsters (as in Clarendon's *History of the Rebellion*, ch. III).
Milton was very much involved with the Civil War, and the first
draft of *Paradise Lost* dates from 1642. As Pandemonium was
erected by the rebel angels after a fierce battle and the subsequent
fall from Heaven, it is quite appropriate—if somewhat fanciful—
for Gandy to endow Satan's high capital with a statue of a lobster
as a sort of collective ensign.

Gandy gives us no idea of the external appearance of Pandemonium, the aspect to which Martin gives his attention (only his
illustration of Satan on his throne has little architectural detail).
Martin created in 'The Choir of Heaven' (*Paradise Lost*, III) a complex of buildings very like those of Pandemonium. But since, as
Milton tells us, Mulciber, the architect of Heaven, fell with the other
rebel angels this is perhaps not surprising. Martin's 'Pandemonium',
which also features in 'The Fallen Angels' (Tate Gallery) (159),
can best be studied in detail in the canvas version of 1841 (175).
Despite the obvious differences, Martin probably knew Gandy's
drawing. Gandy's serpentine balustrade and Death's-head frieze
are a noticeable feature of Martin's 'Pandemonium'. Gandy's sculp-
tured serpent also appears in a more elaborate form as a lampholder.

175 J. Martin, 'Pandemonium'

The frame for this picture, which was probably done according to Martin's design, has decorative monsters of the Gandy type in relief at the corners, and the centres of the long sides.[20]

Martin's Pandemonium is erected on a series of arches hewn out of natural rock similar to those of which the bridge between Hell and Earth is built (167) and similar, also, to those in 'The Fiery Gulf' (170). In all these, and particularly in 'Pandemonium' (175), the edges of the arches have an eroded effect like a seaside cave. It has been suggested that Martin had seen and probably, like Fuseli, made studies of the marine grottoes at Margate and may have based his caves on these.[21] It is certainly clear from Martin's scenes of Hell that he had a particular feeling for caves and underground tunnels. It is interesting that Gandy—whose diary shows him not to have been a very balanced character, though he never developed the serious mental disorders of Martin's family—also shows this predilection for caves and underground places. Sir J. Summerson tells us that 'Gandy had a peculiar interest in caves—in his travel diary he notes particularly the caves of Gibraltar and the Roman catacombs'. In the same diary Gandy recounts his dream of a visit he was compelled to make into Hell in the company of Satan, and Sir J. Summerson believes that 'in the dream the subterranean setting is clearly a symbol of his hampered difficult position in life'.[22]

Gandy and Papworth were architects. Martin occupied himself with aspects of town planning. It is evident that the distinctions during this period between actual architecture and architectural fantasy are tenuous. The qualities demanded of the painter of architectural fantasy are certainly different from those demanded of the architect and many of the designs intended for actual building in this period would have been grotesque had they ever materialized. In 1820 Martin made suggestions for a huge, triumphal arch over Marylebone Road.[23] In France the designs of Boullée, Ledoux and of those published by Vaudoyer in 1806 are close to Martin's and Gandy's architectural fantasies. Even well-established architects tried their hands at this sort of thing. Sir John Soane, architect of the Bank of England, exhibited at the Royal Academy in 1820 'Architectural Visions of Early Fancy in the Gay Morning of Youth; and Dreams in the Evening of Life' and, in 1832, 'Architectural Ruins, a Vision'.

J. Seznec has shown the extraordinary influence which Martin's art had on all ranks of writers in nineteenth-century France.[24] Martin exhibited at the Paris salon in 1834, but his work would be more widely known from engravings, among which would doubtless be the *Paradise Lost* series. Prowett, the publisher, was most probably an American and, according to Martin's son Leopold, the sale of Martin's engravings was even greater in the United States, China and Japan than it was in Britain.[25] Martin's architectural fantasies clearly made a big impact with Frenchmen and Englishmen. It is interesting that the incredible edifices of 'Pandemonium' and 'Balshazzar's Feast' alike, with all their Eastern appurtenances, should have been associated in the minds of viewers with real architecture. J. Seznec tells us that:

A Londres, le 9 août, allant à l'Ambassade de France rendre visite à Talleyrand, il [Michelet] est frappé par la colonnade massive du Quadrant, au bas de Regent Street: il y reconnait 'un monument babylonien à la Martin' . . . Charles Lamb écrivait ironiquement à Barton, le 5 décembre 1828: 'Martin should have been made royal architect. What palaces he would pile . . .'[26]

·Perhaps for the sake of posterity it is as well that Martin's architectural imagination was limited to dealing with the immense proportions of the palaces and temples of the Old Testament and of the architecture of Milton's Hell.

(ii) Milton and English Academic Classicism

Whilst the *Paradise Lost* illustrations of John Martin took up and developed the more romantic aspects of the work of the late eighteenth-century artists of the sublime, the majority of English painters between 1800 and 1860 adopted and conventionalized the more classical side of Barry's and Fuseli's work. The muscular distortions and elongations of Fuseli's figures are softened by the fashionable taste for the gently relaxed grace that characterizes Reynolds's female portraits, and by the attempt to attain a degree of the sort of sentiment and sweetness exemplified in Stothard's work.

William Hamilton (who died in 1801) was a contemporary of Fuseli and, like Westall and Stothard, he inherited from Fuseli a certain delight in elongated, mannerist poses. His work therefore makes him, in a sense, one of Fuseli's 'school', the group of artists including Romney and Westall who adopted features of his style. However, Hamilton, by reason of his complete rejection of the element of force and the violence of gesture and expression which are the hallmark of Westall's and Romney's Milton illustrations, really belongs to the nineteenth-century academic classicists.

Hamilton had the benefit of an artistic training in Rome. A number of his illustrations for Du Rouveray's *Paradise Lost* (he shared the commission with Fuseli) betray a very strict adherence to classical models. 'Eve Tempted' (176), for example, with her abundant tresses, standing with her weight on the right foot, the left foot slightly behind, one hand raised, the other maintaining balance, her face (with eyes looking upward) seen from the three-quarters view, might be a copy from some classically tranquil Roman Venus. Remove the serpent and who would guess that Eve was undergoing the most dire temptation?

In deference to the requirements of the grand style Hamilton's figures are always of supreme importance in his illustrations. In 'Adam and Eve Conversing with Raphael', Hamilton's figure of Adam is almost identical to Stothard's Adam in his treatment of the same subject (1792). This does not necessarily mean that Hamilton used Stothard's design. In view of the inevitable degree of cliché resulting from a system in which all art students spent long periods drawing antique sculpture in the Royal Academy, and similar periods in the life class, it is much more likely that this fairly conventional pose was one which both had studied and adapted to their own use.

A pen, ink and wash drawing of 'The Expulsion' in the Witt

176 After W. Hamilton, 'Eve Tempted'

177 After W. Hamilton, 'Adam and Eve See Michael'

Collection (178) is attributed to Fuseli.[27] This drawing, which
lacks the finesse one would expect from Fuseli, shows Adam and
Eve in the foreground, turning to look up at an angel appearing in
the sky. This is quite different from Fuseli's 'Expulsion' as engraved
by Moses Haughton for the 1802 Du Rouveray *Paradise Lost* (179),
which shows Eve, sorrowing, supported by Adam. However, R.
Rhodes's engraving after William Hamilton's 'Adam and Eve See
Michael Coming' (178) in the same edition is clearly related to the
Witt drawing. In fact the engraver probably used the drawing as
his model (it is certainly by Hamilton not Fuseli), for the two are
the same even to the last detail of the fleeing stag and lion.

A number of new illustrated editions of *Paradise Lost* appeared
around 1805. John Thurston, an artist born in Scarborough in
1774,[28] and Henry Howard, a most prolific Milton illustrator, provided the plates for *The Poetical Works of Milton* in *Aikin's English
Poets* (1805). (Thurston, whose work can only be described as
mediocre, did a further set of plates for an edition of *Paradise Lost*
published by Suttaby, Crosby and Corrall in 1806 and in 1824 exhibited a picture entitled 'Euphrosyne' ('L'Allegro') at the Royal

178 W. Hamilton, 'Adam and Eve See   **179** After J. H. Fuseli, 'The Expulsion'
Michael'

Academy.) Henry Corbould, third son of R. Corbould and a friend of Flaxman and Stothard,[29] followed the example of his father and his friends, all illustrators of Milton's verse. He provided one new illustration to the old 1799 set of Burney illustrations in an edition of *Paradise Lost* published by Mawman in 1817. Henry Corbould's main interest seems to have lain outside book illustration, however, for between 1804 and 1808 he exhibited three *Paradise Lost* scenes at the Royal Academy—all from the first two books of the poem—and a further painting of 'Satan, Sin and Death' in 1834. Two more very minor artists exhibiting subjects of the sublime, melodramatic type during this period, were J. Mowson, an artist who seems to have had a preference for scenes from Spenser, Southey and Gray, and T. M. Simpson who exhibited such subjects as 'Richard I at the Point of Death'. Mowson exhibited 'Satan at the Throne of Chaos' in 1808 and Simpson 'Fallen Angels' in 1809, both at the Royal Academy. No trace can be found of any of these works.

In 1804 M. Craig, another very minor talent, provided illustrations for the Albion Press edition of *Paradise Lost* and in 1812 William Craig—a miniaturist from Manchester[30]—illustrated an edition published by Nuttall. B. J. and R. Johnson's edition of 1808 has one engraving by Tiebout, and Tegg's 1813 edition has a frontispiece engraved by Springsguth. Two members of the Old Water Colour Society[31] exhibited Milton subjects during these early years of the century. John Taylor exhibited a subject from *L'Allegro* in 1813 and S. F. Rigaud in 1801 exhibited a selection of at least six scenes from Milton and a further Milton picture in 1850. There are four drawings by Rigaud from Milton's *Minor Poems* on one mount in the British Museum. These may be the same as one of Rigaud's Academy exhibits. They are in a rather delicate vein of sentiment similar to that seen in Smirke's work. A series of sixteen drawings from *Paradise Lost* and *Paradise Regained* by Rigaud is in the collection of Mr. W. Brandt.

Henry Howard was one of the most prolific Milton illustrators of the period. Born in London in 1769, he had a distinguished early career, winning two medals as a Royal Academy student. His choice of subject from Milton was always such as would suit his delicately linear, classical style. He delighted in subjects like 'The Gardens of Hesperus' (from the end of *Comus*), 'Proserpina' (*Paradise Lost*, IV), 'Circe', 'Sabrina' and many episodes from mythology mentioned in Milton's poetry. Between 1795 and 1846 he exhibited at least twenty-four such subjects at the Royal Academy or the British Institution. His predilection for the soft, fluid, linear quality that could be exploited in the depiction of nymphs and goddesses reveals his dependence on the art of Flaxman. There is a certain degree of abstraction in Howard's art—a rejection of solidity and of any really material background—which is also found in Flaxman's work. This quality, derived originally from Greek vase painting, was admirably exploited by Flaxman for the illustration of the works of classical authors and adapted to ceramic design for Wedgwood's factory. In the case of Howard, this abstract, decorative quality (which he undoubtedly derived from Flaxman)[32] was channelled in a different direction. Howard's designs were in demand for use as decorative ceiling paintings in private houses.

One of Howard's most popular subjects was 'The Planets Drawing Light from the Sun' (*Paradise Lost*, VII), first exhibited in 1796. The same subject was exhibited in 1823 under the title 'The Solar System'. A further duplicate of this picture was painted for a Mr. Morrison and, finally, the composition was adapted to a circle and, at least until the end of the century, adorned the ceiling of the Duchess of Sutherland's boudoir in Stafford House.[33] The Duke of Sutherland must have been one of Howard's best patrons, for he bought 'The Rising of the Pleiades', exhibited in 1839. 'A duplicate of this picture long formed the chief ornament of the Leicester

180 After H. Howard, 'The Rising of the Pleiades'

Gallery'[34] (180). 'The Circling Hours' (*Paradise Lost*, VII), exhibited in 1835, was designed along with 'Pandora' and 'Night
with the Pleiades' for compartments in a ceiling in Sir John Soane's
Museum.[35]

One of the most controversial pictures of the 1820s was Benjamin West's 'Death on a Pale Horse', exhibited in 1817 and representing the opening of the first five seals in Revelations, ch. VI.
West did once venture into Miltonic regions when he painted 'Milton's Messiah from the Sixth Book of *Paradise Lost*' (exhibited in
1809), but he was not in any real sense an illustrator of Milton.
However it was inevitable, in view of the current popularity of
Milton's poetry, that West's 'Death' should be compared to Milton's description of Death in *Paradise Lost*, Book II, a most popular
subject with artists. Fuseli had some fairly harsh words to say about
this picture[36] and poor West was sharply reproached by Hazlitt for
having issued an explanatory pamphlet with the picture.[37] It seems
to have been generally agreed that West made a great mistake in
choosing his subject from Revelations rather than from *Paradise
Lost*. Hazlitt describes West's text accompanying the picture as
'part of a system of self-adulation, which cannot be too much dis-
couraged'.

181 W. Hilton, 'The Creation of Eve'   **182** W. Hilton, 'The Expulsion'

Hazlitt is, no doubt, right to question the increasingly popular habit of providing long explanatory notes for literary paintings. But he writes in a tone which rather implies that West has committed some sort of sacrilege against the memory of Milton by daring to mention his 'visionary Death'.

. . . Mr. West or his commentator should tread cautiously on this ground. He may otherwise commit himself, not only in a comparison with the epic poet, but with the inspired writer, who only uses words. It will hardly be contended, for instance, that the account of Death on the Pale Horse, in the book of Revelations, never produced its due effect of the terrible sublime, till the deficiencies of the pen were supplied by the pencil. Neither do we see how the endowing of a physical form with superhuman strength has any necessary connection with the moral impression of the visionary Death of Milton . . .[38]

One much neglected artist of the early nineteenth century is William Hilton. Bryan's assurance that 'he will stand as a bright star among English historical and poetical painters'[39] has been, sadly, far from realized. Hilton was a friend, and a relation by marriage, of Peter de Wint, the Lincolnshire landscape painter. T. S. R. Boase says of Hilton:

His was a careful, pondered achievement, a reaction against the violence of the mannerist school, and it is sad that much of it, such as his masterpiece, 'Edith finding the Body of Harold', should be such sorry wrecks of corrugated asphaltum. He died in 1839, disappointed by lack of patronage, broken by the death of his wife, Peter de Wint's sister.[40]

In 1823 Hilton exhibited 'Comus with the Lady in the Enchanted Chair' at the Royal Academy. No other Milton pictures are on record, and he did not illustrate any editions of Milton. However, a large folder of unmounted, uncatalogued drawings in the British Museum contains a number of studies for subjects from *Paradise Lost*, as well as a series of drawings of nymphs and naiads, which could have been intended for *Comus*.[41] There are also some drawings of fantastic, rocky landscapes. The existence of the latter, and the figure style in some of the drawings for *Paradise Lost*, indicate that Hilton's 'reaction against the violence of the mannerist school'[42] was not very deep-rooted. Certainly drawings like, for example, 'The Creation of Eve' (181) and 'The Expulsion' (182) exhibit a static quality of monumental tranquillity which is quite alien to mannerist art and which probably derives from the life class of the Royal Academy. But if we examine other drawings, particularly two studies of 'Adam, Eve and Raphael' (one showing the

183 W. Hilton, 'Adam and Eve Converse with Raphael'

three in conversation, the other showing Raphael departing after the meal) (183 and 184), Hilton's indebtedness to Fuseli becomes immediately evident. The elongation of Eve's body and of that of Raphael, the strong, linear outlining of muscles and the stylized curves of the first of these two compositions place Hilton in the tradition of Fuseli (179). In the second drawing the attempt to create from the separate bodies of Adam and Eve one fused, yet dynamic mass in the composition, and the taut vigour with which Raphael leaps from the ground, are both reminiscent of the anglicized mannerism of Fuseli.

Between about 1820 and 1850 two English artists of talent and distinction were using subjects from Milton's poetry in the painting of large-scale, highly finished canvases. These two artists were B. R. Haydon and William Etty. In the case of the former many of his large canvases—including all his Milton subjects—have unfortunately been lost. The only way to deal with this problem in such a survey as this is to reconstruct, as far as possible, from documen-

tary sources, the history and the nature of the artist's corpus of
Milton work.[43]

Haydon's love of Milton's poetry dates from his youth and is
recorded in his journals.[44] We hear how in 1806 Haydon spent the
summer falling 'furiously in love' and riding about the neighbour-
hood, reading 'Milton and Tasso and Shakespeare' in grassy nooks
by the rippling sea'. His first attempt at putting Milton on canvas
seems to have taken place some considerable time after this. On
December 10th, 1823, he writes that he has 'sketched Satan alight-
ing', but this subject does not seem to have progressed any further.
His first exhibited Milton picture was 'Milton and his Daughters',
begun on January 6th, 1835, and shown at the Society of British
Artists in 1840. At about the same time he was working on 'Milton

184 W. Hilton, 'Adam, Eve and Raphael'

at his Organ' and 'Eloisa and Abelard at their Studies'. The latter was probably intended as a partner to 'Milton and his Daughters'. In the same year, 1840, he exhibited 'Samson and the Philistines' at the Society of British Artists, which, like 'Samson and Delilah' on which he was working between 1829 and 1836, may have had either a biblical or a Miltonic source.

'Adam and Eve' was first shown at an Exhibition of Cartoons in Westminster Hall in June 1843. There appear to have been two versions of this, one on which Haydon was working between June 24th and October 4th, 1833, and the exhibited version begun about July 18th, 1842. In view of the fact that Milton was the most common source during the period for subjects concerning Adam and Eve (*Samson Agonistes* being less popular than *Paradise Lost*, there remains some doubt about Haydon's Samson pictures), it seems fairly safe to assume that these pictures were based on *Paradise Lost*. Haydon's habit of meticulously preparing for each work can be seen in a statement he makes on September 19th, 1842, about a study which must have been for 'Adam and Eve': 'At the musaeum [sic] in the morning, I studied reptiles in Cuvier & Russell. Sketched several, & came home & put in my own snake. I find tracing the spine is the secret of drawing snakes.'

Haydon's real success with a subject from Milton came in 1845 when he exhibited 'Uriel and Satan' at the Royal Academy. He had already done a small version of this to which he refers on November 29th, 1829, and after completing the Royal Academy picture he began, on April 9th, 1845, a further 'Satan and Uriel' from a new viewpoint. There are many interesting references to this picture in Haydon's diary. It was his habitual practice to continually alter and repaint sections of a picture. On May 29th, 1844, he copied an angel from Raphael's Bible as a model for Uriel, 'but it was too gentle for an Arch-angel, not sublime enough, tender but not solemn'. On September 10th he writes that his 'Uriel is making a sensation already', and that he thinks the head of Uriel is 'the finest thing I ever did, except the head of Lazarus'. Haydon must have used his muscular model from the Life Guards, for on March 25th, 1845, in connection with the picture he refers to 'my heroic model, Brunskill of the Blues'. But in view of descriptions in contemporary reviews, the soldier probably sat for the figure of Uriel rather than for that of Satan. We discover from an entry dated April 26th, 1846, that Haydon found a purchaser for 'Uriel and Satan' in his friend Dennys, who had a gallery built to house the picture. He paid two hundred and ten pounds for 'Uriel and Satan'.

An entry in Haydon's diary for April 8th, 1845, indicates that the artist was very unhappy about hanging 'Uriel and Satan' in the Academy exhibition. He says that he agreed because his employer (presumably Dennys) insisted, but that he considered it 'an insult to them and a disgrace to me'. *The Times* review of the picture on May 10th, 1845, makes clear the reasons for Haydon's feelings of dissatisfaction.[45] There was always great competition for the best places in the Summer Exhibition and Haydon's picture seems to have been relegated to an ante-room. *The Times* critic describes the picture in some detail, which, since we no longer have the work, is worth quoting fully:

There is one picture which makes us depart from our design of adhering to the great room exclusively on this occasion, that is Haydon's large painting of 'Uriel and Satan' (605) which must arrest even those who are hastening to depart from the Exhibition as a most remarkable work. A striking contrast to the gaudy colouring on which the eye has been feasted, it appears with subdued tone, reminding one of a fresco. The figure of the angel is drawn with a boldness which some might call exaggerated, but with the simplicity and anatomical effect of sculpture, every muscle looking hard and unyielding as iron. The face is noble and ideal and a fine effect is produced by the golden colour of the hair. This huge commanding figure is backed by limitless space, represented by a very dark, positive blue, and the whole conveys the impression of simple vastness. There is a certain crudity about the picture but the impress of genius is unmistakeable.

If we temper such enthusiasm by considering the lively attack against the picture written by Thackeray for *Frazer's Magazine* in June 1845, we may get a reasonably accurate idea of the qualities of 'Uriel and Satan'.[46] Thackeray first of all complains of the size and pretensions of the picture, then goes on to describe it:

A broad-shouldered swaggering, hulking archangel with these rolling eyes and distended nostrils which belong to the species of sublime caricature, stands scowling on a sphere from which the devil is just descending bound earthwards. Planets, comets, and other astronomical phenomena roll and blaze round the pair and flame in the new blue sky.

The intention of Dennys to buy the picture and build a gallery for it was evidently unknown, for Thackeray continues:

. . . It will not do for a chapel; it is too big for a house: I have it—it might hang up over a caravan at a fair, if a travelling orrery were exhibiting inside.

A great many lesser-known artists were exhibiting Milton pictures during the period 1820 to 1850 besides one or two better-known artists whose Milton pictures have since been lost. Among them were M. Dessurne, Charles Baxter, W. D. Kennedy, W. F. D'Almaine, Charles Rolt (who exhibited four between 1847 and 1850), W. P. Frith, C. Earles, C. Lucy, Sir George Patten, G. Danson, C. M. Dubuffe, J. W. Solomon, F. P. Stephanoff (who exhibited three between 1811 and 1844) and J. Wood (who exhibited four between 1825 and 1857).

The history of Etty's Milton paintings is inseparable from the history of the decorations for the garden pavilion in Buckingham Palace grounds in 1841. In November 1841 it was announced that a Royal Commission for promoting the Fine Arts in the United Kingdom was to be established. The first thing that the Commission did was to open, a year later on April 25th, a competition for the decoration of the new Houses of Parliament. Etty was appointed to act as a professional judge for the competition in which competitors were to select subjects from British history or from the works of Shakespeare, Spenser and Milton.[47] The latter was by far the most popular choice of the three poets.[48] The winner of the competition was J. C. Horsley, who had exhibited a picture of 'Milton Dictating *Samson Agonistes*' in 1859. C. W. Cope (whose very sentimental 'L'Allegro' and 'Il Penseroso' are now in the Victoria and Albert Museum, and who also exhibited 'Milton's Dream' in 1850), Daniel Maclise and E. M. Ward were among the artists entrusted with the decorations.

Before the results of the Houses of Parliament competition were announced the Prince Consort commissioned a number of artists to decorate the new summer pavilion in the grounds of Buckingham Palace. The medium chosen was fresco, in which there was a great revival of interest at the time. D. Farr tells us that Etty and Sir William Ross were the last to be asked and that Etty was reluctant to accept the commission in view of his unfamiliarity with the fresco technique.[49] Had more artists voiced the sort of doubts experienced by Etty the consequences of the revival of fresco painting in the Houses of Parliament and elsewhere might have been less disastrous. The garden pavilion was taken down in 1928, by which time the paintings were much ruined by damp.[50] Fortunately, a volume was published 'by command of her majesty' in 1846 which describes the pavilion and includes reproductions of the decorations.[51]

The external appearance of the pavilion was very odd indeed. The 1846 volume describes it as 'picturesque and fantastic'.[52] The main room was an octagon opening onto two smaller rooms, one on either side (185):

The original intention was to decorate only the centre room, and the poem selected for pictorial illustration was *Comus*, in itself like an exquisite many sided gem presenting within a small compass the most faultless proportion and the richest variety . . . *Comus* at once classical, romantic, and pastoral, with all its charming associations of grouping, sentiment, and scenery, was just the thing fitted to inspire English artists . . .[53]

The room on the left was devoted to scenes from Sir Walter Scott and that on the right to Pompeian decoration. The central room had eight lunettes and the rest of the decoration in the room was in stucco and referred either to *Comus*, like the heads of Comus between winged panthers over each door, or to the Royal family, like the cypher of Queen Victoria and Prince Albert 'encircled with

185 'The Buckingham Palace Garden Pavilion: general view of the interior'

186 W. Etty, 'The Gardens of Hesperus'

187 W. Etty, 'Sabrina and her Nymphs'

flowers' beneath each window. All the stucco work was done by
W. G. Nicholl or S. B. Stephens.
For his lunette Etty chose the lines from *Comus*:

. . . *Circe* with the Sirens three,
Amidst the flowry-kirtl'd *Naiades* . . .

Etty's design survives on a large canvas (Art Gallery of Western
Australia, Perth). There is also a panel study for the central figure
of Circe (collection of Mrs. R. Frank, London) and two pen and
ink studies for a naiad (Victoria and Albert Museum). D. Farr
describes Etty's efforts to paint the fresco:

All July was spent struggling with the fresco, at the end of which he
found it as intractable as ever. Maclise recalled how Etty would retouch
upon the dry plaster of a previous day's work with disastrous results.[54]

Etty's ·fresco failed to please and, having paid Etty forty pounds
under the terms of the contract, the Prince Consort offered the
commission to Dyce despite the fact that Etty offered to design a
completely fresh lunette. With this in mind Etty painted 'The
Hesperides' from *Comus* (Lady Lever Art Gallery, Port Sunlight)
(186),[55] a work of considerable distinction which he exhibited in
1844. Etty's central group of Graces and Hours based on the theme
of the dance of the Graces and seen against the golden tree grace-
fully fits the lunette shape. Hesperus can be seen on the left and a
sense of the timeless is established by the dawn on the left and the
moon on the right ('where day never shuts his eye'). Venus and
Adonis are seen to one side of the group and Cupid and Psyche to
the other. A subject involving such a rich accumulation of mythology and offering plenty of scope for the depiction of 'Graces, and
the rosie-bosom'd Howres' was admirably suited to Etty's talent
and he made the most of it.
    Some years before the Buckingham Palace pavilion affair Etty
had painted a large-scale canvas from *Paradise Lost*, Book XI, 'The
World before the Flood' (Southampton City Art Gallery).[56] This
shows a bacchanalian orgy in a Poussinesque vein. The central
group of dancing figures anticipates the Hesperides, but the composition is spoilt by its lack of organization. A great mass of figures
spreads across the lower half of the canvas whilst the upper half
remains devoid of any interest. Another *Paradise Lost* picture,
'Adam and Eve at their Orisons', was commissioned from Etty in
1835 by William Beckford, owner of Fonthill Abbey and author of
Vathek. Unfortunately all that remains of this picture is a sketch in
York City Art Gallery in a totally ruined condition.

About the time of the Houses of Parliament competition in November 1841, Etty painted his most successful Milton picture, 'Sabrina and her Nymphs' (Leicester City Art Gallery) (187). This was a version of a picture which Etty had exhibited at the Royal Academy in 1831, and there was also a version of 1840.[57] The picture illustrates the lines

> Sabrina fair
> Listen where thou art sitting
> Under the glassie, cool, translucent wave,
> In twisted braids of Lillies knitting
> The loose train of thy amber-dropping hair.
> (*Comus*)

Etty's whole picture has an appropriately dreamy, watery quality and one only has to compare it with other attempts to portray this difficult subject to realize Etty's success. Westall illustrated these lines in the 1816 edition of *The Poems of Milton* by drawing a section through the River Severn in order to reveal Sabrina seated on her sandy couch. In Etty's picture, Sabrina's back forms one side of the tight parallelogram of the composition, a pose that is reminiscent of Michelangelo's 'Leda' group. D. Farr suggests that Etty may have studied Rosso Fiorentino's large cartoon after Michelangelo's 'Leda' which was presented to the Academy by William Locke the younger in 1821. D. Farr also notices

> . . . a marked difference in conception between the solidly modelled figure done from the Life with its robust spontaneity, and the slim elegant creatures in the Sabrina. This inconsistency may be explained by the gradual change in Etty's use of his Life Studies.[58]

One other Milton picture, 'Delilah before the Blinded Samson' (York City Art Gallery), completes the group of works by Etty. It is a very rich, Titianesque picture in which the artist has laid great emphasis on the sumptuous quality of Delilah's clothing and on surface variety generally, using a great deal of white highlighting. It is untypical of most of Etty's work and probably dates from the 1830s when Etty painted an unlocated 'Samson' from Judges XVI.

The lunette supplied in the Buckingham Palace garden pavilion by William Dyce was in place of Etty's 'Circe'. It illustrates the return of the two brothers and the Lady to their parents' house at the end of *Comus* and, for some extraordinary reason, Dyce portrays all the figures in medieval costume (188). The lunette is designed very much as a final tableau from a stage version of the mask, but it completely lacks any scenic or background interest.

188 After W. Dyce, 'The Bridgewater Family Re-united'

A drawing for the figure of the Attendant Spirit in a private collection is more skilfully executed than the fresco appears to have been.[59]

The other seven lunettes in the pavilion were painted by Sir Charles Eastlake (who exhibited a picture based on the concluding lines of *Comus* in 1845), Edwin Landseer, C. R. Leslie, Daniel Maclise (who exhibited another scene from *Comus* in 1844), Sir William Ross, Clarkson Stanfield and Thomas Uwins. The latter was known primarily as a book-illustrator and had already provided a design of 'Samson Agonistes' for an 1806 edition of *Milton's Poetical Works* (published by Suttaby, Crosby and Corrall), as well as a title page illustrating a scene from *Paradise Lost*, Book II, for the volume of *Paradise Lost* in the 1839 English Classics series.

189 After Sir Charles Eastlake, 'Virtue Ascending'

190 After C. R. Leslie, 'Comus Tempts the Lady'

The artists contributing to the decorative scheme were allowed absolute liberty in the selection of subjects and the consequence was a high degree of repetition. It is a frequent fault of communal productions of this period (like the Etching Club edition of *Milton's Minor Poems*) that no co-ordinator was appointed and the result is repetition of subject and a confusing *mélange* of styles in design and costume. C. R. Leslie, W. Ross and Daniel Maclise all represented the Lady on the throne in Comus's palace. Admittedly they all show different stages in the narrative; Leslie shows Comus trying to persuade the Lady to drink his 'cordial julep' (190), Ross shows the brothers attacking Comus (191), and Maclise shows Sabrina freeing the Lady from the enchantment of the throne (192). However, the general effect created by all three compositions is similar. This is not surprising, since this episode of the mask was clearly the favourite not only because it is the most dramatic part of the poem but because it is logical for the artist to show the Lady seated on a raised throne and thus a compositional solution to the lunette form is readily available. Maclise's composition is over-crowded; Leslie's evokes the lascivious atmosphere of an Eastern potentate's tent. Ross's composition built up of tense diagonals and full of fierce action is perhaps the most successful of the three. Stanfield's lunette (193) contains an innocuous moonlit landscape with a river valley in which the Attendant Spirit appears in the foreground and Comus and his crew are seen dancing on the river bank. All the figures are so small that it seems doubtful whether anyone seeing it from floor level would recognize in the lunette a representation from *Comus*. Uwins shows a rather heavily drawn

191 After W. Ross, 'The Brothers Attack Comus'

192 After D. Maclise, 'Sabrina Sets the Lady Free'

193 After C. Stanfield, 'The Dell in *Comus*'

194 After T. Uwins, 'Comus Spies on the Lady'

Lady being spied on by Comus (194). Landseer's lunette (195) contains a somewhat baroque composition showing Comus and his rout of monsters. The whole thing is a reasonably successful depiction of the grotesque medley, but it is unfortunate that Landseer should have decided to fill the spandrels with the three-quarter face portraits of individual monsters. Seen in isolation these reveal Landseer's lack of imagination and resemble what one might imagine to be the appearance of ancestors of Winnie the Pooh.

In 1843 the publisher Tilt issued a new edition of *Milton's Poetical Works* packed with a vast number of illustrations, all of which are by William Harvey. There are forty-three plates in all, but they are all very conventional, biblical and almost totally without artistic merit.

195 After E. Landseer, 'Comus and his Rout'

Another artist who joined in the competition for the decoration of the Houses of Parliament was W. E. Frost. He won a prize of a hundred pounds for his cartoon. Frost was a most prolific artist, particularly in the field of Milton subjects. Between 1845 and 1877 he exhibited eleven Milton subjects. Like Henry Howard he delighted in subjects involving mythical personages from *Comus* and the *Minor Poems*. Sabrina, Panope, the Daughters of Hesperus, Andromeda and the Syrens, all from Milton's poetry, were depicted by W. E. Frost in a pleasantly gentle, classical style. Like Etty his particular talent lay in the depiction of the nude female form—hence his choice of subject—and his work doubtless owes quite a lot to the more original and polished work of Etty.

(iii) Pastoral Idylls (1848–1885)

Despite the invention during the nineteenth century of new processes of reproducing pictures the art of etching survived. Members of amateur groups like the Art Union and the Etching Club cooperated to produce lavishly illustrated editions of the classics which contributed to the general revival of book illustration in the '60s. Many imaginative publishing ventures were initiated during this period by designers and illustrators who combined enterprise and technical skill, like the brothers Dalziel.

Paradise Lost loses its supremacy in the field of illustration after the 1830s and its place is taken by the minor poems, particularly *L'Allegro* and *Il Penseroso*. These two poems have always appealed greatly to illustrators because they are written in pictorial form and approximately every seven lines provides a new tableau in which the rustic and the mythological are pleasantly mingled. This distinctive form enabled the Etching Club and the Art Union to cut the poems into fragments and distribute one piece to each member artist participating in the scheme. The result, of course, is a heterogeneous assortment of ill-matching designs. Most of them are very dull, but some, especially the straightforward landscape scenes, which do not involve so many incongruities of period and style, are relatively successful.

In 1848 *L'Allegro* and *Il Penseroso* were published with thirty illustrations designed for the Art Union of London. Among the illustrators were F. W. Hulme, F. R. Pickersgill, J. Phillip, A. Warren, W. C. Thomas, T. F. Marshall, Hablot K. Browne, W. L. Leitch and many others. The Dalziels were among the engravers.

F. R. Pickersgill was a fairly prolific illustrator of Milton. He exhibited two subjects from *Comus* at the Royal Academy in 1844

196 After F. R. Pickersgill, 'Orpheus Singing to Pluto'

197 After E. H. Wehnert, 'And Join with Thee Peace and Quiet'

198 After A. C. Selous, 'Towered Cities'

and 1849, and one subject from *Samson Agonistes* in 1859. However, his style, with its rather effete reminiscences of Flaxman and Henry Howard, is not at all suited to the varied and constantly changing natural background of *L'Allegro* and *Il Penseroso*. His illustration for the Art Union edition shows 'Orpheus Singing to Pluto' (*Il Penseroso*) (196). E. F. Wehnert's 'And join with thee Peace, and Quiet' (197), showing three large, classically draped female forms, uses a completely different figure style more reminiscent of G. F. Watts. Yet another style, this time one of detailed medieval archaism, characterizes H. C. Selous's 'Towered Cities' (*L'Allegro*) (198).

There is no doubt that the only really successful illustrations in this edition are the landscape scenes like F. W. Hulme's 'The Arched Walls of Twilight Groves' (199), which are, by and large, much better executed than the scenes including figures and which avoid a confusion of styles. Admittedly these idyllic English landscape scenes can become repetitive, but this is less the fault of the individual artist than the mistake of the editor in organizing a volume in which every few lines of the poem are illustrated.

199 After F. W. Hulme, 'The Arched Walk's of Twilight Groves'

200 After Birket Foster, 'By Hedgerow Elms'

In 1849 a very similar edition was published by J. Cundall and illustrated by the Etching Club. Most of the designs were done by J. C. Horsley, Thomas Creswick, H. J. Townsend and R. Redgrave and comprise a series of little landscape vignettes, often two to a page, with the text in between. The fact that fewer artists participated in the scheme means that there is more unity but, as with the Art Union edition, the poem is really used as a framework on which to hang as many illustrations as possible.

The impression of banality created by the Etching Club edition is also characteristic of the charming but repetitive illustrations by Birket Foster in the edition of 'L'Allegro' and 'Il Penseroso' published by David Boyne in 1855 (200). Here again, there are a vast number of plates and one cannot help thinking that had the artist contented himself with fewer illustrations the whole production would have been better. Three years later Birket Foster co-operated with Pickersgill, Harrison Weir and others on an edition of Comus published by Routledge. The general standard, despite the fact that the designs were engraved by the Dalziels, is very low. Even more of a mixed assortment are the illustrations for Ode on the Morning of Christ's Nativity published in 1868. Numbers of different artists including W. Small and Albert Moore designed plates for this production.

It is encouraging to turn to the Milton illustrations of one member of the Etching Club whose work rises above this general mediocrity. Samuel Palmer's most comprehensive series of etchings—had he completed them—would have been those illustrating Milton. R. G. Alexander has written of Palmer's etching 'The Willow', his probationary work on election to the Etching Club in 1850, that it 'was rather a trial than an attempt to express his real aims as an etcher . . . Palmer had no scheme for a definite "series" in mind when etching his first plates; or, indeed, until later in life he came to put upon copper his meditations on the poetry of Milton and Virgil'.[60] One would expect Palmer, as a disciple of Blake, to have been a lover of Milton's poetry and, as a member of the Etching Club working in the 1860s, he might be expected to show a preference for Milton's pastoral poetry. In fact Palmer did illustrate the minor poems of Milton but not until the end of his life, between 1860 and 1880. Yet G. Grigson has written: 'Milton in poetry—especially the pastoral Milton of moonlight and tufted trees—and Claude in painting are parallel as two prime influences on Palmer, in his moonlights and twilights.'[61] Palmer's best moonlights and twilights belong to his early Shoreham years and, despite the fact that he executed his Milton etchings late in life, there is ample evidence in Palmer's letters that Milton was a source of inspiration to him from his earliest youth. On January 26th, 1872, Palmer wrote to P. G. Hamerton a letter in which he says: I had a little Milton bound with brass corners that I might carry it always in my waistcoat-pocket; after doing so for twenty years it was all the fresher for the porterage.'[62] In 1880 Palmer wrote on July 27th to C. W. Cope thanking him for the gift of a *Life of Milton*. He says: 'Many thanks for the Milton, a model of condensation.

201 S. Palmer, 'The Skylark'

This makes the sixth life of him which I remember to have read. Each was a whet for the next . . .'[63]

In 1831–2 Palmer painted a sepia sketch of 'The Skylark', a subject which he repeated in 'The Rising of the Lark' after his Italian visit and also in his etching 'The Skylark' of 1850 (201).[64] All these were most probably based on Milton's lines in *L'Allegro*:

> To hear the Lark begin his flight,
> And singing startle the dull night,
> From his watch-towre in the Skies,
> Till the dappled dawn doth rise.

Even before the first version of 'The Skylark' Palmer had already set his hand to evoking in paint a mood described in poetry. 'Late Twilight' (Ashmolean Museum) of 1825 had inscribed on its original mount the lines from *Macbeth*: 'The West yet glimmers with some streaks of day' (202). There is evidence, moreover, that

202 S. Palmer, 'Late Twilight'

Palmer had planned his Milton series for many years before he actually got the opportunity to begin to execute it. In view of all these considerations it seems justifiable to discuss Palmer's Milton illustrations here although most of them belong outside the chronological limits of this work.

The sources for our evidence that Palmer had long planned to illustrate Milton's pastoral poems are his own letters and the *Life* that his son wrote. Palmer's chance to illustrate his favourite poet came in the autumn of 1863 when a small drawing 'Twilight: the Chapel by the Bridge', exhibited by Palmer at the Old Society of Water Colour Painters, was bought by T. R. Valpy. Palmer's son, A. H. Palmer, describes Valpy as

a man of a strangely-combined character. A serious and sensitive devoutness which suggested that of the old Puritans, a business-like shrewdness and caution worthy of a veteran merchant, and the astuteness of an experienced equity lawyer—these attributes seemed inconsistent with an ardent love of art and of poetry . . .

but, A. H. Palmer continues:

He was a man who could revel in the tints of a dying bramble-leaf, and who could fling his law, and his caution, and his seriousness behind him, before a beautiful landscape or a resplendent sunset.[65]

We do not have Valpy's letters to Palmer, but, judging by Palmer's replies, Valpy seems to have allowed Palmer a free hand over the designs and he does not appear to have become impatient over the long delays caused by Palmer's illness and his meticulous methods of work.

Valpy's commission was for a set of designs illustrating *L'Allegro*, *Il Penseroso*, *Lycidas* and *Comus*. A. H. Palmer tells us that his father had long been contemplating such a venture. Referring to Valpy's commission he says:

Many years before this, my father had left London for the purpose of attempting in country retirement, a series of designs from *L'Allegro* and *Il Penseroso*, but had attempted them vainly.

Here and there in his portfolios I have come across slight sketches bearing the titles of the two poems, and he had occasionally painted other Miltonic subjects and even sold them.[66]

Unfortunately A. H. Palmer had a habit of destroying 'slight sketches' by his father,[67] but a letter to Valpy from Palmer, dated June 1864, bears out what his son says:

Now only three days have passed since I did begin the meditation of a subject which, for twenty years, has affected my sympathies with seven-fold inwardness though now, for the first time, I seem to feel in some sort the power of realizing it. It is from one of the finest passages in what Edmund Burke thought the finest poem in the English language.[68]

Palmer then quotes a passage from *Il Penseroso*. Later in the same letter he says:

I carried the Minor Poems in my pocket for twenty years, and once went into the country expressly for retirement while attempting a set of designs for L'Allegro and Il Penseroso, not one of which I have painted . . . But I have often dreamed the day-dream of a small sized set of subjects (not however monotonous in their shape yet still a set; perhaps a dozen or so), half from the one and half from the other poem. For I never artistically know 'such a sacred and homefelt delight' as when endeavouring in all humility to realize after a sort the imagery of Milton.

Palmer lived until 1881 but his illustrations to Milton were only published posthumously, in *The Shorter Poems of John Milton* (1888) with an introduction by A. H. Palmer. Virgil's *Eclogues* were also published with Palmer's illustrations (1883) and in both cases Palmer's etchings were supplemented with reproductions or engravings by A. H. Palmer. One commentator has said that these two productions 'seem like ghosts from the past . . . In many of the etchings, except for those in which the photomechanical process intervenes too obviously, there is still a touch of the old enchantment'.[69]

In fact Palmer completed only two of his eight intended etchings from *L'Allegro* and *Il Penseroso*; 'The Bellman' and 'The Lonely Tower'.[70] Drawings for the eight etchings to *L'Allegro* and *Il Penseroso* and for the two to *Comus* and one to *Lycidas* were exhibited at the Royal Society of Painters in Watercolour. Some of these are now in the Victoria and Albert Museum, presumably bequeathed by Mrs. Valpy, who owned them when A. H. Palmer was writing the introduction to *The Shorter Poems*. Unlocated are the drawings for 'The Prospect' (*L'Allegro*), 'Morning (*L'Allegro*), 'The Curfew' (*Il Penseroso*), 'The Lonely Tower' (*Il Penseroso*), 'The Dell of Comus' and 'Lycidas'. Of these, 'The Lonely Tower' is one of the two that Palmer etched, but for the rest we are dependent on A. H. Palmer's reproductions from the drawings which have disappeared. A. H. Palmer writes of his father in the Preface to *The Shorter Poems of Milton*: 'As he did not live to complete more than two of the etchings, and these differed so considerably from the drawings as to be practically other versions, I saw no reason against attempting

to reproduce the whole series.'[71] Obviously A. H. Palmer's reproductions are far from satisfactory material to work on. However,
Palmer's etching 'The Bellman' (214) is virtually identical to the
squared-up drawing in the Victoria and Albert Museum (213),
which would suggest that the two etchings were based very closely
indeed on the drawings. It may be that A. H. Palmer was hoping
to gain for himself more of the credit for the series than he deserved.
He does not tell us exactly what process of reproduction is used but
makes a general statement about orthochromatic photography and
the process of M. Dujardin. The final effect fairly closely resembles
a mezzotint.

R. G. Alexander has written of Palmer's choice of subjects from
Milton: 'I do not think of him as an illustrator; an artist may find
his starting-points wherever he chooses—and these were his.
Sometimes they were no more than his excuses.'[72] This is a very
misleading statement, for although the originality and independence of Palmer's Milton illustrations are indisputable, his own
writings make it clear that he thought long and deeply, not only
about the significance of the lines of verse he was illustrating, but
also about the relationship between poetry and painting. It is from
his writing that we also learn of Palmer's personal attitude to the
poet Milton.

In a letter to Valpy dated June 3rd, 1865, Palmer writes:

It seems to me evident that poetry, being successional as to time and to
suggestion of space, and as it can turn and look all round it, admits more
objects than picture; but that picture, although tied to the unity of one
moment and one aspect, gives incomparably more illustration to each of
the images.[73]

Another letter to Valpy, dated August 27th, 1866, indicates that
Palmer's enjoyment of the natural scene was very much bound up
with what he had read and seen in works of art. His attitude is less
akin to the 'emotion recollected in tranquillity' of his contemporary
Wordsworth[74] than Archibald Alison's 'nature embellished and
made sacred by the memory of Theocritus and Virgil'.[75] Palmer
writes that he,

having got through the hard work, can now hope, D.V. for a little Miltonic solace; for, exquisite as are some of the favoured aspects of nature,
no facts nor representation of facts alone can give rest to the mind which
has humbly dwelt on the works of the ideal masters. Though sight is the
most refined of the senses, yet sight of colour and shade is a sensual
pleasure, unless the visible suggest the historic and poetic.[76]

In an early letter to Linnell, dated December 21st, 1828, Palmer calls Milton 'that arch-alchemist' and describes how Milton can transform any matter of history or dogma into 'poetic gold'. Palmer's admiration for the poet has no bounds. For him Milton is as sacred a subject as he was for Blake: 'I must be called mad to say it but I do believe that his stanzas will be read in Heaven.'[77] Much later, in August 1864, Palmer wrote to Valpy: 'I am never in a "lull" about Milton in the abstract, nor can tell how many times I have read his poems, his prose, his biographers. He never tires. He seems to me to be one of the few who have come to full maturity of manhood.'[78]

For Palmer, Milton was a nature poet and his own active experience of nature (described in theory in the letter to Valpy of August 27th, 1866, and quoted above), was certainly greatly enhanced by his intimate knowledge of Milton's pastoral verse. In one of his most ecstatic descriptive letters about his mystical experience in the natural scene, written to Julia Richmond on December 9th, 1872, Palmer describes 'the glistering of the stars through the loop holes in the thick woven canopy of ancient elm trees'. Palmer then ponders on some lines of Milton:

I cannot help thinking that Milton intended his 'Shady roof, of branching elm star-proof' as a double stroke—as he tells of the impervious leafy gloom glancing at its beautiful opposite—'Loopholes cut through thickest shade' and in them socketed the gems which sparkle on the Ethiopic forehead of the night.[79]

We also learn from remarks in his letters of the very slow gestation of Palmer's work and of the methods he employed on the Milton illustrations. He describes his aims in a letter to Valpy on October 20th, 1864, soon after he received Valpy's commission. He writes:

I saw . . . a set of highly finished etchings the size of Turner's *Liber Studiorum*; and as finished as my moonlight with the cypresses; a set making a book—a compact block of work which I would fain hope might live when I am with the fallen leaves.[80]

A. H. Palmer tells us that at about this time Palmer made himself a portfolio which he inscribed 'MIL' into which he put all kinds of sketches from among the classified divisions in his other portfolios.[81] It was evidently Palmer's habit to incorporate into the Milton designs studies he had made at some earlier date. In an undated letter to Valpy about 'The Haunted Stream' Palmer mentions that he has among his studies a very suitable sky.

203 After S. Palmer, 'Morning'

204 S. Palmer, 'The Eastern Gate'

205 After S. Palmer, 'Lycidas'

206 After S. Palmer, 'The Prospect'

The first illustration to *L'Allegro* is 'Morning', for which we only have A. H. Palmer's reproduction. As in so many of Palmer's Milton illustrations (drawings, etchings and reproductions) the predominantly dark foreground is occupied by cattle and the light floods from a hidden source behind the distant hills. The second design, 'The Eastern Gate' (204) illustrating Milton's description of the sunrise, is very similar both in the drawing and the reproduction. The theme of cattle at dawn or twilight was a favourite with Palmer, for he repeats it in 'The Bellman' (213), in 'Lycidas' (205) and in his small etching of 'The Early Ploughman' (Victoria and Albert Museum; this is not an illustration to Milton but it is very close in concept to these designs for the minor poems).

'The Prospect' (206) illustrates the lines from *L'Allegro* beginning 'Streit mine eye hath caught new pleasures'. Palmer rightly perceived that Milton's description here is really little more than an accumulation of all the set features that the period would expect to find in a landscape formula. Writing to Valpy concerning this subject on October 21st, 1867, he says:

It is a very curious subject for there seems no medium between a mappy Buckinghamshire treatment and a genial poetic swoon. Between ourselves, and trembling to say it, I think that Milton (with him a most exceptional case) was a little halting between the two. The mountain's 'barren breast' and the 'meadows trim with daisies pied' seem to jar a little.[82]

Palmer's solution to the problem of Milton's unnaturalistic landscape description is an essentially formal and conventional, Italianate view (known only from the reproduction), with hard, volcanic-looking mountains in the background and an umbrella pine in the right foreground. This is combined with a much more English-looking stone bridge and wall in the left foreground. The total effect is not unpleasing but inevitably rather artificial, especially when compared with Runciman's interpretation of this scene (60).

'A Towered City' (207) is less Italianate than 'The Prospect' but repeats the repoussoir tree and the bridge. Certain elements of composition, however, notably the tree and the seated figures on the left (the latter are more clearly seen in the reproduction (208)), the tower on the hill, the deep valley bordered by a stone wall and the general quality of light are repeated in 'The Lonely Tower' (209). Palmer liked to introduce a reclining figure in the corner foreground of his work and there are several studies for such figures in his sketch book of 1824[83] (210).

207 S. Palmer, 'A Towered City'

208 After S. Palmer, 'A Towered City'

One of the first designs that Palmer attempted for *Il Penseroso* was for the lines:

Some still removed place will fit,
Where glowing Embers through the room
Teach light to counterfeit a gloom.

Fuseli had painted a picture based on these lines between 1796 and 1799, but Palmer had little success with them.[84] He wished the fire to be the sole source of light, which led to endless difficulties, recorded in his letters, and all that remains of his efforts is a very brief charcoal sketch in the Victoria and Albert Museum.

Palmer's illustration to 'The Curfew' (*Il Penseroso*) is only known to us from his son's reproduction (211). There is, however, in the Victoria and Albert Museum a watercolour sketch signed and dated 1864 which must be related to 'The Curfew'. It is called 'Going Home at Curfew Time' and has a number of features which appear in an almost identical form in A. H. Palmer's reproduction: the mass of trees on the right, the building in the distance, the sickle moon and the cattle being driven home. This seems to

209 After S. Palmer, 'The Lonely Tower'

be one of the occasions when Palmer drew on earlier sketches for ideas in composing the Milton illustrations. 'The Curfew'—even as we know it from the reproduction—would have been one of the most successful designs of the series. Although the foreground figure is almost a repeat of that in 'The Lonely Tower' (207) and there are suggestions of a Mediterranean cypress tree on the right, the design is one of Palmer's least mannered and one most reminiscent of the fruitful Shoreham period. This is not surprising since it appears to be based on another early work, a sketch entitled 'The Haunted Stream' (212) illustrating Milton's lines from *L'Allegro*:

210 S. Palmer, 'Country Boy Reclining'

Such sights as youthful Poets dream
On Summer eeves by haunted stream.

'The Bellman' (*L'Allegro*) is one of Palmer's only two completed mezzotints (214) and follows closely the rough, watercolour sketch (213). Like 'The Lonely Tower' (209) 'The Bellman' is very dark in tone with much high-lighting of surfaces. The glow of light from behind the hill and the cattle in the foreground are, by now, familiar features of Palmer's Milton designs. It seems that Palmer must have executed most of the enormous amount of detail and finish onto the plate itself, for it is absent in the sketch and there does not appear to have been any intermediate stage. It is evident

211 After S. Palmer, 'The Curfew'

212 S. Palmer, 'The Haunted Stream' (from a reproduction)

from Palmer's correspondence that he was accustomed to spending long hours reworking the smallest detail and it is probably true to say that vacillation and indecision were the chief faults in Palmer's later work. Nevertheless, 'The Bellman', despite the over-intricacy of detail, is one of Palmer's most successful Milton designs. The softness of the contours and the gentle mysteriousness of the evening light are enhanced by the velvet texture of the engraving. Palmer's success in this design makes one regret that he did not try his hand at engraving earlier, in his Shoreham days.

'The Water Murmuring' (*Il Penseroso*) (216) the sketch for which is in the Victoria and Albert Museum shows a rocky river valley with an enormous oak tree in the foreground under which the nymphs mentioned in the poem are seen at play. This composition bears a close resemblance to two of Palmer's illustrations to *Comus* (217) which also include valleys and large trees. It is a pity that Palmer weakened his designs as a set by a tendency to reproduce two or three established formulae, for example the pattern of design involving a castle on a hill and a river valley, or that featuring cattle in the foreground.

Palmer had been thinking about the lines from *Il Penseroso* describing the valley of 'The Water Murmuring' long before he made

213 S. Palmer, 'The Bellman'

Valpy's acquaintance. On December 21st, 1828, he wrote to John
Linnell, saying:

Milton by one epithet, draws an oak of the largest girth I ever saw, 'Pine
and *monumental* oak:' I have just been trying to draw a large one in
Lullingstone; but the poet's tree is huger than any in the park: there the
moss, and rifts and barkey furrows, and the mouldering grey (tho' that
adds majesty to the lord of the forests) mostly catch the eye, before the
grasp and grapple of the roots, the muscular belly and shoulders, the
twisted sinews.[85]

Milton's epithet to which Palmer refers is as follows:

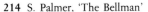

And shadows brown that *Sylvan* loves
Of Pine, or monumental Oake,
Where the rude Ax with heaved stroke,
Was never heard the Nymphs to daunt.
(*Il Penseroso*)

When Palmer came to illustrate 'The Water Murmuring' (the
next scene) he looked back to his 1828 sketches from Lullingstone
Park (215). Even in A. H. Palmer's reproduction, something can
be discerned of the sinewy quality, the familiar girth and texture of

214 S. Palmer, 'The Bellman'

the old oak which the artist describes so vividly in his letter to Linnell. In two of the drawings (collection of Mrs. E. A. C. Druce and collection of Sir K. Clark (215)) we can see that Palmer made a much more successful attempt at reproducing the monumental quality of the oak than one would imagine from the diffident tone of his letter.

Finally we come to Palmer's designs for *Comus*. These represent 'The Brothers Lingering under the Vine' (217), 'The Dell in *Comus*' and 'The Brothers Led by the Attendant Spirit'. The first of these (for which we have Palmer's own sketch) is an almost exact copy of a small etching entitled 'The Morning of Life' (218) which Palmer had completed some time earlier. There are differences in detail, but the general design with the sun shining through a network of branches with dark masses on either side and one long branch sweeping horizontally across the page is basically the same. 'The Dell in *Comus*' is based on the same general pattern in reverse, with the branch leaning from left to right and the same glow of light filtering through a tunnel of branches. As always with Palmer the figures are very small and the great variety of tree forms is stressed. Palmer's illustrations cover the whole range of forest growth from the great oak of 'The Water Murmuring' to the poplars and slender birch trees of 'The Brothers and the Attendant Spirit'. In addition to these three *Comus* illustrations, Palmer exhibited 'Sabrina' at the Royal Society of Painters in Watercolour in 1880, but the whereabouts of this picture is not now known.

M. Butlin has said:

Today Palmer's career after the Shoreham period is perhaps excessively decried: a few cool-toned water-colours of the later 1830s, a number of the works done in Italy between 1837 and 1839, and some of the etchings of his later years reveal a continuing creative ability. But his early directness of vision had gone: nature, together with his memories of Shoreham and Italy became a source of pictorial effects rather than a vital experience to which he could give visual expression.[86]

Palmer's Milton illustrations, despite their incomplete state, despite the reworking of earlier themes and the use of formulae in design, must be considered a great achievement. They do lack the immediacy of Palmer's Shoreham work and this is not surprising considering that, according to Palmer's son, the artist would many a time 'pause just as his brush touched the card-board, and then quite unconsciously lay brush and palette aside for hours together, his eyes remaining fixed upon the drawing'.[87] Palmer himself realized his tendency to overwork his designs. In a letter to Valpy of

215 S. Palmer, 'Oak Tree in Lullingstone Park'

216 After S. Palmer, 'The Water Murmuring'

217 S. Palmer, 'The Brothers Lingering under the Vine'

218 S. Palmer, 'The Morning of Life'

December 1865 Palmer says: 'Danger is likely to accrue rather from my own over-fastidiousness than otherwise, and in art that is sometimes more dangerous than rashness.'[88] But his designs comprise, nevertheless, one of the most carefully considered, lovingly composed and poetically faithful sets of Milton illustrations in English art. Palmer—even though the designs may not be the acme of his artistic career—was the only English artist to seriously attempt and to achieve with a considerable measure of success the illustration of Milton's pastoral poetry.[89]

Palmer's illustrations reveal a love of nature through which this artist's position as one of the last of the great school of English nineteenth-century landscape painters is revealed.

(iv) Conclusion

This book originated as an art-historical survey of a particular field of pictorial art: literary painting and book illustration as related to their poetic source, Milton. However, during the process of studying in chronological order a representative selection of artists, light has been thrown on many other aspects of English art during the period 1688 to 1860. We have seen how an illustrator like Medina, working at the end of the seventeenth century, works in an idiom which is still in many ways rooted in the Middle Ages. We have noticed how Hogarth's work reflects the style of international baroque and how in Hayman's illustrations a link is formed between England and the rococo art of France and Italy. In Fuseli's Milton pictures we have recognized the emotional, tumultuous fervour of the early years of the Romantic Movement and by contrast Etty's Milton pictures appear as part of the laboured and conscientious endeavour of artists of the time to establish an English school of history painting. It is to be hoped therefore, that the study of Milton and English art has not demonstrated a development somewhere outside the mainstream of English art but has revealed a phenomenon which is essentially a part of English art history and in which many major as well as minor English artists were involved.

We have seen that Milton's poetry provided a controversial talking point as well as a source of inspiration (religious, political or artistic) not only for painters but also for sculptors (and even architects), writers, poets and people who can claim little other distinction apart from that of having survived in memory through the preservation of their letters or journals. We have seen, in fact, how the fascination exercised by the poetry of Milton permeated many levels of society and most fields of culture.

One of the most important things to have been established is the clear demonstration of the radical way in which the pictorial concept of a poet's work can change from one age to the next. We have seen at one extreme Milton's poetry completely and unashamedly transformed into the personal idiom of the graphic artist; at the other extreme we have seen Milton's philosophy and poetic imagery most faithfully and imaginatively translated into pictorial symbolism.

The existence of a tradition of Milton illustration cannot be denied. In this study we have seen (despite the widely different concepts of the poetry in the work of different artists) the gradual establishment of this tradition, the process of its liberation from the fetters of Bible illustration, and its development to a point at about the year 1800 after which a clear current involving an established selection of subjects and frequently a familiar system of iconography can be easily recognized. Milton's poetry today is less widely read than at any other time in history, but apart from Shakespeare no English creative writer has had such a deep and widespread influence on artists.

Notes to Chapter IV

1. T. Balston, *John Martin: His Life and Works* (1947), pp. 95–6, p. 99.
2. The oil sketches for *Paradise Lost* used to be in the possession of T. R. Laughton, C.B.E., of Scarborough. All but two—which were retained by Mr. Laughton— were sold at Sotheby's on March 18th, 1964. One was bought by Mr. John Prickett (I am indebted for this information to Miss Miranda Strickland-Constable, Keeper, City Art Gallery, Leeds) and one is in the possession of Mrs. R. Frank. From what I have seen of the sketches the mezzotints appear to be based very closely on them.
3. T. Balston, 'John Martin, Illustrator and Pamphleteer', *The Library*, XIV (1934), p. 389.
4. Balston, *John Martin*, p. 99. No original source is given.
5. J. Seznec, *John Martin en France* (1964), p. 48. The practice of B. R. Haydon later in the century in hiring a room specifically to exhibit one mammoth-sized picture may be seen as part of this trend towards regarding a picture as a sort of theatrical spectacle. Gericault's 'Raft of the Medusa' was exhibited in London in 1840 and from the start the exhibition was planned on a popular level. When taken to Dublin its popularity suffered from competition with Messrs. Marshall's 'Marine Peristrephic Panorama, accompanied by music'. L. Johnson, 'The "Raft of the Medusa" in Great Britain', *B. Mag.*, 1954.

6. According to Seznec, op. cit., p. 20 (n.), the frontispiece to *Vathek* after Isaac Taylor anticipates 'Satan Presiding in the Infernal Council' by Martin. The latter was entertained at Fonthill by Beckford in 1823 and drew the abbey.
7. F. D. Klingender, *Art and the Industrial Revolution* (1947), p. 103.
8. In 1813 'The Expulsion' was shown at the B.I. and 'Adam's First Sight of Eve' (Glasgow City Art Gallery) at the Royal Academy. In 1841 Martin exhibited 'Pandemonium' and 'Celestial City and River of Bliss' at the Royal Academy (both in collection of Mr. Hugo Huntington-Whitely). In 1844 he exhibited at the Royal Academy 'The Morning Hymn' and 'Evening in Paradise'.
9. See *Paradise Lost*, Book IV:
   . . . and over head up grew
   Insuperable highth of loftiest shade,
   Cedar, and Pine, and Firr, and branching Palm,
   A Silvan Scene, and as the ranks ascend
   Shade above shade, a woodie Theatre
   Of stateliest view.
10. Svendsen, p. 67.
11. Ibid., pp. 66–7.
12. Macaulay's review of Southey's edition of *Pilgrim's Progress*, 1886. T. Balston, *John Martin*, p. 99.
13. F. D. Klingender, op. cit., p. 104.
14. Ibid., pp. 106–7.
15. W. G. Rawlinson, *The Engraved Work of J. M. W. Turner R.A.* (1908), I, p. lviii (Introduction).
16. Ibid., p. li.
17. Balston, *John Martin*, p. 267 (App. 3).
18. Sir J. Summerson, 'The Vision of J. M. Gandy', *Heavenly Mansions* (1949).
19. The first of these was destroyed in an air raid in 1940, the second is in the possession of Dr. Eric Gandy. See Summerson, op. cit., p. 132, nn. 1 and 2.
20. See R. James, 'Two Paintings by John Martin', *B. Mag.* (Aug 1952), pp. 234–7. This work, along with the Tate Gallery 'Fallen Angels' and one of the oil sketches for the Prowett mezzotints, was exhibited at Manchester City Art Gallery, May 31st to July 14th, 1968, as part of 'Art and the Industrial Revolution'.
21. Schiff, p. 55.
22. Sir J. Summerson, op. cit., p. 128.
23. See J. Seznec, op. cit., pp. 29–30.
24. Ibid.
25. M. L. Pendered, *John Martin, Painter, His Life and Times* (1923), p. 156.
26. J. Seznec, op. cit., pp. 29–30.
27. The Witt Collection, London University. The Courtauld Institute Handlist of Drawings, no. 3393.

28. Bryan.
29. Ibid.
30. Collins-Baker, *The Library* (June 1948), p. 103, n. 1.
31. Bryan, and Boase, *English Art*, p. 41.
32. Bryan says that in Italy Howard joined Flaxman and Deare in making a set of outlines of antique sculpture.
33. Bryan.
34. Ibid.
35. Graves, *R.A.*
36. E. C. Mason, *The Mind of Henry Fuseli* (1951), p. 345.
37. B. West, 'Death on a Pale Horse' or 'The Opening of the First Five Seals' (catalogue, 1821).
38. W. Hazlitt, 'West's Picture of Death on the Pale Horse', in *Essays on the Fine Arts*, ed. C. Hazlitt (1873).
39. Bryan.
40. Boase, *English Art*, p. 153.
41. Case 243. See drawings nos. 707, 1323, 1324, 1352, 1404, 1560, 1571, 1627,
42. Boase, *English Art*, p. 153.
43. Yvonne Ffrench, in 'Some Unrecorded Haydon Drawings', *Apollo*, VII to VIII (Nov. 1958), p. 148, says that: 'There is clearly no existing corpus to which the student quarrying for details of his lost compositions might successfully turn.' The writer then goes on to speak of the 'twenty-six volumes of bulky parchment-bound, ledger-like folios' of Haydon's unpublished journals now in America. The text of these was published in 1963 but the drawings contained in the text still have not appeared in any publication. The collection of Haydon drawings in the British Museum consists almost entirely of studies from the Elgin marbles.
44. For all references to Haydon's pictures and writings, see *The Diary of B. R. Haydon*, ed. W. B. Pope (Cambridge, Mass., 1963).
45. Reprinted, ibid., V, p. 438.
46. Ibid.
47. D. Farr, *William Etty* (1958), pp. 95–6.
48. T. S. R. Boase, 'The Decorations of the New Palace of Westminster', *J.W.C.I.*, XVII (1954).
49. D. Farr, op. cit., pp. 95–6.
50. Boase, *English Art*, p. 214n.
51. L. Gruner, *The Decorations of the Garden Pavilion in the grounds of Buckingham Palace* (1846). The descriptive introduction is by Mrs. Jameson.
52. Ibid. Introduction.
53. Ibid.
54. D. Farr, op. cit., pp. 95–6.
55. Another version is in the possession of M. A. M. Clark, Providence, Rhode Island, and there are three studies in the Victoria and Albert Museum.

56. A sketch on millboard for this picture is in York City Art Gallery. There are also studies for the picture in the Victoria and Albert Museum.
57. See D. Farr, op. cit., p. 62.
58. Ibid.
59. The Detroit Institute of Arts and the Philadelphia Museum of Art, *Romantic Art in Britain* (exhibition catalogue) (1968), no. 189.
60. R. G. Alexander, *A Catalogue of the Etchings of Samuel Palmer* (The Print Collectors Club, 1937), p. 120.
61. G. Grigson, *Samuel Palmer: The Visionary Years* (1947), p. 23.
62. A. H. Palmer, *The Life and Letters of Samuel Palmer, Painter and Etcher* (1892).
63. Ibid.
64. The sketch is now unlocated, but a photograph of it appears in G. Grigson, op. cit.
65. A. H. Palmer, op. cit., pp. 148–9.
66. Ibid., p. 149.
67. See M. Butlin, *Samuel Palmer's Sketch Book* (1824) (facsimile), 1962, Introduction.
68. A. H. Palmer, op. cit.
69. D. Bland, *The Illustration of Books* (1962, 3rd enlarged edition), p. 253.
70. See R. G. Alexander, op. cit., p. 19.
71. *The Shorter Poems of John Milton Illustrated by Samuel Palmer* (1888). Preface, pp. xix–xx.
72. R. G. Alexander, op. cit., p. 15.
73. A. H. Palmer, op. cit.
74. Preface to the second edition of the *Lyrical Ballads*. Wordsworth, *The Poetical Works* (1847).
75. A. Alison, *Essays on the Nature and Principles of Taste* (1810) (6th ed., Edinburgh, 1825), p. 64.
76. A. H. Palmer, op. cit.
77. Ibid.
78. Ibid.
79. Ibid.
80. Ibid.
81. Ibid., p. 153.
82. Ibid.
83. Victoria and Albert Museum, published in facsimile by the Trianon Press for the William Blake Trust, ed. M. Butlin (1962).
84. Fuseli's picture was exhibit no. xxxiii in the Milton Gallery and showed a man and a woman seated on either side of a hearth.
85. A. H. Palmer, op. cit.
86. M. Butlin, op. cit., p. 11.
87. A. H. Palmer, op. cit., p. 152.
88. Ibid.

89. Subjects from Milton do not seem to have been very popular among Palmer's associates from his Shoreham days. However, George Blake Richmond's 'The Creation of Light' was based on lines from *Paradise Lost* (VII) and John Linnell exhibited 'The Eve of the Deluge' (*Paradise Lost*, XI) in 1848.

Illustrations of Milton's Poetry from the 1870s to the Present Day

W. E. Frost and Samuel Palmer as well as many lesser-known artists such as B. W. Leader, Charles Rossiter, John Wood, Charles Rolt and Charles Lucy continued to exhibit works based on Milton's poetry well into the 1880s. However, there were no new illustrators working in this field and few designs of distinction appeared in published work (apart from Palmer's designs for *The Minor Poems*) until the 1890s when there was a sudden revival in the illustration of Milton's poetry. All the artists concerned in this revival seem to have been influenced to some extent by the decorative style of Art Nouveau and by the designs of Aubrey Beardsley.

In 1896 the first of the illustrated editions of Milton of this era was published by Hacon and Ricketts. *The Early Poems* was illustrated by Charles Ricketts in a highly eclectic and decorative style. The title page with its thickly laid border of strap-work and fleur-de-lys, its elongated, sinuous figures and the linear treatment of the background cliffs, shows at once a debt to medieval manuscript illumination and the school of William Morris, to Aubrey Beardsley and to the art of the Japanese woodcut. The artist shows little awareness of the text and the whole production is over-rich in decorative detail.

In 1897 Emily J. Harding and T. H. Robinson illustrated *Ode on the Morning of Christ's Nativity*. The designs are rather sentimental and some of them are adorned with unpleasantly heavy, floral frames. R. Anning Bell's illustrations to the 1903 edition of *Lycidas and the Minor Poems* (published by G. Bell), like those of Charles Ricketts, are very much in the style of Art Nouveau. Some of the better designs in this edition, however, have a certain dramatic dignity. See, for example, the gesture of the poet rejecting Melancholy in favour of Mirth in the illustration to *L'Allegro*, which is reminiscent of some of Rossetti's work.

One artist among this group of illustrators who owes nothing to the production of Art Nouveau is William Hyde, who illustrated *The Works of Milton* published by the Astolat Press in 1904. Hyde's work is a continuation of the pastoral, idyllic concept of Milton established by Samuel Palmer. It is varied in quality and Hyde makes little attempt at interpretation. However, in his etchings (see, for example, that to *Il Penseroso*, 'Kerchieft in a Comely Cloud') he manages to represent a fine variety of natural texture and a great deal of movement in wind-swept trees and clouds. When using the mezzotint medium, as in his illustration to *Lycidas*, 'So Sinks the Day Star', Hyde fully exploits the possibility of attaining a blurred, soft and mellow effect.

In 1905 William Strang illustrated *Paradise Lost*, published by Routledge. Some of the etchings were actually issued on their own without any text, which reinforces the impression they give of having been designed individually rather than as part of a book. The following year Jessie M. King's very exotic Beardsley-influenced set of illustrations to *Comus* were published in photogravure. The text of *Comus* is very short, has little variety of scene and little action and does not therefore justify so many designs. The result is inevitably a certain monotony, and an additional problem is created by the fact that the pages are overcrowded and the figure drawing very stylized. It is sometimes very difficult to distinguish which is the Lady and which is Sabrina. Nevertheless, despite all these faults Jessie King's designs frequently establish the characteristic mood of the text. There is a sense of evil and fey mystery as well as exotic languor in Jessie King's 'The Ladye Set in the Enchanted Chair' which is absolutely appropriate to *Comus* and which no other illustrator of the poem ever really achieves.

There is a gap of some years after Jessie M. King's edition before another series of illustrated editions of Milton's poetry were produced in the 1920s and 1930s. Most of these belong to the genre of the gift book or the 'edition de luxe'. *Comus* published by Doubleday Page in 1921 and illustrated by Arthur Rackham is a very splendid production containing black and white woodcuts alternating with colour reproductions. Like Jessie M. King, Arthur Rackham exploits the qualities of evil in the poem and the night threats of the wood in his drawing of twisted roots and branches which appear in the shapes of wicked faces.

Many of the editions of Milton published during the 1920s and 1930s make practically no concession to the poetry at all. Productions like *Paradise Regained* illustrated by Thomas Lowinsky in 1924, *Paradise Lost and Paradise Regained* illustrated by D. E. Galanis or *Comus* illustrated by Edmund Dulac are really little more than fancy gift books. But one progressive aspect of the illustrative art of this period is the introduction of new techniques into the field and some of these are seen in the work of artists illustrating Milton's poetry. In 1937 Nonesuch published an edition of *Comus* with most attractive coloured lino-cuts by Mildred Farrar which pre-dates the real revival of this medium instigated by Matisse in France during the years after 1944. In addition, there were several editions of Milton's poetry with very effective woodcuts by Blair Hughes Stanton published in these years. *Four Poems* published by the Gregynog Press, Newtown, has a most original illustration to *Lycidas* showing the huge figure of Neptune, impassive at the event of the shipwreck (the event which inspired the poem) and at the sight of the tiny drowning figures. In such a work we see a suggestion of a return to the concept of interpretative illustration as Blake would have understood it.

Sculpture on Miltonic Themes

During the eighteenth century there were probably many portrait busts and statues of Milton besides those by Roubiliac and Rysbrack (see pp. xxxiii and 46), but not until right at the very end of the century do sculptors seem to have taken a great deal of interest in subjects from Milton's poetry. This is not surprising, as one would not imagine Milton's poetry—with all its vivid and detailed background—to be particularly suited to the requirements of the sculptor. What does surprise is the enormous popularity enjoyed by the poet among sculptors working between 1840 and 1880.

Allowing for the fact that some of the works exhibited by sculptors were sketches in which the sculptor was liberated from the three-dimensional limits of his work, we can see in the first group of Miltonic works by sculptors around the 1800s, the subjects which were to dominate the sculpture displays at the Royal Academy exhibitions during the latter half of the nineteenth century. All seem to have been single figures or small groups and the subjects chosen concern only events in which the major figures of *Paradise Lost* participate. Charles Felix Rossi (son of an Italian practising medicine in Nottingham) exhibited a 'Model of Eve as Described by Milton' at the Royal Academy in 1796. His 'Eve at the Fountain', exhibited in 1822, was sold in 1835 for two hundred guineas.[1] Mrs. Siddons, the actress, tried her hand at sculpture and exhibited 'A Bust of Adam from Milton's *Paradise Lost*, Book IV, line 300' at the Royal Academy in 1802. Joaquim Smith exhibited 'An Angel Casting Satan into the Abyss' in 1803 and in 1814 F. A. Legé exhibited 'Satan: "So stretched out, huge in length, the arch fiend lay" '. This work was also exhibited in Edinburgh and was, evidently, not favourably received, for the *Scot's Magazine* (1815, p. 334) reported that 'some intrusive Goth had dared to mutilate it!'[2] H. W. Peck and V. Gahagen both exhibited Milton works in 1817 and Josephus Kendrick exhibited three sculptures between 1819 and 1826.

Flaxman's work has been discussed in detail (p. 79), so it is not necessary to say anything further about him here. Between 1817 and 1840 we see the same subjects as were exhibited around 1800 repeated again and again: 'Eve at the Fountain', 'Satan Cast out of Heaven', 'Falling Angels' (a subject popular with Flaxman and his painter associates) and many statues of Adam or Eve with various quotations added. E. H. Baily's 'Eve at the Fountain' (1820) (Bristol City Art Gallery) was originally designed as the handle of a cover for a soup tureen, but when executed in marble it gained him a European reputation.[3] Baily followed up his success with other sculptures on Miltonic subjects, one of which, 'Eve Listening to the Voice', is now in the Bethnal Green Museum. Other sculptors exhibiting Milton subjects at this time were A. Rouch, S. W. Arnald (better known as a painter), F. S. Archer and William Pitts.

During the 1830s we have some of the first examples of sculpture on subjects from the minor poems, for example John Francis's 'Il Penseroso'

(1837) and Sir Robert Westmacott's 'Euphrosyne' (1837). Subjects such as these which could be treated as general personifications were favourites with sculptors of the 1850s and the pastoral poems of Milton were generally popular in the middle and later years of the nineteenth century.

The Great Exhibition (1851) was undoubtedly one cause of the enormous quantity of Miltonic sculpture executed between 1847 and 1860. We are told that sculpture was more largely represented than painting at the exhibition partially because it was 'of much assistance' to the general appearance. ' "The happy and judicious arrangement of objects of plastic art in the great structure forms one of its most interesting features", said a contemporary account; the bishops, on the other hand, had written to the Queen protesting that they could not attend the opening ceremony unless some of the nakedness were decently covered.'[4] In view of the success of the sculpture at the Great Exhibition, the Corporation of London decided to commission works of statuary to decorate the Egyptian Hall in the Mansion House. As in the Houses of Parliament scheme (p. 208) the subjects 'were vaguely drawn from English literature or history',[5] which naturally provided an extra incentive to sculptors with a leaning towards subjects from Milton's poetry.

The most striking characteristic of the Milton sculpture of the 1850s is the overwhelming predominance of 'Sabrinas', closely followed by 'Il Penserosos' and 'L'Allegros', these being, presumably, personifications of Melancholy or Mirth. The appeal of such poetic female personifications to the nineteenth-century sculptor working in the style of the Greek revival is understandable. However, the immense vogue of *Comus* at this time must be due—at least in part—to the nature of the poem's subject-matter. The concept of chastity as the most powerful of virtues, assailable but not to be overcome, would naturally appeal to the moralistic inclinations of the Victorian artist and the Victorian public. In view of the enormous number of artists involved in Milton sculptures during the period it seems most appropriate and helpful to conclude simply with a list of sculptors exhibiting Milton subjects from the 1840s to the end of the century at the Royal Academy or elsewhere.[6]

This account does not in any way pretend to be a comprehensive survey of Miltonic sculpture, but even a very rough guide to the way in which the themes of painting recur in sculpture may be found helpful.

Armstead Henry Hughes, 'Satan Beguiling Eve', 1851, R.A.
Bell John, 'A Daughter of Eve', 1853, R.A.
— 'Lost Paradise', 1879, R.A.
Brown Alfred, 'Satan Falling from Heaven', 1847, R.A.
Calvi Pietro, 'Lucifer', 1879, R.A.
Cardwell H., 'Sabrina', 1856, R.A.
Drury Alfred, 'Il Penseroso', 1888, R.A.
Earle Thomas, 'L'Allegro' (2), 1852, R.A.
— 'Sin Triumphant', 1846, B.I.
— 'L'Allegro', 1850, B.I.

— 'Il Penseroso', 1853, B.I.
— 'Sin Triumphant', 1855, B.I.
Fontana Aristide, 'The Pensierosa', 1882, R.A.
— 'The Allegra', 1882, R.A.
Foley John Henry, 'The Elder Brother in *Comus*' (Diploma Gallery, Burlington House), 1860, R.A.
Glassby Robert E., 'Satan', 1867, R.A.
Griffith James Milo Ap, 'Sabrina', 1884, R.A.
— 'Sabrina', 1886, R.A.
Hale Lawrence, 'The Lady in *Comus*', 1862, R.A.
Hancock John, 'Comus Listening to the Lady', 1845, R.A.
— 'Youth and Joy' (*Comus*), 1851, R.A.
— 'Penserosa' (Osborne), 1858, R.A.
— 'Penseroso', 1862, R.A.
— 'Penseroso' (Egyptian Hall, Mansion House), 1864, R.A.
Legrew James, 'Milton Dictating his Address to Light . . .', 1845, R.A.
Leifchild Henry S., 'Il Pensiero', 1865, R.A.
Lough J. G., 'St. Michael Triumphing over the Devil' (*P.L.*? exhibited Great Exhibition, 1851), R.A.
— 'Comus' (Egyptian Hall, Mansion House), 1856
Lynn Samuel F., 'Sketch for a Bust of Eve', 1862, R.A.
Marshall W. Calder, 'Eve', 1846, R.A.
— 'Sabrina Fair', 1846, R.A.
— 'Sabrina', 1847, R.A.
— 'Eve's Dream', 1868, R.A.
— 'Sabrina Thrown into the Severn', 1881, R.A.
— 'Eve', 1885, R.A.
Miller Felix M., 'The Translation of Milton' ('one of a series of 120 designs in outline from the works of Milton'), 1847, R.A.
— 'The Attendant Spirit in *Comus*', 1848, R.A.
— 'Sabrina', 1849, R.A.
— 'The Brothers and Sister in *Comus*', 1850, R.A.
— 'Virtue may be assailed but never hurt' (*Comus*), 1850, R.A.
— 'The Brothers in *Comus*', 1850, R.A.
— 'Lycidas is dead . . .', 1850, R.A.
— 'The Lady in *Comus*', 1863, R.A.
Montford Horace, 'Sabrina Rising from the Water', 1876, R.A.
— 'Sabrina and the Water Nymphs', 1890, R.A.
Papworth Edgar G. Junr., 'Paradise Regained', 1865, R.A.
— 'Morning' (*Paradise Lost*), 1867, R.A.
Rogers Mark, 'L'Allegro', 1902, R.A.
Ruddock Samuel, 'Sabrina Disenchanting the Lady', 1869, R.A.
Thrupp Frederick, 'Death Triumphing over the Saviour' (*Paradise Lost*), 1871, R.A.
— 'Prevenient Grace Descending', 1874, R.A.
Wade C., 'Il Penseroso', 1890, R.A.
Wall J., 'Sabrina', 1868, R.A.

Westmacott J. S., 'L'Allegro', 1862, R.A.
— 'Eve', 1865, R.A.
— 'Eve Listening to the Serpent', 1871, R.A.
— 'Eve', 1885, R.A.
Woodington W. F., 'Milton Dictating to his Daughter' (exhibited Westminster Hall), 1844
— 'The Lady in the Enchanted Chair', 1865, R.A.

Appendix C

Pictures of Milton's Life

The question of pictures based on events taken from biographies of Milton has already been discussed to some extent in the introduction to this work. Our aim here is to cite specific examples of such pictures and to assess in what way artists were particularly interested in Milton's life.

Engraved portrait busts of Milton were very numerous from the middle of the eighteenth century to the middle of the nineteenth (see p. 42 n. 15). Engravings after pictures of Milton's life seldom occur in editions to Milton's poetry, although a number of editions are adorned with frontispieces portraying Milton, usually inscribed with lines from the poetry which might be thought to have autobiographical significance. See, for example, J. Thurston's frontispiece showing Milton with a lyre in the 1806 edition of *Paradise Lost*. This follows roughly the pattern of Cheron's 'Milton Inspired' (the title page of the 1720 edition of *The Poetical Works*) or J. H. Mortimer's illustration to *Ode on the Morning of Christ's Nativity* which portrays Milton and is inscribed with the lines: 'My muse with angels did divide to sing . . .' (Bell's *Poets of Great Britain* 1777). There are also a few illustrations to autobiographical poems, in particular 'Milton's Dream'; 'Methought I saw my late espoused Saint . . .' Westall illustrated this poem in the 1797 edition of *The Works of Milton* and Charles West Cope exhibited a canvas on this subject at the Royal Academy in 1850.

Formal portraits of Milton such as that by Jonathan Richardson of himself and his son in the presence of Milton (collection of Lieutenant Colonel and Mrs. W. H. Bromley-Davenport) or 'Shakespeare, Milton and Spenser, with Nature Dictating to Shakespeare' exhibited by Joseph Strutt at the Royal Academy in 1784 are frequently to be found during the period. However, the anecdotal picture of Milton's life is a phenomenon which seems to originate in the 1790s and to be confined to the genre of the large exhibited canvas. There are one or two such pictures which pre-date Fuseli's Milton Gallery (1799), but the great majority were painted after the turn of the century. The fact that Fuseli incorporated three anecdotal pictures into his Milton Gallery is some indication that by this time an interest in the details of Milton's life was an accepted accompaniment to an interest in Milton's poetry. The reasons for the fascination which Milton the man—poet, politician and private citizen—held for writers and artists at the turn of the eighteenth century has already been discussed (p. 95–6). It is possible to divide the anecdotal portraits of Milton into three main groups (each symptomatic of one particular aspect of the Milton cult): pictures portraying Milton composing, those with a particular sentimental or romantic appeal and those in which the interest is political or historical.

Milton the poet and writer was, naturally, the most popular subject with painters. We know that numerous *Lives* of Milton were published and these were evidently read avidly by the general public. Samuel Palmer, for example, was quite a connoisseur of *Lives* of Milton (see

p. 236). 'Milton Dictating *Paradise Lost*' or 'Milton and his Daughters' was the most popular of all the anecdotal subjects. Most accounts of the life of the poet are based on the first *Life of Milton* by the poet's nephew, Edward Phillips. One such is Dr. Johnson's *Life of Milton*[7] and, if we take this as fairly typical it is interesting to note how very closely many artists followed the account of incidents as given in the biography. Dr. Johnson describes Milton's habits of composition as follows: 'He composed much in the morning, and dictated in the day, sitting obliquely in an elbow-chair, with his leg thrown over the arm.' Romney's picture of 'Milton and his Daughters' (1793) (collection of Major Samuel Whitbread)[8] shows Milton in exactly the pose described by Johnson, reclining in a chair with one leg thrown over the arm. Fuseli, in his painting 'Milton's Wife Pleading and Imploring for his Pardon' (Walker Art Gallery) and in 'Milton Dictating to his Daughters', depicts the poet in a similar posture. Joseph Lionel Williams, exhibiting 'Milton Dictating *Paradise Lost*' at the Royal Academy in 1845 actually quotes these lines from Johnson as an accompaniment to his picture.

Richard Paye Morton exhibited 'Milton Composes his *Paradise Lost*' in 1800 but this has been lost. Westall, in his depiction of the same scene (R.A. 1802, Sir John Soane's Museum), gives his picture a rural setting (presumably intended to be Chalfont St. Giles). James Barry shows Milton dictating to a male scribe in a pleasantly studious interior whilst the poet's daughter is seen sorting his books on a shelf by the organ (drawing and engraving, 1807, British Museum). Other versions of this subject were painted by Henry Joseph Fradelle (1817), who also painted 'An Incident in Milton's Life when a Student at Cambridge' (1839), and by B. R. Haydon (1835–9) (Haydon was also at work on 'Milton at his Organ' in 1835).

Another group of anecdotal Milton pictures are those which depict episodes from Milton's life which might be interpreted as being full of pathos or sentiment. Westall's 'Milton when a Youth Discovered Sleeping in a Wood by an Italian Lady of Quality' (R.A. 1830, engraved by F. Engleheart, 1816) shows Milton lying under a tree and a lady about to drop a note onto his breast. Fuseli's 'Milton when a Youth' (Milton Gallery XXXIX) depicts the same subject. Here a lady dressed in the high-waisted 'directoire' style looks down admiringly on the sleeping form of the boy. Frederick Newenham (1807–59) painted a similar subject, 'Milton at the Age of Twelve'. The romantic appeal of such a subject, with its 'plein air' setting and its suggestion of the infant prodigy, is clear.

Fuseli's 'Milton's Wife Pleading and Imploring for his Pardon' (not included in the Milton Gallery, sent to Roscoe 1800, collection of the Walker Art Gallery, Liverpool) has similar sentimental appeal. The poet sits with lowering visage whilst his wife, on her knees, grasps his hand in supplication. Again, the artist closely follows Johnson's account of the episode,[9] in which we are told that the poet resisted his wife's entreaties for a while and that there was 'strong intercession of friends on both sides'. Fuseli shows the poet resisting and also shows the friends looking through the doorway at what is going on. The same subject was exhibited by Sir William Boxall in 1829, and a similar subject, 'Milton's First Meeting with Mary Powell, Accompanied by her Brother', was exhibited by Alfred Rankley in 1862.

'Milton as a Boy with his Mother' (Milton Gallery XXXVIII) is another picture by Fuseli with great sentimental appeal. It is interesting to note that the subject of 'Milton Dictating *Paradise Lost*' could be given a similar sense of pathos and an emotional quality simply by reference to Milton's blindness. Although we no longer have the pictures, this must certainly have been the case in Callcott's and Horsley's pictures of this subject if the titles are anything to judge by. Sir Augustus Wall Callcott exhibited in 1840 'Milton Dictating to his Daughters'. The Royal Academy catalogue entry is accompanied by the following description: 'He is represented as he describes Samson in the "Agonistes" "dark amid the blaze of noon" and at the moment when dictating these lines: "Seasons return, but not to me return . . ." etc.' J. C. Horsley exhibited the same subject in 1859 at the Royal Academy.

The third group of pictures of Milton's life are those in which the subjects were clearly chosen for their political interest or because they could be classified as episodes of British history and thus be considered suitable subjects for depiction in the grand manner as a contribution to the English school of history painting. Romney's 'Milton and his Daughters' has already been discussed, but it is necessary to mention it again here as, when considered with its companion piece 'Newton Making Experiments with the Prism', it really belongs in this category. Romney clearly intended these pictures as portrayals of two great episodes from English creative history, the one literary, the other scientific. For the eighteenth century there was no great distinction between the literary and scientific but Milton and Newton were seen as two great explorers and inventors whose work was equally exciting. However, were any further connection needed to justify the partnership Romney could have found it. Indeed he may have known of Archibald Alison, who must have had a familiar source since he speaks of his anecdote as 'well known', writing in 1810: 'The anecdote of the late celebrated mathematician is well known, who read the Paradise Lost, without being able to discover in it anything that was sublime, but who said that he could never read the queries at the end of Newton's Optics without feeling his hair stand on end and his blood run cold.'[10]

The most popular of all the historical or political subjects involving Milton concerns the poet's meeting with Galileo. This is ironic since it seems very doubtful whether Milton could ever have met the great astronomer as his visit to Italy (as it is recorded) would have been too late. However, the combined fascination of an alien country, early scientific pioneer and prison setting—not to mention the implications of English progressive liberty opposed to Italian, Popish tyrannical intolerance—clearly exerted a strong influence on nineteenth-century artists. Versions of this subject were exhibited by Charles Lucy (1840), Solomon Hart (1847) and Eyre Crowe (1859), all with long descriptions and explanations attached. Milton's association with Cromwell is a much more obvious choice of subject. Frederick Newenham exhibited 'Cromwell Dictating to Milton' at the British Institution in 1850 and four years later Samuel Blackburn exhibited 'Cromwell, Milton and Mary Powell his Wife' at the Royal Academy.

It is significant that, as far as one can tell from titles, all these anecdotal pictures of Milton's life give a most sympathetic portrayal of a poet who was a revolutionary and a potential regicide as well as (to judge by all accounts) a most cantankerous person. This is, perhaps, the surest indication of the tendency of nineteenth-century painters of history to gloss over realities and to romanticize personalities.

Notes to Appendixes B and C

1. R. Gunnis, *A Dictionary of British Sculptors 1660–1851* (1953).
2. Ibid.
3. Ibid.
4. Boase, *English Art*, p. 266.
5. Ibid., p. 268.
6. Sources: R. Gunnis, op. cit. Graves, *R.A.* Graves, *B.I.*
7. Dr. S. Johnson, *The Lives of the English Poets* (1783). Edited by H. S. Scott (Oxford, 1905).
8. There are four sketches for this picture in the Fitzwilliam Museum and one in the possession of G. D. Lockett, Esq. It was engraved by Benjamin Smith in 1795.
9. Dr. S. Johnson, op. cit.
10. A. Alison, *Essays on the Nature and Principles of Taste* (1810) (6th edition, Edinburgh, 1825), p. 88.

Appendix D

J. H. Fuseli's Milton Gallery, 1799

Sources

The Milton Gallery. A Catalogue of the first series of pictures and sketches from the poetic works of John Milton by Henry Fuzli, R.A. (1799); J. Knowles, *The Life and Writings of Henry Fuseli* (1831); and G. Schiff, *J. H. Füssli's Milton Galerie* (Zurich, 1963).

I 'Satan Summons His Host'
Paradise Lost, I.
Oil on canvas. 365·8 × 442.
Collection of the Duke of Wellington, Stratfield Saye.
Engraved by P. W. Tomkins for *The Works of the British Poets*, 1805–8.

II 'Satan Risen from the Flood, Beelzebub Rising'.
Paradise Lost, I.
Oil on canvas. 365·8 × 396·2.
Collection of the Duke of Wellington, Stratfield Saye.
Engraved by W. Bromley for Du Rouveray's edition, 1802.

III 'Satan Haranguing his Host'.
Paradise Lost, I.
Sketch. c. 365·8 × 426·8.
Unlocated.

IV 'Figures from a Simile in Allusion to the Contracted Form of the Spirits Assembled in the New-raised Hall of Pandemonium'.
(Fairy Elves . . .)
Paradise Lost, II.
Oil on canvas.
Unlocated.

V 'Satan Encountering Death, Sin Interposing'.
Paradise Lost, II.
Oil on canvas. 304·8 × 396·2.
Unlocated.
(Other versions: Feigen collection, Chicago; Bollag collection, Zurich; Sergel collection, Stockholm National Museum; British Museum; Ashmolean Museum; Los Angeles County Museum.)
Engraved by A. Smith.
Engraved by James Neagle for Du Rouveray's edition, 1802.

VI 'The Birth of Sin'.
Paradise Lost, II.
Oil on canvas.
Unlocated.
Engraved by Abraham Raimbach, 1806.

VII 'Sin Pursued by Death'.
Paradise Lost, II.
Oil on canvas. 127×118·8.
Kunsthaus, Zurich.
Engraved by Moses Haughton, 1804.
Drawing, British Museum.

VIII 'Lapland Orgies, the hell-hounds round Sin compared to those that . . . follow the night long . . .', etc.
Paradise Lost, II.
Oil on canvas.
Unlocated.
cf. Drawing, 'The Night Hag': British Museum.

IX 'Satan's Ascent from Hell'.
Paradise Lost, II.
Oil on canvas. 304·8×396·2.
Unlocated.

X 'A Gryphon Pursuing an Arimaspian. A comparison of Satan's exertion to force his way through the realm of Chaos'.
Paradise Lost, II.
Oil on canvas.
Unlocated.

XI 'Satan Bursts from Chaos'.
Paradise Lost, II.
Oil on canvas. 396·2×304·8.
Collection of Dr. Ulrich, Zurich.
Drawing (attributed to Fuseli) (collection of Mrs. W. M. Crane, New York).
Drawing, 1821.
Pencil and wash.
Auckland City Art Gallery, New Zealand.

XII 'Ulysses between Scylla and Charybdis. An exemplification of Satan straitened in his passage to Light'.
Paradise Lost, II.
Oil on canvas—sketch.
Kunstmuseum, Aarau.

XIII 'Adam and Eve First Discovered by Satan'.
Paradise Lost, IV.
Oil on canvas. 304·8×396·2.
Unlocated.

XIV 'Satan Starting from the Touch of Ithuriel's Spear'.
Paradise Lost, IV.
Oil on canvas. 365·8×396·2.
Unlocated.

(Version exhibited R.A. 1780, versions: collection of Dr. Ulrich, Zurich; National Museum, Stockholm.)
Engraved by A. Smith for Du Rouveray's edition, 1802.

XV 'Satan Discovering his Fate in the Scale Aloft, Flying from Gabriel and the Angelic Squadron'.
Paradise Lost, IV.
Sketch.
Unlocated.

XVI 'A Dream of Eve, Fancying to have Tasted the Fruit from the Tree of Interdicted Knowledge . . .'
Paradise Lost, V.
Oil on canvas.
Collection of Dr. Von Bourg, destroyed during war.
Engraved by Moses Haughton, c. 1805.

XVII 'The Creation of Eve as Related by Adam'.
Paradise Lost, VIII.
Oil on canvas. 213·4×304·8.
Collection of Dr. Burg, Lausanne.
(Watercolour study, Kunsthaus, Zurich.)
Engraved by Moses Haughton, 1803.

XVIII 'Eve New Created Led to Adam'.
Paradise Lost, VIII.
Oil on canvas.
Unlocated.
Sketch in Huntington Library.

XIX 'Eve at the Forbidden Tree'.
Paradise Lost, IX.
Oil on canvas. 213·4×304·8.
Unlocated.
Engraved by P. W. Tomkins, 1805, for *The Works of the British Poets*.

XX 'Adam Resolved to Share the Fate of Eve: the Guardian Angels Leaving the Garden'.
Paradise Lost, IX.
Oil on canvas. 132×167·6.
Unlocated.
Engraved by Moses Haughton, 1806.

XXI 'Eve after the Sentence and Departure of the Judge, Despairing, Supported by Adam'.
Paradise Lost, X.
Oil on canvas.
Unlocated.
Version in private collection, Basle.
Engraved by Moses Haughton, 1805.

XXII 'Death and Sin Bridging the Waste of Chaos and Met by Satan
on his Return from Earth'.
Paradise Lost, X.
Oil on canvas. 304·8 × 335·3.
Galerie Neupert, Zurich.
Drawing c. 1819–21.
Pencil, pen and watercolour.
Auckland City Art Gallery, New Zealand.

XXIII 'Satan Discovered on his Throne after his Return from Earth'.
Paradise Lost, X.
Oil on canvas.
Unlocated.

XXIV 'The Vision of the Lazar House'.
Paradise Lost, XI.
Oil on canvas.
Unlocated.
(Versions: Kunsthaus, Zurich; British Museum.)
Engraved by Holloway, 1791.

XXV 'The Vision of the Deluge'.
Paradise Lost, XI.
Oil on canvas. 205·7 × 274·3.
Unlocated.
(Versions: Reinhart collection, Winterthur; Kunstverein,
Winterthur.)

XXVI 'The Vision of Noah'.
Paradise Lost, XI.
Oil on canvas. 304·8 × 396·2.
Luton Church, Bedfordshire.
(Sketch: Kunsthaus, Zurich.)

XXVII 'The Dismission of Adam and Eve from Paradise'.
Paradise Lost, XII.
Oil on canvas.
Unlocated.
Engraved by A. Smith for Du Rouveray's edition, 1802.

XXVIII 'Christ on the Pinnacle of the Temple'.
Paradise Regained, IV.
Oil on canvas. 213·4 × 304·8.
Unlocated.

XXIX 'Ode on the Morning of Christ's Nativity: Mary and Jesus, the
Ruin of Paganism'.
Oil on canvas.
Unlocated.

XXX 'L'Allegro: Faery Mab'.
Oil on canvas.
Unlocated.
(Version in private collection, Basle.)
Engraved by W. Raddon, 1834.

XXXI 'L'Allegro: The Friar's Lanthorn'.
Canvas. 86·4×111·8.
Collection of Lieutenant Colonel J. L. B. Leicester-Warren,
Tabley House, Knutsford.
Engraved by Moses Haughton, 1806.

XXXII 'L'Allegro: The Lubbar Fiend'.
Canvas.
Unlocated.
Engraved by Moses Haughton, 1806.

XXXIII 'Il Pensieroso—Silence: "some still removed place"'.
Oil on canvas.
Private collection, Basle.
Engraved by J. Rogers, 1844, for Chidley edition.
(Study for female figure in Belfast Museum.)

XXXIV 'Il Pensieroso: Cremhild Meditating Revenge over the Sword
of Sigfrid'.
Canvas.
Unlocated.
(Fuseli exhibited four pictures of Cremhild at the Royal
Academy in 1807, 1814, 1817 and 1820.)

XXXV 'Comus; The Palace and the Rout of Comus; the Lady Set in
the Enchanted Chair to whom he Offered his Glass, the
Brothers Rushing in with Swords Drawn Wrest the Glass out
of his Hand; his Rout Flying'.
Unlocated.
Drawing once owned by Akermann, now unlocated, reproduced in G. Schiff, op. cit.

XXXVI 'The Orgies of Cotytto'.
Unlocated.
Copy attributed to a student in private collection, Zurich.

XXXVII 'Lycidas' Solitude, Morning, Twilight'.
Canvas. 75·1 × 109·2.
Collection of Dr. Ulrich, Zurich; loaned to Kunsthaus.
(Other versions in collection of Dr. Ulrich; Kunsthaus.)
Engraving by Moses Haughton, 1803.

XXXVIII 'Milton as a Boy with his Mother'.
Canvas. 101·6×172.
Unlocated.
Larger unfinished duplicate in Hotel Euler, Basle.
(Drawing: Belfast Museum, undated engraving by Perry.)

XXXIX 'Milton when a Youth'.
Canvas. 65·9×91·2.
Unlocated.
Old photograph in Courtauld Institute.

   XL 'Milton Dictating to his Daughter'.
Canvas. 86·4×110·5.
Unlocated.
Version in Bollag collection, Zurich.
(Undated engraving by Moses Haughton.)

Additional Pictures Exhibited in 1800

  XLI 'Sin Receiving the Key of Hell'.
Paradise Lost, II.
Canvas.
Unlocated.

 XLII 'Satan's First Address to Eve'.
Paradise Lost, IV.
Canvas.
Unlocated.
Version in Auckland City Art Gallery.
(Engraved by Tomkins between 1805 and 1808.)

XLIII 'Adam and Eve Meeting after her Seduction'.
Paradise Lost, IX.
Canvas.
Unlocated.

XLIV 'Elegy on the Death of a Fair Infant: Winter Carrying off a
Maid'.
Canvas.
Unlocated.

 XLV 'L'Allegro: Euphrosyne or Mirth with Fancy and Moderation
Hovering over her, Tripping forward . . .'.
Canvas.
Kunsthaus, Zurich (on loan from private collection).
Drawing c. 1780.
Pencil heightened with white.
Auckland City Art Gallery.

XLVI 'Il Pensieroso: Melancholy Reclining on her Throne'.
Canvas.
Destroyed accidentally.
Engraved by Sharpe, 1804, title page to *The British Theatre*, III.

XLVII 'Sonnet III; the Shepherdess of the Alps Watering her Plants'.
Canvas.
Unlocated.

Blake's Illustrations to *Paradise Lost*

Sources

C. H. Collins-Baker, *Catalogue of William Blake's Drawings and Paintings in the Huntington Library* (San Marino, California, 1938); M. Peckham, 'Blake, Milton and Edward Burney', *The Princeton University Library Chronicle*, XL (Spring 1950); and *Romantic Art in Britain* (Detroit Institute of Arts and the Philadelphia Museum of Art, 1968).

Satan Summons his Legions
(a) Watercolour. 21·1×25·1. c. 1807.
    Huntington Library.
(b) Drawing. 39×51·4. Signed and dated 1808.
    Victoria and Albert Museum. (Roughly corresponds to centre part of (a).)
(c) Tempera. 40·6×52·3.
    Collection of Lord Leconfield, Petworth. (Differs in composition from (a) and (b).)
(d) Tempera sketch for (c). 41·9×53·9.
    Graham Robertson collection (Victoria and Albert Museum).

Satan, Sin and Death
(a) Watercolour. 20·8×24·8. 1807–8.
    Huntington Library.
(b) Watercolour. 38·6×49·5. 1807–8.
    Huntington Library.
(c) Pencil, pen and watercolour sketch for (a) and (b). 19·7×24·9.
    Collection of Mr. and Mrs. J. W. Garrett (U.S.A.).

Christ Offers to Redeem Man
(a) Watercolour. 20·9×25·7. c. 1807.
    Huntington Library.
(b) Watercolour. 38·8×48·7. c. 1808.
    Boston Museum.

Satan's and Raphael's Entries into Paradise
    Watercolour. 20·3×25·1. c. 1807.
    Huntington Library.

Satan Watching the Endearments of Adam and Eve
(a) Watercolour. 21·4×25·9. c. 1807.
    Huntington Library.
(b) Watercolour. 38·8×48·7. c. 1808. (Satan in reverse from (a).)
    Boston Museum.
(c) Pencil drawing on f. 18 of album of Blake's sketches.
    British Museum (study for (a) and (b)).
(d) Drawing on the back of a portion of a letter, 4·4×6·4, repeats (a), (b) and (c) but without the figure of Satan.

(*e*) Drawing. 25·4×39·4.
National Gallery, Melbourne.
(*f*) Drawing. 20·3×26·7. Dated 1806.
Sold in the Sidney Morse sale, July 26th, 1929, bought by Bunbaum.

Satan as a Toad at the Ear of Eve
(*a*) Watercolour. c. 1808.
Boston Museum.
(*b*) Drawing.
Collection of Mrs. Bateson.

Raphael Talks to Adam
(*a*) Watercolour. 20·9×25·7. c. 1807.
Huntington Library.
(*b*) Watercolour. 38·8×48·7. c. 1808. (Earlier stage in episode than (*a*).
Boston Museum.
(*c*) Pencil drawing on f. 19 of album of Blake's sketches.
British Museum.

The Creation of Eve
(*a*) Watercolour. 20·8×25·4. c. 1807.
Huntington Library.
(*b*) Watercolour. 38·8×48·7. c. 1808. (Elaboration of (*a*).)
(*c*) Drawing 40·6×50·8. (Replica of (*b*).)
National Gallery, Melbourne.
(*d*) Drawing.
British Museum.

The Rout of the Rebel Angels
(*a*) Watercolour. 20·8×25·9. c. 1807.
Huntington Library.
(*b*) Watercolour. 38·8×48·7. c. 1808. (Minor differences of detail from (*a*).)
(*c*) Tempera on copper. Lot 75 in the Aspland sale, January 1885, bought by Gray.
(*d*) Indian ink and wash drawing. (Related to (*a*) or (*b*).)
Exhibited Boston 1891, lent by Charles E. West.
(*e*) Pencil sketch of fighting angels. 30·2×25·1.
British Museum.

The Fall of Eve
(*a*) Watercolour. 20·9×25·4. c. 1807.
Huntington Library.
(*b*) Watercolour. 38·8×48·7. c. 1808. (Minor differences from (*a*).)
Boston Museum.
(*c*) Pencil drawing. 12·7×22·9. Signed and dated 1808. (Preliminary study for (*b*).)
Victoria and Albert Museum.

(*d*) Watercolour. 'The Fall of Man'. Signed and dated 1807.
Victoria and Albert Museum.

So Judged He Man
(*a*) Watercolour. 20·3×25·1. c. 1807.
Huntington Library.
(*b*) Watercolour. 38·9×49·5. c. 1808.
Harvard College Library. (Almost identical to (*a*).)
(*c*) Indian ink drawing, 'God Speaking to Adam and Eve'. 15·2×18·7.
British Museum. (Differs radically from (*a*).)

The Lazar House of Milton
Watercolours over oils. 59×47·3. Signed and dated 1795.
Tate Gallery.

Michael Foretells the Crucifixion
(*a*) Watercolour. 25·4×20·3. c. 1807.
Huntington Library.
(*b*) Watercolour. 37·8×48·7. c. 1808. (Slight differences from (*a*).)
Boston Museum.
(*c*) Drawing. 38·7×49·2.
Collection of Mrs. T. H. Riches.

The Expulsion
(*a*) Watercolour. 20·5×25·1. c. 1807.
Huntington Library.
(*b*) Watercolour. 37·8×48·7. c. 1808. (Slight difference in attitude of
Adam and Eve.)
Boston Museum.

There are many other works which, though strictly imaginative or biblical in subject-matter, show the influence of Milton on Blake. One typical example is the pen and watercolour 'Satan in his Original Glory' (Tate Gallery), which is a rendering of a subject from Ezekiel.

Classified Bibliography

Works on Illustrations of Milton's Poetry

C. H. Collins-Baker, 'Some Illustrators of Milton's *Paradise Lost*, 1688–1850', *The Library*, III, no. 1 (June 1948).

Helen Gardner, 'Milton's First Illustrator', *Essays and Studies*, N.S. IX (1956).

M. Y. Hughes, 'Some Illustrators of Milton: the Expulsion from Paradise', *Journal of English and Germanic Philology*, LX, 4 (1961).

D. Irwin, 'Fuseli's Milton Gallery', *Burlington Magazine* (Dec. 1959).

M. Peckham, 'Blake, Milton and Edward Burney', *The Princeton University Library Chronicle*, XI (Spring 1950).

G. Schiff, *Johann Heinrich Füssli's Milton Galerie* (Zurich, 1963).

K. Svendsen, 'John Martin and the Expulsion Scene in *Paradise Lost*', *Studies in English Literature 1500–1900*, I (1961).

C. B. Tinker, 'Blake: Dreams of Milton', *Art News* (1950).

Biographies and Works on Individual Artists and Writers

R. G. Alexander, *A Catalogue of the Etchings of Samuel Palmer* (The Print Collector's Club, 1937).

F. Antal, *Fuseli Studies* (1956).

— *Hogarth and his Place in European Art* (1962).

Arts Council, *James Gillray 1756–1815. Drawings and Caricatures* (exhibition catalogue) (1967).

Auckland City Art Gallery, *A Collection of Drawings by Henry Fuseli* (1967).

T. Balston, *John Martin, his Life and Works* (1947).

— 'John Martin, Illustrator and Pamphleteer', *The Library*, XIV (1934).

J. Beer, *Blake's Humanism* (Manchester, 1968).

W. Blake, *The Letters of William Blake*. Edited by Sir G. Keynes (1956).

— *Complete Writings*. Edited by Sir G. Keynes (1925).

Sir A. Blunt, *The Art of William Blake* (New York, 1959).

— 'Blake's Pictorial Imagination', *J.W.C.I.*, VI (1943).

A. E. Bray, *Reminiscences of Thomas Stothard* (1851).

M. Butlin, *Samuel Palmer's Sketch Book (1824)* (facsimile) (1962).

R. Cohen, *The Art of Discrimination: Thomson's 'The Seasons' and the Language of Criticism* (1964).

C. H. Collins-Baker, *An Exhibition of William Blake's Water-color Drawings of Milton's 'Paradise Lost'*, Huntington Library and Art Gallery exhibition catalogue (San Marino, California, 1938).

— *A Catalogue of William Blake's Drawings and Paintings in the Huntington Library* (San Marino, California, 1938).

— 'The Sources of Blake's Pictorial Expression', *Huntington Library Quarterly*, IV, no. I (Oct. 1940).

— 'Sir James Thornhill as Bible Illustrator', *Huntington Library Quarterly*, X (1946–7).

W. G. Constable, *John Flaxman* (1927).

A. C. Coxhead, *Thomas Stothard. R.A.* (1906).

A. Crookshank, 'The Drawings of George Romney', *Burlington Magazine* (Feb. 1957).

S. F. Damon, *William Blake. His Philosophy and Symbols* (1924).

— 'Blake and Milton', *The Divine Vision*. Edited by V. Da Sola Pinto (1957).

Helen Darbishire, *The Early Lives of Milton* (1932).

G. W. Digby, *Symbol and Image in William Blake* (Oxford, 1957).

J. Farington, *The Farington Diary*. Edited by J. Greig (1923).

D. Farr, *William Etty* (1958).

Yvonne Ffrench, 'Some Unrecorded Haydon Drawings', *Apollo* (Nov. 1958).

J. Flaxman, 'An Account Book of John Flaxman, R.A.', *The Walpole Society*, XXVIII (1940).

N. Frye, *Fearful Symmetry. A Study of William Blake* (Princeton, 1947).

— 'Notes for a Commentary on "Milton"', *The Divine Vision*. Edited by V. Da Sola Pinto (1957).

P. Ganz, *The Drawings of Johann Heinrich Füssli* (translated into English, 1949).

W. Gaunt, *Arrows of Desire. A Study of William Blake and his Romantic World* (1956).

J. F. Gilliam, 'Scylla and Sin', *Philological Quarterly*, XXIX (1950).

G. Goodwin, *Thomas Watson, James Watson and Elizabeth Judkins* (1904).

G. Grigson, *Samuel Palmer. The Visionary Years* (1947).

L. Gruner, *The Decorations of the Garden Pavilion of Buckingham Palace* (1846).

J. Hagstrum, *William Blake, Poet and Painter* (Chicago University, 1964).

B. R. Haydon, *The Diary of B. R. Haydon*. Edited by W. B. Pope (Cambridge, Massachusetts, 1963).

W. Hazlitt, 'West's Picture of Death on the Pale Horse', *Essays on the Fine Arts*. Edited by C. Hazlitt (1873).

D. Hill, *Mr. Gillray the Caricaturist. A Biography* (1965).

J. Illo, 'Animal Sources for Milton's Sin and Death', *Notes and Queries*, CCV (1960).

R. James, 'Two Paintings by John Martin', *Burlington Magazine* (Aug. 1952).

L. Johnson, 'The "Raft of the Medusa" in Great Britain', *Burlington Magazine* (1954).

Dr. S. Johnson, *Prose and Poetry*. Edited by M. Wilson (1963, 1st ed. 1950).

T. Jones, 'The Memoirs of Thomas Jones, 1774–1775', *The Walpole Society*, XXXII (1946–8, published 1951).

J. F. Kerslake, 'The Richardsons and the Cult of Milton', *The Burlington Magazine* (Jan. 1957).

Sir G. Keynes, *Pencil Drawings by William Blake* (1927) and *Blake's Pencil Drawings* (2nd series, 1956).

J. Knowles, *The Life and Writings of Henry Fuseli* (1831).

E. C. Mason, *The Mind of Henry Fuseli* (1951).

J. Milton, *The Poetical Works*. Edited by Helen Darbishire, 2 vols. (Oxford, 1952, 1955).

The Milton Gallery, *A Catalogue of the First Series of Pictures and Sketches from the Poetic Works of John Milton by Henry Fuzli* [sic], *R.A.* (London, 1799?).

C. Mitchell, 'Benjamin West's "Death of General Wolfe" and the Popular Military Piece', *England and the Mediterranean Tradition* (Oxford, 1945).

J. Nichols and G. Steevens, *The Genuine Works of William Hogarth* (1808).

B. Nicolson, 'Two Companion Pieces by Wright of Derby', *Burlington Magazine* (March 1962).

A. H. Palmer, *The Life and Letters of Samuel Palmer, Painter and Etcher* (1892).

— *The Minor Poems of John Milton*, preface (1888).

R. Paulson, *Hogarth's Graphic Works* (1965).

M. L. Pendered, *John Martin, Painter. His Life and Times* (1923).

A. Pope, *Works*. Elwin-Courthorpe edition (1871–89).

— *The Poems of Alexander Pope*. Edited by J. Butt (1963).

N. Powell, *The Drawings of Henry Fuseli* (1951).

W. G. Rawlinson, *The Engraved Work of J. M. W. Turner, R.A.* (1908).

J. Richardson (father and son), *Explanatory Notes and Remarks on Milton's 'Paradise Lost' with the Life of the Author, and a Discourse on the Poem* (1734, reprinted in Helen Darbishire, op. cit.).

J. Romney, *Memoirs of the Life and Works of George Romney* (1830).

J. Seznec, *John Martin en France* (1964).

Sir J. Summerson, 'The Vision of J. M. Gandy', *Heavenly Mansions* (1949).

J. Toland, *The Life of John Milton* (1698, reprinted in Helen Darbishire, op. cit.).

G. Vertue, The Notebooks of George Vertue, *The Walpole Society* (XVIII, XX, XXII, XXIV, XXVI, XXX).

J. Warton, *Odes on Various Subjects* (1746).

B. West, 'West's Gallery', *A Catalogue of Pictures Painted by the Late Benjamin West . . . etc.* (1821).

Whitechapel Art Gallery, *An Exhibition of Paintings and Drawings by John Martin. 1789–1854* (September 23rd to November 1st, 1953).

W. Wordsworth, *The Poetical Works* (1847).

Historical Surveys and General Works of Criticism

J. Addison, 'Essays on the Pleasures of Imagination', in *The British Essayists*, XII (1823).

A. Alison, *Essays on the Nature and Principles of Taste* (1810, 6th ed. Edinburgh, 1825).

Arts Council, *The Romantic Movement* (exhibition catalogue, 1959).

D. Bland, *A History of Book Illustration* (1958).

— *The Illustration of Books* (1962, 3rd ed. enlarged).

T. S. R. Boase, *English Art 1800–1870* (Oxford, 1959).

— 'The Decoration of the New Palace of Westminster', *J.W.C.I.* (1954).
— 'Macklin and Bowyer', *J.W.C.I.* (1963).
E. Burke, *A Philosophical Enquiry into the Origin of our Ideas of the Sublime and Beautiful* (1757. Edited by J. T. Boulton, 1958).
Courtauld Institute, London University, *Handlist of Drawings in the Witt Collection.*
E. Croft-Murray, *Decorative Painting in England 1537–1837*, I (1962).
A. Cunningham, *The Lives of the Most Eminent British Painters, Sculptors and Architects* (1829–33, 2nd ed. 1837).
The Detroit Institute of Arts and the Philadelphia Museum of Art, *Romantic Art in Britain* (exhibition catalogue, 1968).
A. Dobson, *Eighteenth Century Vignettes* (1st series, 1892).
— *At Prior's Park and Other Papers* (1912).
J. Flaxman, *Lectures on Sculpture* (1829, new ed. 1865).
N. Frye, 'Romanticism Reconsidered', *English Institute Essays* (1962).
W. Gilpin, *Three Essays: On Picturesque Beauty, On Picturesque Travel and On Sketching Landscape* (3rd ed. 1800).
M. Girouard, 'English Art and the Rococo', *Country Life* (Jan.–Feb. 1966).
J. W. Good, 'Studies in the Milton Tradition', *University of Illinois Studies in Language and Literature*, I (1915).
L. Gowing, 'Hogarth, Hayman and the Vauxhall Decorations', *Burlington Magazine* (Jan. 1959).
G. Grigson, 'Painters of the Abyss', *The Architectural Review* (1950).
Jean Hagstrum, *The Sister Arts: the Tradition of Literary Pictorialism from Dryden to Gray* (Chicago, 1958).
R. D. Havens, *The Influence of Milton on English Poetry* (Harvard, 1922).
P. Hofer, *Baroque Book Illustration* (Harvard, 1951).
W. Hogarth, *The Analysis of Beauty* (1753. Edited by J. Burke, Oxford, 1955).
A. R. Humphreys, *The Augustan World* (1954, ed. 1964).
C. Hussey, *The Picturesque. Studies in a Point of View* (1927).
D. Irwin, *English Neo-Classical Art: Studies in Inspiration and Taste* (1966).
Dr. S. Johnson, *The Lives of the English Poets* (1783. Edited by H. S. Scott, Oxford, 1905).
Lord Kames, *The Elements of Criticism* (1762, 8th ed. 1807).
F. D. Klingender, *Art and the Industrial Revolution* (1947, revised by A. Elton, 1968).
T. Macklin, *The Poets' Gallery* (1790).
E. Mâle, *The Gothic Image* (1961, 1st ed. 1913).
E. Malins, *English Landscaping and Literature, 1660–1840* (1966).
M. Merchant, *Shakespeare and the Artist* (1959).
H. N. Morriss, *Flaxman, Blake, Coleridge and Other Men of Genius influenced by Swedenborg* (1915).
E. Panofsky, *Studies in Iconology* (Oxford, 1939).
E. Panofsky, Klibansky and Saxl, *Saturn and Melancholy* (1964).
N. Pevsner, *Academies of Art Past and Present* (Cambridge, 1940).
M. Praz, *The Romantic Agony* (1933).

W. H. Pyne (pseudonym E. Hardcastle), *Wine and Walnuts* (2nd ed. 1824). Reprinted in *The Somerset House Gazette* (1824).

R. and S. Redgrave, *A Century of British Painters* (1947, 1st ed. 1866).

Sir J. Reynolds, *Discourses on Art*. Edited R. Wark (Huntington Library publications, 1959).

J. Richardson, *The Theory of Painting* (1719. In *Works*, 1792 ed.).

J. G. Robertson, *Studies in the Genesis of Romantic Theory in the Eighteenth Century* (Cambridge, 1923).

R. Rosenblum, *Transformations in Late Eighteenth Century Art* (Princeton, 1967).

J. Seznec, *Literature and the Visual Arts in Nineteenth Century France* (University of Hull, 1962).

Earl of Shaftesbury, *Charakteristicks* (1710, 3rd ed. 1723).

P. B. Shelley, *A Defense of Poesy* (1822). *The Complete Works* (1965).

Dr. A. Von Gertsch, *Der Steigende Ruhm Miltons* (Leipzig, 1927).

E. K. Waterhouse, *Painting in Britain 1530–1790* (Harmondsworth, 1953).

D. Webb, *Remarks on the Beauties of Poetry* (1762).

M. Whinney, *Sculpture in Britain 1530–1830* (Harmondsworth, 1964).

W. Whitley, *Artists and their Friends in England 1700–1799* (1928).

Works of Reference

L. Binyon, *Catalogue of Drawings by British Artists in the British Museum* (1898).

Dr. M. Bryan, *A Biographical and Critical Dictionary of Painters* (1873).

A. Graves, *The Royal Academy of Arts. A Complete Dictionary of Contributors . . . etc. 1769–1904* (1906).

— *The Society of Artists of Great Britain 1761–1791 and The Free Society of Artists 1761–1783. A Dictionary . . . etc.* (1907).

— *Exhibitors at the British Institution 1806–67* (1908).

R. Gunnis, *A Dictionary of British Sculptors 1660–1851* (1953).

A. M. Hind, *A History of Engraving and Etching* (1923).

Editions of the Bible

The Holy Bible, The Theater (Oxford, 1679).

The Holy Bible, J. Baskett (Oxford, 1717).

Illustrated Editions of the Poetry of Milton

1688, *Paradise Lost*, R. Bentley and J. Tonson, illustrated by J. B. Medina.

1713, *Paradise Regained*, J. Tonson, 5th ed., illustrations attributed to J. B. Medina.

1720, *The Poetical Works*, J. Tonson, illustrations by Cheron and one by Thornhill.

1749, *Paradise Lost and Paradise Regained (and Minor Poems)*, T. Newton, illustrated by F. Hayman.

1777, *The Poetical Works*, Bell's *Poets of Great Britain*, illustrated by J. H. Mortimer.

1781, *Paradise Lost*, The Poetical Magazine, illustrated by Dodd.

1794, *Paradise Lost*, J. and H. Richter, illustrated by H. Richter.

1794–7, *The Poetical Works*, J. and J. Boydell, illustrated by R. Westall.

1795–6, *The Poetical Works*, C. Cooke, illustrations by Kirk and one by Brown.

1796, *Paradise Lost*, J. Parsons, illustrated by H. Singleton and R. Corbould.

1796, *Paradise Regained and the Minor Poems*, Longman, Law and associates, illustrated by E. F. Burney.

1799, *Paradise Lost*, C. Whittingham, illustrated by E. F. Burney.

1802, *Paradise Lost*, Du Rouveray, illustrations by J. H. Fuseli and W. Hamilton.

1804, *Paradise Lost*, The Albion Press, illustrated by M. Craig.

1805–8, *The Poetical Works*, T. Park (*The Works of the British Poets*), illustrated by J. H. Fuseli and R. Westall.

1805–6, *The Poetical Works*, J. Heath and G. Kearsley (vols. 12–15, Aikin's *English Poets*), illustrated by J. Thurston and H. Howard.

1806, *Paradise Lost*, W. Suttaby and associates, illustrated by J. Thurston.

1806, *The Poetical Works*, W. Suttaby and associates, illustrations by Fuseli, Stothard and Uwins.

1808, *Paradise Lost*, B. J. and R. Johnson, one illustration anon. engraved by C. Tiebout.

1808, *The Latin and Italian Poems of Milton Translated into English Verse*, J. Johnson, illustrated by J. Flaxman.

1812, *Paradise Lost*, published in Liverpool, illustrated by W. M. Craig.

1813, *Paradise Lost*, T. Tegg, one illustration by S. Springsguth.

1816, *Paradise Regained and the Minor Poems*, J. Sharpe, illustrated by R. Westall.

1817, *Paradise Lost*, C. Whittingham, illustrated by R. Westall.

1817, *Paradise Lost*, J. Mawman and associates, illustrations by E. F. Burney and one by H. Corbould.

1821, *The Poetical Works*, Suttaby, Evance and Fox, frontispiece by H. Howard.

1825–7, *Paradise Lost*, S. Prowett, illustrated by J. Martin.

1829, *Paradise Lost*, 'Printed for the booksellers', one illustration attributed to Corbould.

1835, *The Poetical Works of John Milton*, J. Macrone, illustrated by J. M. W. Turner.

1839, *Paradise Lost*, English Classics, one illustration by T. Uwins.

1843, *Paradise Lost*, Tilt, illustrated by W. Harvey.

1848, *L'Allegro and Il Penseroso*, with thirty illustrations designed for the Art Union of London.

1849, *L'Allegro*, J. Cundall, illustrated by members of the Etching Club.

1855, *L'Allegro and Il Penseroso*, D. Boyne, illustrated by Birket Foster.

1858, *Comus*, Routledge, illustrations by Pickersgill, Birket Foster, Harrison Weir and others.

1888, *The Shorter Poems*, illustrated by S. Palmer.

Index

Illustrations are listed at the front of the book and are not included in the index